W9-AUK-396

FIRST AID
MANUAL

PRINCIPLES OF THE RED CROSS

Nationally and internationally, the Red Cross bases its actions on seven principles.

Humanity

The Red Cross, born of a desire to bring assistance without discrimination to the wounded on the battlefield, endeavors – in its international and national capacity – to prevent and alleviate human suffering wherever it may be found. Its purpose is to protect life and health and to ensure respect for the human being. It promotes mutual understanding, friendship, co-operation and lasting peace amongst all peoples.

Impartiality

It makes no discrimination as to nationality, race, religious beliefs, class or political opinions. It endeavors to relieve the suffering of individuals, being guided solely by their needs, and to give priority to the most urgent cases of distress.

Neutrality

In order to continue to enjoy the confidence of all, the Red Cross may not take sides in hostilities or engage at any time in controversies of a political, racial, religious or ideological nature.

Independence

The Red Cross is independent. The National Societies, while auxiliaries in the humanitarian services of their Governments and subject to the laws of their respective countries, must always maintain their autonomy so that they may be able at all times to act in accordance with Red Cross Principles.

Voluntary service

The Red Cross is a voluntary relief organisation not prompted in any manner by desire for gain.

Unity

There can be only one Red Cross Society in any one country. It must be open to all. It must carry on its humanitarian work throughout its territory.

Universality

The Red Cross is a world-wide institution in which all Societies have equal status and share equal responsibilities and duties in helping each other.

FIRST AID
MANUAL

**The Authorised Manual of
the Australian Red Cross Society.**

An imprint of HarperCollins*Publishers*

AN ANGUS & ROBERTSON BOOK

An imprint of HarperCollinsPublishers

First published in Australia in 1984 by
William Collins Pty Ltd

Reprinted in 1984, 1985, 1986, 1987, 1989, 1990

This edition published in 1990 by
CollinsAngus&Robertson Publishers Pty Ltd
A division of HarperCollinsPublishers (Australia) Pty Ltd
4 Eden Park, 31 Waterloo Road, North Ryde NSW 2113
Reprinted in 1991

A Dorling Kindersley book
Original title First Aid Manual
Copyright © 1982 by
**St Andrew's Ambulance Association
The British Red Cross Society**

Revisions to text and illustrations made by
and copyright © 1983, 1990 by
The Australian Red Cross Society

National Library of Australia
Cataloguing-in-Publication data:

First aid manual
 Includes index
 ISBN 0 207 16917 9

 1. First aid in illness and injury —
 Handbooks, manuals, etc. I. Dunne,
 Jemima. II. Australian Red Cross
 Society.
616.02'52

Printed in Hong Kong by Wing King Tong

FOREWORD

The need for First Aid Training is greater than ever. Road accidents in Australia are still increasing and the use of mechanical and electrical appliances and chemicals at home, at work and at leisure, increases the risk of injury. There is an ever-increasing demand for First Aid training for personal use in addition to the demand for certificated First Aiders in industrial, agricultural and commercial establishments.

The *First Aid Manual* is both an instructional and a reference book designed to meet the needs of those interested in First Aid as well as those who require an acknowledged qualification. It provides the necessary material for instructional courses.

Great care has been taken in the preparation of this First Edition of the Australian Red Cross Society First Aid Manual to obtain the views of many of those who render First Aid, as well as those who see the results of it, to ensure the Manual is as widely accepted as possible. This has involved consultation with authorities in many fields and the Society is grateful for this help. However, the Editorial Committee realises that it is impossible to produce a definitive work in any technical field which will secure the immediate and unreserved approval of all readers, and First Aid is no exception. A new edition of this Manual is produced regularly. The Society would welcome comments or suggestions on this manual and these should be forwarded to the Red Cross Divisional Headquarters in your State or Territory.

The Australian Red Cross Society

CONTENTS

HOW TO USE THIS BOOK

The Australian Red Cross Society First Aid Manual contains all the information which is necessary for standard First Aid courses. *The Society will award First Aid certificates after careful assessment of the theoretical and practical knowledge of each candidate, following a recognised course of instruction.*

The information in the *First Aid Manual* is divided into three main sections and each section is denoted by different page borders. The major First Aid techniques, those which are vital to save lives, are contained in one chapter at the front of the book; these pages are marked by a wide, red border. Here you will find the techniques for resuscitation and the control of bleeding.

The main section of the book, marked by thin red page borders, contains chapters which deal generally with situations such as *Action at an Emergency* and *Procedure at Major Incidents*, and others which deal specifically with conditions relating to the major classifications such as *Unconsciousness, Emergencies Which Cause Lack of Oxygen, Wounds and Bleeding, Circulatory Disorders* and *Fractures*. In each case the condition is defined and the possible symptoms and signs and recommended treatment are described. The treatments are all set out in simple step-by-step form and are accompanied by descriptive illustrations to make them easier to follow. It is also important to realise that all the symptoms and signs listed as part of any condition may not occur in the order given and may not all be present in every condition.

Towards the end of the book are two chapters — *Dressings and Bandages* and *Handling and Transport* — which contain information relevant to all conditions. These chapters are denoted by wide, grey page borders.

As a general principle, information on the structure and function of parts of the body have been included in some of the chapters in order to aid understanding of the treatment described.

The chapter on *Emergency Childbirth* at the end of the book is included to provide the necessary information should the emergency arise without normal facilities being immediately available. This subject, however, does *not* form part of a Standard First Aid course and is therefore *not* required for any examination purposes.

The First Aid Manual can be used as a guideline for treatment by the untrained person. However, skills such as Expired Air Resuscitation and External Cardiac Compression *must* be taught by qualified instructors using approved training manikins. The Australian Red Cross Society offers a range of First Aid and Resuscitation training courses through the National Health and Safety Education Program. For information on these courses please contact the nearest Red Cross Divisional Headquarters.

In this manual the techniques of cardiopulmonary resuscitation (CPR) and life-supporting first aid are based on the policy statements of the Australian Resuscitation Council.

THE PRINCIPLES AND PRACTICE OF FIRST AID

First Aid is the skilled application of the accepted principles of treatment when an injury or sudden illness occurs, using the facilities or materials available to you at the time. It is the approved method of treating a casualty until responsibility is assumed by an ambulance officer, nurse or doctor.

Basic Life Support is a set of emergency procedures that consist of recognition of airway obstruction, failure of breathing or circulation and the use of the appropriate resuscitation techniques until the casualty recovers or is transferred to the care of an ambulance officer, nurse or doctor.

WHY IT IS GIVEN

First Aid is given to a casualty:
- To preserve life.
- To protect the unconscious.
- To prevent the condition worsening and relieve pain.
- To promote recovery.

THE RESPONSIBILITY OF THE FIRST AIDER

Because of the frequency and serious nature of many accidents, the role of the First Aider is very important.

In the management of a casualty, your responsibility as a First Aider is to:
- Assess the situation.
- Identify a life-threatening condition and establish priorities of treatment.
- Give immediate, appropriate and adequate treatment, bearing in mind that a casualty may have more than one injury, and that some casualties will require more urgent attention than others.
- Arrange without delay for the casualty to be transferred to a doctor, hospital or home, according to the severity of the injury or condition.

Your responsibility ends when the casualty is handed over to the care of an ambulance officer, nurse or doctor, or other appropriate person. Before you leave the incident, make your report to whoever is in charge and ascertain whether you could be of any further help.

DEFINITIONS

Medical aid means treatment by a doctor.
Advanced Life Support describes the performance of more specialised resuscitation techniques by highly trained personnel.
First Aider is the term which describes any person who has received a certificate from an authorised body indicating that he or she is qualified to render First Aid. It was first used in 1894 by the Voluntary First Aid Organisations in the United Kingdom.

First Aid certificates issued by the Australian Red Cross Society are awarded to candidates who have attended a course of theoretical and practical work and who have passed a professionally supervised examination.

The certificate awarded is valid for three years ensuring that First Aiders are:
- Highly trained.
- Regularly examined.
- Kept up-to-date in knowledge and skill.

BASIC LIFE SUPPORT TECHNIQUES

Skilled First Aiders can save lives by maintaining a casualty's vital needs. In any emergency you should always stay with the casualty and, where there is more than one person needing care, attend to the unconscious casualty first. The priorities in the care of the unconscious casualty are the care of *Airway*, *Breathing* and *Circulation*; commonly abbreviated as A B C. For life to continue, a person must be able to take oxygen into his or her lungs. This is in turn distributed throughout the body by the blood. While it is possible for some parts of the body to survive for a time without oxygen, other parts such as the vital nerve cells in the brain, can die or suffer permanent damage very quickly when deprived of oxygen.

DANGER

You must assess the situation quickly to ensure your own safety and that of the casualty. Where danger exists either move the cause from the casualty or, if that is not possible, move the casualty from the cause.

RESPONSE

The most important initial observation to be made is whether the casualty is conscious or unconscious. Shake the casualty gently and shout a simple command, e.g., "Squeeze my hand; let it go". The unconscious casualty will fail to respond to the spoken word or to obey a shouted command.

The conscious casualty should be allowed to assume the position in which he or she is most comfortable.

Control any severe bleeding to prevent or reduce serious blood loss so that an adequate circulation can be maintained.

AIRWAY

The unconscious casualty is in danger because of the risk of a blocked airway (see p. 16). Turn him or her over into the Lateral Recovery Position to drain fluids and ensure a clear passage of air to the lungs (see p. 22).

BREATHING

Check breathing: watch for movement in the lower chest and abdomen; listen and feel for air escaping from the nose and mouth. If the casualty stops breathing, quickly turn him or her on to the back and begin Expired Air Resuscitation (E.A.R.) (see p. 18).

CIRCULATION

Check the carotid pulse to determine whether effective circulation is present (see p. 23). If the pulse is present, stop any obvious bleeding and continue E.A.R. If the pulse is absent, begin External Cardiac Compression (see p. 24) and continue E.A.R.

Throughout this text the emphasis will be on Basic Life Support without equipment. It is important to practise these techniques under trained supervision as a text book description is no substitute for practical knowledge and experience.

RESPIRATION

Oxygen is vital to support life. The aim of breathing is to transfer oxygen from the air to the lungs where it can be picked up by the blood and circulated throughout the body, and to allow carbon dioxide, a waste product, to be expelled.

When you breathe, air enters the nose or mouth and flows down the main airway, the windpipe (trachea), through smaller passages (bronchi), and finally reaches the air sacs (alveoli) in the lungs where an exchange of gases is made. In these small sacs, oxygen is picked up by the blood and carbon dioxide is given up by the blood to be breathed out.

Air is a mixture of gases: 21% of it is oxygen. Only 5% of the oxygen is used up in breathing, so that when we exhale, we breathe out 16% in addition to a small amount of carbon dioxide. The amount of oxygen breathed out is therefore adequate to resuscitate another person.

In the mouth and throat, food and air share the same passage, but at the top of the main airway is the voice box (larynx). This structure not only serves as the organ of speech but also acts as a valve which closes whenever you swallow, thus preventing the inhalation of food or drink. However, in an unconscious person, this protective mechanism works less well and becomes increasingly ineffective as unconsciousness deepens.

The Respiratory System

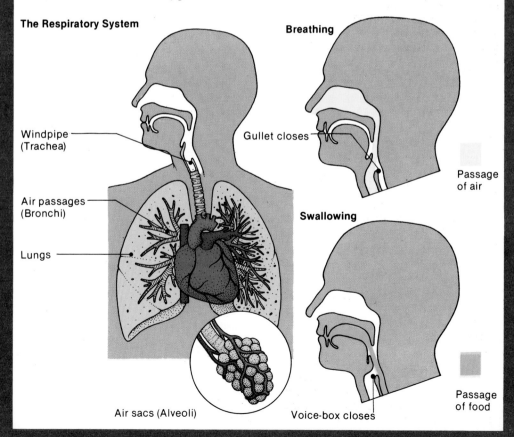

Windpipe (Trachea)

Air passages (Bronchi)

Lungs

Air sacs (Alveoli)

Breathing

Gullet closes

Passage of air

Swallowing

Voice-box closes

Passage of food

HOW WE BREATHE

Breathing is divided into three phases: breathing-in (inspiration), breathing-out (expiration) and pause. When you breathe in, the chest muscles pull the ribs upwards allowing the chest to expand in width and height. The diaphragm, a strong muscular partition which separates the chest cavity from the abdominal cavity, contracts and flattens increasing the chest's capacity from below. This combined action causes air to flow into the lungs so that the exchange of gases can take place. When breathing out, the diaphragm and the rib muscles relax and resume their position at rest. A short pause follows before the cycle starts all over again.

A breathing control centre in the brain determines the rate and depth of breathing; the average adult normally breathes 16—18 times per minute and children and infants breathe 20—30 times per minute. This rate increases during stress, exercise, injury or fever and it is accompanied by an increase in the heart rate so that extra oxygen can be carried around the body.

HOW OXYGEN IS CIRCULATED BY THE BLOOD

Every cell in the body needs oxygen as well as food and water. Our oxygen supply is obtained from the air we breathe and the oxygen supply to the cells is dependent on several factors. For example: the amount of oxygen in the air may be reduced when the environment is polluted by noxious gases; the efficient function of the breathing control centre in the brain can be damaged by head injury, disease, drugs or foreign material; the diaphragm and the muscles of the chest wall, which are essential for efficient breathing, can be paralysed following injury to the spinal cord in the neck; disease may cause inefficient exchange of gases in the lungs, particularly the passage of oxygen into the bloodstream and/or an inefficient heart to pump the oxygenated blood to the vital organs of the body, in particular the heart and the brain.

Oxygen is carried around the body by the red cells in the blood (see pp. 28—9). Blood is circulated in a continuously repeated cycle by the contraction-relaxation movements of the heart. Each time the muscle contracts, blood is forced out of the pumping chambers, when the muscle relaxes, replacement blood flows into the collection chambers. In the average adult at rest, the heart "beats" about 72 times each minute.

Deoxygenated blood flows back from the tissues into two main veins, then into the right side of the heart. It is then forced out of the heart to the lungs where the exchange of gases takes place. The oxygenated blood returns to the left side of the heart and is then pumped out again into the main artery, and from here it is distributed to all parts of the body (see pp. 28–9). Valves in the heart ensure that blood continues to flow around the body in the right direction.

Human red cells contain a special iron-carrying pigment called haemoglobin which has the ability to combine with oxygen. Each 100ml of blood contains approximately 15g of haemoglobin. As the red cells give up their oxygen to the tissues, the blood loses its bright red appearance; the blood in the veins is darker than that in the arteries. If more than 5g of the haemoglobin is no longer combined with oxygen, the blood assumes a bluish colour which is reflected in the colour of the skin, the tongue and inside the mouth (cyanosis). If cyanosis occurs and is associated with airway obstruction, or other emergencies such as smoke inhalation, the casualty has severe oxygen lack and urgent treatment is necessary.

A casualty will be pale when the total number of red cells is diminished, e.g., when the casualty is anaemic or when the blood vessels to the skin are constricted.

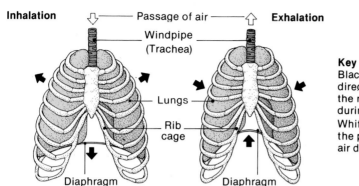

Inhalation — Passage of air — **Exhalation**

Windpipe (Trachea)

Lungs

Rib cage

Diaphragm — Diaphragm

Key
Black arrows indicate the direction of movement of the rib cage and diaphragm during breathing.
White arrows indicate the passage of air during breathing.

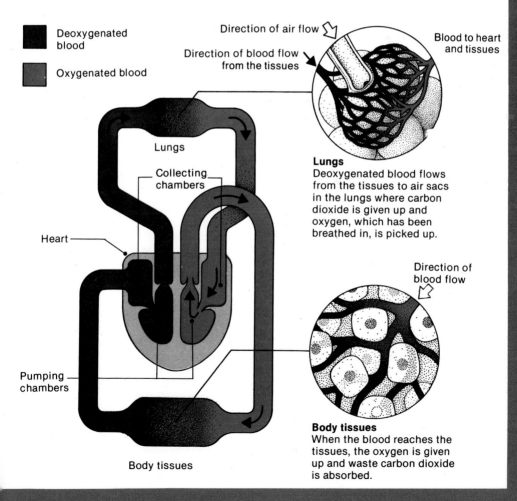

Deoxygenated blood

Oxygenated blood

Direction of air flow

Direction of blood flow from the tissues

Blood to heart and tissues

Lungs

Collecting chambers

Heart

Pumping chambers

Lungs
Deoxygenated blood flows from the tissues to air sacs in the lungs where carbon dioxide is given up and oxygen, which has been breathed in, is picked up.

Direction of blood flow

Body tissues

Body tissues
When the blood reaches the tissues, the oxygen is given up and waste carbon dioxide is absorbed.

RESUSCITATION

Resuscitation is the preservation of life by the establishment and/or maintenance of Airway, Breathing and Circulation — A.B.C. — and related emergency care. The objective of modern resuscitation techniques is to ensure an adequate supply of oxygen to the brain, not only to preserve life, but to prevent the damage to brain cells that results from lack of oxygen.

It is generally agreed that resuscitation should always be attempted when a person collapses or suffers injury when apparently in good health (e.g., following near-drowning, head injury, electric shock or heart attack), or where the medical condition is reversible such as self-poisoning. Many seemingly hopeless cases have been revived with no apparent brain damage, especially children who have been immersion victims. Resuscitation is not performed on a person who has been dying of a fatal disease and whose death is expected.

If there is any doubt about the duration of collapse, the casualty should be given the benefit of the doubt and resuscitation must be commenced immediately.

In this section we discuss the principles and practice of resuscitation as they apply to any casualty who is unconscious following a head injury, near-drowning, poisoning, electric shock, convulsions, suffocation, smoke inhalation or stroke, or to any casualty whose breathing or circulation has failed.

Resuscitation priorities
In all emergencies, as a First Aider you must act quickly to assess the situation to ensure your own safety and that of the casualty. It is important to remain with the casualty, call for help and to begin the appropriate treatment according to the Basic Life Support Flow Chart (see opposite). Where there is more than one person requiring treatment, any unconscious casualty must be treated first.
Unnecessary movement of any casualty may make injuries worse and treatment more difficult. A person who has collapsed or been injured should only be moved if: he or she is in immediate danger, e.g., from road traffic, hot road surfaces, fire, surfing conditions or marine animals; or if it is necessary to carry out life-saving treatment, e.g., to establish and ensure a clear airway and perform Expired Air Resuscitation (see p. 18) or Cardio-pulmonary Resuscitation (see p. 26) when the casualty needs to lie on a firm surface. Except in life-threatening situations, always splint a fracture before moving a casualty.

The most experienced person present should assume overall responsibility for management of the emergency. However, once an ambulance officer arrives, the bystander should offer assistance and work under the direction of the ambulance officer. If a doctor is present ambulance officers and bystanders work under the supervision of the doctor who will accept clinical responsibility for the care given to the casualty.

When resuscitation is required and it is started in the absence of a doctor, continue until any of the following applies:
● Breathing and circulation return.
● Resuscitation is continued by another responsible person.
● A doctor assumes responsibility.
● The casualty is transferred to the care of ambulance officers.
● The First Aider is exhausted and unable to continue.

Modern resuscitation techniques
Research has shown that manual chest compression/arm lifts do not achieve adequate oxygenation of the blood to maintain life and prevent brain damage.

NB Remember, do not stand by and let the casualty die. Turn him or her on to the side, keep the airway clear and ensure that breathing is satisfactory.

BASIC LIFE SUPPORT FLOW CHART

This flow chart sets out the procedure which should be followed in any emergency where a casualty collapses. All the techniques required are described on the following pages together with clear concise diagrams which help you to understand them. Where relevant, we have colour-coded the headings in this section so that they tie-in with the chart.

COLLAPSE
Check response to
SHAKE AND
SHOUT

UNCONSCIOUS
Turn casualty on side
CLEAR AIRWAY
(see p. 16)
HEAD TILT (see
p. 17) with jaw
support
Turn face slightly
downwards
CHECK
BREATHING (see
p. 17)

CONSCIOUS
Make the casualty
comfortable
Observe: AIRWAY
(see p. 16)
BREATHING
(see p. 17)
CIRCULATION
(see p. 23)

NOT BREATHING
Turn casualty on to
back
E.A.R. (see p. 18)
 – 5 full breaths in
10 seconds
CHECK PULSE
(see p. 23)

BREATHING
Leave on side in
LATERAL
RECOVERY
POSITION (see
p. 22).
Observe:
 AIRWAY
 BREATHING
 CIRCULATION

Key
E.A.R. Expired air
resuscitation
E.C.C. External

PULSE ABSENT
C.P.R. (see p. 26)
 (E.A.R. AND
 E.C.C.)
Check breathing
and pulse after 1
minute and then at
least every 2
minutes.

PULSE PRESENT
Continue E.A.R.
Check pulse and
breathing after 1
minute and then
every 2 minutes

cardiac com-
pression
C.P.R. Cardio-
pulmonary resus-
citation, i.e.,
Expired air resus-
citation together
with External
cardiac com-
pression

DANGER
The unconscious casualty cannot protect him or herself from any danger and you may also be at risk of immediate injury. If possible, remove the danger from the casualty, otherwise remove the casualty and yourself from danger such as fire, surf or oncoming traffic.

RESPONSE
Once it is safe to do so, you must determine whether the casualty is conscious or unconscious. To do this, assess the casualty's response to "Shake and shout" by shaking the casualty firmly but not roughly by the shoulders and asking his or her name. Give a simple command such as: "Open your eyes, squeeze my hand, let it go.".

The casualty is conscious if he or she responds to the spoken word and obeys a shouted command. If there is no response the casualty is unconscious.

CONSCIOUS CASUALTY

If the casualty is conscious, help him or her to adopt a comfortable position: a person who is short of breath or who has chest pain may wish to sit up; a person who feels faint may wish to lie down. Do not move the casualty for 10–15 minutes, observe him or her closely to make sure that the condition remains satisfactory; be prepared to commence resuscitation while you are waiting for the ambulance or other medical assistance. Any subsequent treatment given will depend on the cause of the collapse.

UNCONSCIOUS CASUALTY

When looking after an unconscious casualty it is important to maintain an open *airway* and adequate *breathing* and *circulation*. *Always remember that an open airway takes precedence over all fractures, including suspected spinal injuries*.

Turn the casualty on to his or her side and remove any foreign material from the mouth. Open the airway using head tilt with jaw support (see opposite) otherwise breathing may stop and the lack of oxygen may also result in heart failure.

AIRWAY

If a casualty is unconscious, the airway may be narrowed or blocked making breathing difficult or impossible. This can occur for several reasons: the head may tilt forward narrowing the air passage; loss of muscular control may allow the tongue to slip back and block the airway; and, because the reflexes are impaired, saliva or vomit may lie in the back of the throat and block the airway.

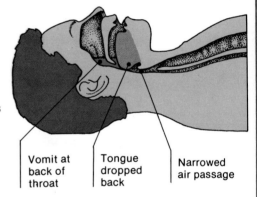

Vomit at back of throat | Tongue dropped back | Narrowed air passage

RECOGNISING AIRWAY OBSTRUCTION

If the casualty is breathing there will be:
● Noisy breathing.
● Laboured breathing (the chest will suck in and the abdomen will push out instead of both rising together).
● Flaring of the nostrils.
● Drawing in of the chest wall between the ribs and of the soft spaces above the collar-bone and breastbone. (The latter two are commonly seen in children with croup).

CLEARING THE AIRWAY

Quickly turn the casualty on to his or her side into the Lateral Recovery Position (see p. 22) with the face turned slightly downwards to enable fluid to drain from the mouth. Clear the mouth of vomit, or

any other foreign material that you can see, using your fingers if necessary. Leave firmly-fitting dentures in place but remove loose dentures.

NB If two First Aiders are present, one should support the head; the other should look into the casualty's mouth and remove any foreign material.

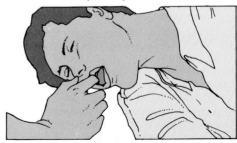

OPENING THE AIRWAY

If the casualty is lying on his or her back for Expired Air Resuscitation, kneel beside the head and place the palm of one hand on top of the casualty's head with your thumb lying along the hairline. Place your other hand on the casualty's chin using the *"Pistol grip"*. Place the knuckle of your middle finger under the point of the casualty's chin. Place your thumb along the front of the lower jaw between the lower lip and the point of the chin, and place your index finger along the line of the lower jaw. Curl your other fingers in towards the palm of the hand. *Keep all fingers clear of the soft tissues of the neck*. Position the index finger and thumb so that you can open the casualty's mouth. Maintain an open airway by keeping the head tilted back and supporting the jaw.

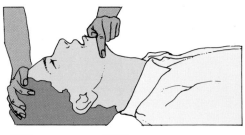

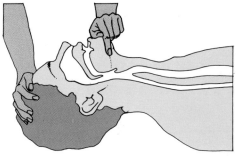

CHECKING BREATHING

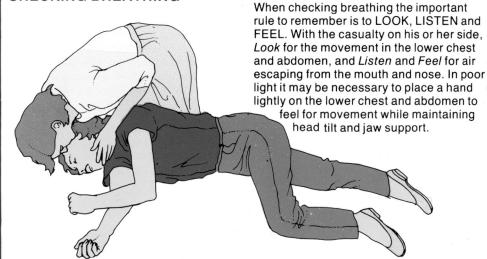

When checking breathing the important rule to remember is to LOOK, LISTEN and FEEL. With the casualty on his or her side, *Look* for the movement in the lower chest and abdomen, and *Listen* and *Feel* for air escaping from the mouth and nose. In poor light it may be necessary to place a hand lightly on the lower chest and abdomen to feel for movement while maintaining head tilt and jaw support.

BREATHING

If the casualty is breathing, leave him or her in the Lateral Recovery Position and await the arrival of the ambulance or other medical help and observe Airway, Breathing and Circulation. All unconscious casualties should be transported in the Lateral Recovery Position.

NOT BREATHING

If the casualty is not breathing, quickly turn the casualty onto his or her back. Tilt the head back (see above) and support the jaw. Begin Expired Air Resuscitation immediately. Give 5 full breaths in the first 10 seconds then check the pulse.

Expired Air Resuscitation

There are two basic methods for giving Expired Air Resuscitation: Mouth-to-mouth and Mouth-to-nose methods. Although Mouth-to-mouth is the more commonly used method, both are equally effective provided the airway is clear, the seal is efficient and enough force is used to make the chest rise.

The mouth-to-nose method is generally used when it is the First Aider's preferred method and when resuscitation is performed in deep water (see p.50). Remember that if a blockage in the nose prevents adequate lung inflation you must change to the mouth-to-mouth method.

When resuscitating children under two years old, a combination, mouth-to-mouth-and-nose, should be used.

POSSIBLE PROBLEMS

If the chest does not rise or there is resistance to your efforts to blow air into the casualty's chest, it may indicate several things. To find out where the problem lies you should systematically check the following.
● Check the mouth for any foreign material, vomit or blood. If there is anything there, roll the casualty on to his or her side and clear the airway (see p. 16).
● Make sure that the head tilt and jaw support are adequate (see p. 17).
● Check the air seal; can you hear any air escaping from the mouth or nostrils as you blow. If you can, block the nostrils again and open your mouth wider to cover the casualty's mouth.
● Make sure you are blowing hard enough. Blow a little harder if necessary.

Distended stomach
If Expired Air Resuscitation is performed without a clear airway or if you blow too hard into the casualty's mouth, air will be forced into the casualty's stomach. If this occurs, the abdomen will swell and there will be no air escaping from the mouth and nose when you stop blowing. If distension appears, check the airway but DO NOT APPLY PRESSURE TO THE STOMACH because this may cause regurgitation.

Regurgitation and vomiting
If regurgitation or vomiting occur, turn the casualty on to his or her side and clear the airway (see p. 16). Then continue resuscitation as before, ensuring that head tilt and jaw support are adequate and that you do not blow too hard.

Clenched jaws
If the jaws are clenched, do not try to prise the mouth open. Peel the lips apart and blow through or around the teeth. Alternatively, use the mouth-to-nose method.

MOUTH-TO-NOSE METHOD

Follow the same sequence as for Mouth-to-mouth, opposite, but to obtain a seal, open the airway using the pistol grip and backward tilt (see p. 17), and push the lower lip up against the upper lip with your thumb. During inflation place your mouth over the casualty's nose so that it covers the bridge of the nose but take care not to compress the soft part of the nostrils. During exhalation peel down the casualty's lower lip to expose the teeth — it is not necessary to open the casualty's mouth.

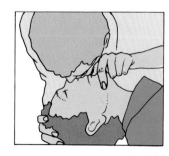

MOUTH-TO-MOUTH METHOD

1 With casualty on his back on a firm surface, open the airway using the "Pistol grip" and the backward tilt (see p. 17). Open your mouth wide, take a deep breath and seal the casualty's nose to prevent air escaping by placing your cheek against the nostrils as you place your mouth over the casualty's mouth. Alternatively you can seal the nose by pinching the casualty's nostrils. This method is not as satisfactory because some head tilt may be lost.

2 Looking along the casualty's chest, blow into the casualty's lungs until you can see the chest rise.

Do Not over-inflate because excessive pressure will force air into the casualty's stomach and this may cause regurgitation.

3 Remove your mouth from the casualty's and, leaving the casualty's mouth open for exhalation, turn your head so that your ear is about 25mm from the casualty's mouth and you are looking along the *lower chest and abdomen*. Look, listen and feel for air escaping from the mouth and nose. At the same time ensure that the casualty's stomach is not distended with air.

4 Give five full breaths as quickly as possible, these should take about 10 seconds.

5 Check the casualty's carotid pulse (see p. 23) to make sure that the heart is still beating. If it is present, continue E.A.R. at a rate of 15 breaths per minute or one breath every four seconds until breathing returns.

If there is only one First Aider, check the pulse again for five seconds after one minute and at least every two minutes thereafter. If the pulse disappears, CPR must be commenced immediately (see p.26).

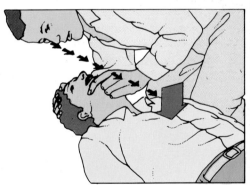

If there are two First Aiders, it is not necessary to interrupt lung inflations because the second First Aider can continue to monitor the pulse at least every two minutes (see p. 23).

NB If there are two First Aiders you should change over every few minutes to avoid fatigue. Remember that the airway must be kept open during the change over.

E.A.R. for a Laryngectomy

A laryngectomee is a person who has had his or her voice-box (larynx) removed as part of the treatment for cancer; he or she will be left with an opening (stoma) in the front of the neck, through which breathing takes place either totally, or in some cases, partially.

Where there is no connection between the lungs and the nose or mouth the person is a total neck breather; when there is a connection between the windpipe (trachea) and the back of the mouth, the person is a partial neck breather because some breathing takes place through the mouth and nose.

Many laryngectomees wear a cravat,

scarf or choker around their neck to hide the stoma, so if a casualty collapses and is wearing one of these, remove it quickly to check. If the stoma is not revealed immediately, it will become obvious when the head is tilted.

If you find a casualty in this condition follow the normal procedure for any casualty who collapses according to the Basic Life Support Flow Chart (see p. 15), but if E.A.R. is required direct Mouth-to-Stoma Resuscitation will be necessary. When breathing returns, turn the casualty over into the Lateral Recovery Position and ensure that the stoma remains clear.

Total neck breather

Breathing through stoma

Surgical tie-off

Air flow to lungs
(plastic or metal
tube may be present)

Partial neck breather

Breathing through mouth,
nose and stoma

Windpipe (trachea)
Air flow to lungs
(plastic or metal
tube may be present)
Gullet
Lungs

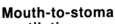

Mouth-to-stoma ventilation

1 If the casualty is not breathing turn him on to his back, kneel beside him and support the head in a backward tilt, place your mouth over the stoma and blow until the chest rises. Lift your mouth away, turn your head towards the casualty's chest and hold your ear 25mm away from the stoma and listen and feel for air escaping from the stoma.

If the chest fails to rise when you breathe into the stoma, and air escapes from the mouth and nose, it is likely that the casualty is a partial neck breather. Place the palm of your hand over the casualty's mouth and nose, seal the nostrils between your index and middle fingers and use your thumb to press the chin upwards and backwards.

Resuscitation for Infants and Children

Children need to be handled very gently at all times. Follow the procedure set out for adults in the Basic Life Support Flow Chart (see p. 15). Check response by using "Shake and Shout". Older children should be treated in the same way as adults. Children and infants under 8 years old should be treated as described below.

AIRWAY

If unconscious, turn the child over on to his or her side and quickly clear the mouth and nostrils of foreign matter. However, to secure an open airway in babies and young children under one year old, DO NOT use the head tilt.

The upper airway in babies and very young children is easily obstructed because: the tongue is large; the neck is short; the windpipe is very soft and easily compressed by over-enthusiastic head tilt; and the adenoids can be large and may block the air passages in the nose.

BREATHING

Expired air resuscitation should be given at a normal rate of 20 breaths per minute to young children 1–8 years old but great care should be taken not to over-inflate – give small puffs with sufficient force to make the chest rise. With babies and small children under one year old, use the mouth-to-mouth-and-nose method and give breaths at a rate of 20 puffs per minute or one breath every three seconds.

CIRCULATION

Check the carotid pulse as for adults after the first five breaths, again after one minute and then at least every two minutes thereafter (see p. 23). If it is absent begin Cardio-pulmonary Resuscitation as described on p. 26. When breathing commences turn the casualty into the Lateral Recovery Position (see p. 22).

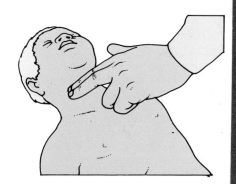

The Lateral Recovery Position

If the casualty is unconscious but breathing, or when a casualty begins to breathe again, after E.A.R., he or she must be rolled over on to his or her side with the head tilted backwards, the jaw supported and the face pointed slightly downwards. This position is known as the Lateral Recovery Position.

The advantages of this position are that:
● It provides a good, safe airway; the tongue will fall forward away from the back wall of the mouth.
● Vomit or other foreign material will drain out of the mouth or into the lower cheek allowing easy removal.
● It is easy to observe the casualty's airway, breathing and circulation.
● The casualty is completely stable.
● The casualty can be turned on to his or her right or left side.
● The casualty can be turned on to his or her back quickly and easily if resuscitation is required.

Here we describe how to turn a casualty or to the left side; reverse instructions to turn the casualty on to the right side.

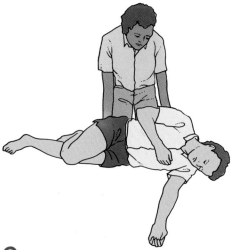

1 Kneel beside the casualty's right side, level with the waist. Place the left arm out at right angles to the trunk and place the right arm across the chest with fingers pointing to the left shoulder. Lift the right knee so that the thigh is at right angles to the trunk and the foot is still in contact with the ground.

2 With your left hand under the casualty's right shoulder and your right hand under the right hip, roll the casualty away from you on to his left side.

MODIFICATIONS

If there are obvious fractures of the upper or lower limbs, it may not be possible to stabilise the casualty using bent limbs as props. In such cases, the Lateral Recovery Position can be maintained by placing a rolled blanket or similar bulky material along the body. If necessary, place bulky padding between the upper arm or leg and the ground to stabilise the casualty without placing undue pressure on the limb.

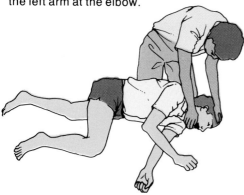

3 Lift the casualty's right leg to keep the thigh at a right angle to the trunk and the knee joint at a right angle (this prevents the casualty rolling on to his face), and fold the casualty's right arm across the left arm at the elbow.

4 Put the casualty's head in a backward tilt with the face slightly downward to ensure that vomit or foreign material will drain from the mouth, and support the jaw.

5 Keep checking the casualty's condition, making sure that the airway remains open and that breathing and circulation are maintained.

6 Keep the casualty's temperature as close to normal as possible. Most unconscious casualties are already cold and will lose body heat quickly if not covered. Avoid covering the casualty with anything that makes it difficult to observe airway breathing and circulation.

Checking Circulation

The carotid arteries are the major blood vessels in the neck. There is one on each side of the windpipe and they carry blood to the brain. If a pulse can be felt in the carotid arteries, it confirms that the heart is beating. The carotid pulse is felt because they are large arteries and usually easily accessible.

Check the carotid pulse after the first five breaths of E.A.R. while the head is still tilted. Slide your middle and index fingers from the casualty's adam's apple, over into the groove between the windpipe and large muscle of the neck. Always feel for the pulse with pads of your fingers not your fingertips or thumb; do not press firmly; and feel for about five seconds.

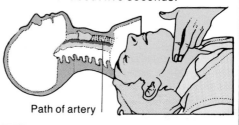

Path of artery

IF THE PULSE IS PRESENT

If the casualty's heart is beating but he or she is still not breathing, continue E.A.R. at the normal rate. Check the carotid pulse again after one minute and thereafter every two minutes.

IF THE PULSE IS ABSENT

If the casualty has no carotid pulse, commence Cardio-pulmonary Resuscitation (C.P.R.), a combination of E.A.R. and External Cardiac compression (E.C.C.), because the casualty has suffered Cardiac Arrest. However, the following criteria must *all* apply before E.C.C. is commenced. The casualty must be: unconscious; not breathing even after the airway has been cleared; and have no carotid pulse.

External Cardiac Compression

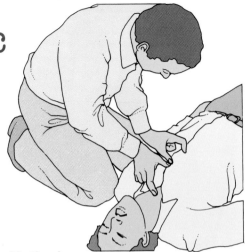

When the heart stops, circulation of the blood stops (see p. 12). However, it is possible for the First Aider to provide an artificial blood circulation by exerting rhythmic pressure at regular intervals over the breastbone (sternum) to compress the heart between the breastbone and the spinal column. The rhythmic pressure is known as External Cardiac Compression (E.C.C.).

Correctly performed, External Cardiac Compression provides enough movement of blood to sustain life and prevent brain damage. External Cardiac Compression may restart the normal action of the heart, but even if the heart does not restart spontaneously, E.C.C. may keep the heart and brain alive so that advanced life-support techniques may successfully restart the heart later. However, inefficient technique is less likely to be successful.

It is also important to note that External Cardiac Compression by itself does not result in any oxygenation of the lungs and therefore the blood. It is only one part of the technique of Cardio-pulmonary Resuscitation (see p. 26) which involves artificial inflation of the lungs together with compression of the heart, in order to provide oxygenated blood to keep the brain alive.

It is essential for adults, children and infants that you determine the correct compression site for each individual casualty as described right and opposite. For children and infants we have taken 1–8 years and under one year as a guide-line for the different hand and pressure positions. However, because children of the same age vary in size, these specifications should be used only as a guide-line. **NB** *Never practise E.C.C. on a living person.*

Method

1 Turn the casualty on to the back on a firm surface and kneel right up against him or her. Locate the correct compression point by identifying:
● The lower end of the breastbone: working from the outside inwards, locate the lowest rib on each side and run your fingers along it until they meet in the middle. Leave your index finger on this point.
● The upper end of the breastbone: feel for the groove between the collar-bones and place your other index finger on this point.
● The midpoint of the breastbone: extend the thumbs of each hand equal distances and continue until they meet in the middle.

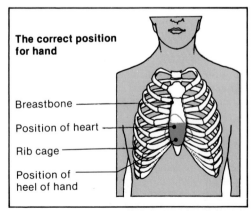

The correct position for hand

Breastbone —

Position of heart —

Rib cage —

Position of heel of hand —

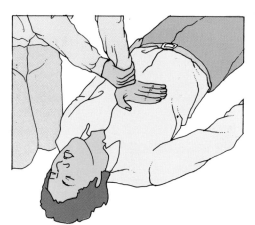

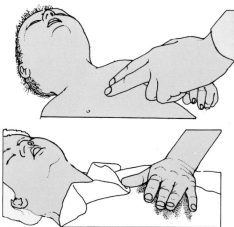

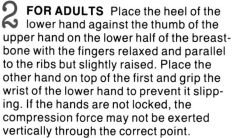

2 **FOR ADULTS** Place the heel of the lower hand against the thumb of the upper hand on the lower half of the breastbone with the fingers relaxed and parallel to the ribs but slightly raised. Place the other hand on top of the first and grip the wrist of the lower hand to prevent it slipping. If the hands are not locked, the compression force may not be exerted vertically through the correct point.

3 Kneel with one knee against the casualty's chest and the lower knee slightly back so that your shoulder is directly over the breastbone. Use your body weight as the compression force, exerting pressure through the heel of the lower hand. The compressions must be rhythmic with the compression and relaxation phases of equal duration – avoid rocking movements, thumps or jabs. For adults give 60 compressions per minute at the rate of 80 per minute. For children or infants give 90 compressions at the rate of 100 per minute. (For synchronisation of inflations and compressions see overleaf.)

NB The soft pliable chest wall of a child means that less pressure must be used when giving E.C.C.

FOR INFANTS AND CHILDREN UNDER 8
Place the hand directly below the midpoint of the breastbone. For children aged 1–8 years use one hand only to exert pressure. For infants and babies under one year you must only use two fingers to exert pressure.

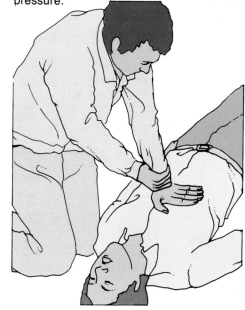

DEPTH OF COMPRESSION

Casualty	Compression Site	How	Depth
Adult	Lower half of sternum	2 hands	40–50mm (1½–2in)
Child 1 – 8	Middle of sternum	1 hand	25mm (1in)
Infant under 1	Middle of sternum	2 fingers	15mm (½in)

Cardio-Pulmonary Resuscitation

If the casualty is not breathing and there is no pulse present, you will have to give Cardio-Pulmonary Resuscitation. This is a combination of Expired Air Resuscitation and External Cardiac Compression given at specific ratios. The ratio of inflations to compressions will depend on whether there are one or two First Aiders.

ONE FIRST AIDER

For adults the sequence must be 15 compressions followed by two inflations in 15 seconds, and there should be four complete cycles per minute.
For babies and children under 8, the sequence should be 15 compressions followed by two inflations in 10 seconds and there should be six complete cycles per minute.

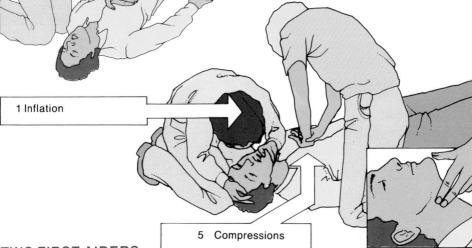

15 Compressions

2 Inflations

1 Inflation

5 Compressions

TWO FIRST AIDERS

The sequence for adults when two First Aiders are working together should be five compressions to one inflation in five seconds and 12 complete cycles should be given per minute. For infants and children the cycle must be five compressions to one inflation in three seconds and 20 cycles should be completed per minute. There should be no pause in E.C.C. to give E.A.R. — the inflation must be interposed between the last compression of one cycle and the first compression of the next.

The most experienced First Aider should begin performing E.A.R. because it is important to maintain a clear airway and interpose the lung inflations correctly.

To make sure you get no break in the sequence the First Aider performing the E.C.C. should call from 1–5 as he or she gives the compressions so that the other person can interpose the inflations. Perfect synchronisation requires practice.

RECOVERY CHECKS

The casualty's pulse should be checked after a minute and then at least every two minutes thereafter. The First Aider performing External Cardiac Compression should cease compression for 5 seconds while the pulse is checked. If the pulse has returned, watch for the return of breathing and turn the casualty in to the Lateral Recovery Position immediately.

When the casualty regains consciousness, check the state of consciousness every two minutes (see p. 95). Watch carefully for any change in the condition. If the casualty has regained consciousness and later becomes quiet or unconscious, check the airway, breathing and circulation and begin treatment following the Basic Life Support Flow Chart (see p. 15).

CHANGE-OVER TECHNIQUES

These must be as smooth as possible with minimum interference. If you are by yourself and a second First Aider arrives, you should continue compressions and indicate when you are ready to change over to the Two First Aider method. When you are ready, observe the following:

1 Check for effective compression: the second First Aider should feel the carotid pulse.

2 If there is no pulse with compression he or she should advise the other First Aider that more effective compression is needed.

3 If there is a pulse with compression ask the first person to stop compressions and check the pulse for 5 seconds.

4 If spontaneous pulse is present, the second First Aider should give a full inflation and the first person should monitor the radial pulse at the wrist. If this cannot be felt, the carotid pulse must be checked again at least every two minutes.

5 If there is no pulse, the second First Aider should give one inflation and the first person should change to giving the casualty 60 compressions per minute without a pause and continue as opposite.

CHANGING OVER WITH THE TWO FIRST AIDER METHOD

If the First Aider performing E.C.C. is exhausted you should change duties with minimal interference to resuscitation. The First Aider performing cardiac compression should indicate readiness to change, the other First Aider should complete the next breath of E.A.R. and move to the casualty's side ready to take over the third and subsequent compressions. Both First Aiders should then continue the cycle calling each compression in the normal way.

Summary

In any situation when a person collapses it is important that you care for the Airway, Breathing and Circulation using the techniques described in this section following the order laid out in the Basic Life Support Flow Chart (see p. 15). Remember: don't stand by and let a person die and don't give up too soon.

The need for training and retraining
Proficiency in some resuscitation techniques such as feeling the pulse, finding the correct hand positions and use of the Lateral Recovery Position can be achieved by practising on colleagues. However, you must never practise C.P.R. on a living person: chest inflations and heart compressions must be practised on approved training manikins.

Supervision by trained instructors is essential and regular training is needed.

BLOOD AND THE CIRCULATION

There are approximately 6 litres (10 pints) of blood in the normal adult's circulatory system. Blood carries oxygen and other nutrients to the tissues, and carbon dioxide and other waste products away from them. It flows through a network of flexible tubes called blood vessels.

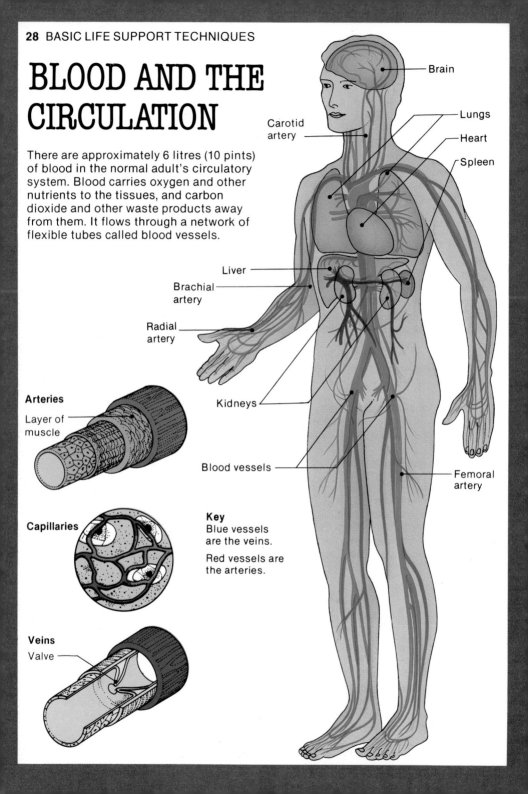

Brain

Carotid artery

Lungs

Heart

Spleen

Liver

Brachial artery

Radial artery

Kidneys

Blood vessels

Femoral artery

Arteries

Layer of muscle

Capillaries

Key
Blue vessels are the veins.

Red vessels are the arteries.

Veins

Valve

Arteries carry blood away from the heart. They are the strongest of the blood vessels and their walls contain elastic and muscular tissue. As the blood is forced along the arteries by the action of the heart, the muscular wall expands and then returns to its normal size. This wave of pressure is called the *pulse* and it can be felt wherever an artery is close to the surface and can be pressed against a bone, at the neck or wrist, for example (see p. 85). Arteries divide becoming smaller and thinner as they reach the tissues until they become capillaries.

Capillaries are very small blood vessels, consisting only of a thin layer of cells through which the exchange of fluids and gases to and from the tissue cells of the body can be made. Having done this, the tiny capillaries gradually join up and become veins.

Veins carry blood back to the heart. Smaller veins unite, gradually becoming larger until they end in two large veins which return the blood to the right collecting chamber of the heart. Veins have no muscular layer, and they rely on "back" pressure and the squeezing action of the body muscles to make blood flow through them. Because of this, veins in the lower part of the body have one-way "cup-like" valves which help to control the flow of blood back to the heart.

Severe Bleeding

When you cut yourself you bleed because pressure inside the blood vessels forces blood out. In arterial bleeding, bright red-coloured blood pumps out in time with the heart; in venous bleeding, the blood is a darker red and gushes out with less pressure; in capillary bleeding, blood oozes out.

The body contains certain inbuilt mechanisms to slow down or stop bleeding spontaneously. When a wound occurs

the cut ends of a blood vessel contract to reduce the loss of blood and blood pressure falls. Blood clots form and plug up damaged vessels. The more slowly blood flows from a wound, the easier it is for a clot to form; the faster blood flows, the more likely it is that any clots will be washed away.

The Dangers of Blood Loss

Normally the loss of 500ml (one pint) of blood in an adult is barely noticeable (e.g., blood donor), but by the time that 1½ litres (3 pints or about a third of the blood volume) is lost, the results can be serious because there is not enough blood left to provide sufficient flow around the body. If you do not act quickly to stop severe bleeding, there is a danger that shock, and even loss of life may result.

The symptoms and signs of severe blood loss are due partly to the blood loss itself, and partly to the body's reaction to that loss; they may not all be apparent in every casualty. The face and lips become pale and the skin feels cold and clammy as the vessels which supply blood to the skin constrict in order to divert blood to the vital organs. To compensate for the blood loss, the pulse becomes faster, but weaker. If bleeding is prolonged, there may be a reduction in the flow of blood to the brain, resulting in blurring of vision, giddiness, clouding of consciousness and fainting. In addition, the casualty may become anxious, restless and talkative for the same reason. (see also *Shock*, p. 86).

Blood loss can also cause a feeling of thirst resulting from the body's natural urge to replace lost fluid, and a hunger for air to replace lost oxygen.

You should act quickly to stop any bleeding but, urgently if:
● A large amount of blood is being lost.
● The bleeding appears to be arterial — bright red and spurting regularly.
● The bleeding has continued for an abnormally long time.

Controlling Blood Loss

Blood loss is controlled in three ways: by pressure, elevation and rest. There are two kinds of pressure: direct pressure over the wound and indirect pressure on the artery which supplies the area.

Direct pressure must always be used first; indirect pressure must only be used if direct pressure fails and as a last resort.

Direct Pressure

In order to stop bleeding without interfering with the rest of circulation, you should apply pressure directly on a wound immediately. This pressure compresses the blood vessels in the area and helps to slow down the flow of blood so that a clot can form. Pressure has to be maintained for five to 15 minutes because it takes time to halt the flow of blood. If there is a foreign body embedded in the wound, pressure has to be applied alongside it (see p. 62).

If the wound is on a limb, you should also raise the injured part above the level of the casualty's heart and support it in this position. This will slow down the flow of blood by lowering the local blood pressure.

Method

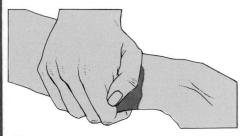

1 Apply direct pressure on the wound with thumb and/or fingers.

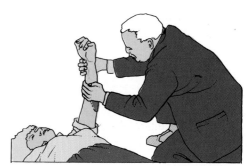

2 Help the casualty to lie down in a comfortable position. If possible raise the injured part above the level of the heart. Keep the injured part, and the casualty, at rest.

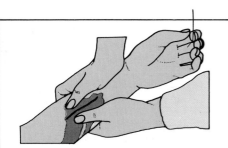

If the wound is large, squeeze the sides of the wound together gently but firmly and maintain pressure.

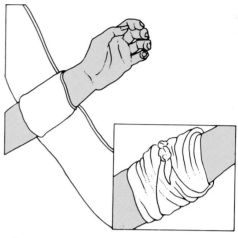

3 Place a sterile or clean bulky unmedicated dressing over the wound
making sure that it extends well beyond
the edges of the wound.

If no suitable dressing is available, an
improvised dressing can be made
from any suitable clean material which can
be used as a bulky pad (see p. 175).

4 Hold the dressing in place securely
with a bandage tied firmly enough to
control bleeding but not so tight as to cut
off circulation (see p. 178). Use a folded
triangular bandage and tie the knot over
the pad. Immobilise the injured part (see
Fractures, pp. 104–125).

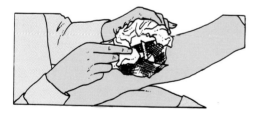

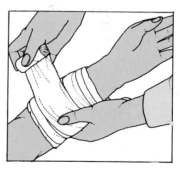

If a foreign body is present, build up
dressings and padding around the
wound until they are high enough to
prevent pressure on the object (see p. 62).
Secure the dressings with a diagonally-
applied bandage (see p. 187).

If you are using a roller bandage
secure ends as described on p. 186.

5 If bleeding continues, reassess the
method of application of the dressing.
If it is not applied correctly, the pad may
need to be either relocated or replaced
until the bleeding stops.

Uncontrolled Bleeding

If bleeding cannot be controlled by direct pressure or if it is impossible to apply direct pressure successfully (e.g., after a shark attack or extensive power boat injuries), as a *last resort* you may need to use indirect pressure. This is applied by tying a roller bandage around a limb to compress an artery against an underlying bone. This is known as an arterial tourniquet. However, since an arterial tourniquet cuts off the blood supply to the tissues of the entire limb, an arterial tourniquet MUST ONLY BE USED AS A LAST RESORT.

There are two main pressure points used to control severe bleeding, one is on the *brachial* artery in the arm, and the other is on the *femoral* artery in the thigh.

The brachial artery runs along the inner side of the upper arm between the muscles and its course roughly follows the seam of the sleeve. To apply pressure, pass your fingers under the casualty's arm and slide them between the muscles. Press upwards and inwards pushing the artery against the bone.

The femoral artery passes into the lower limb at a point corresponding to the centre of the fold of the groin and runs along the inside of the thigh. To apply pressure, lay the casualty down with knee bent. Locate the artery in the groin and press it against the rim of the pelvis with your fist or the heel of your hand.

Method

1 Tie a broad (5–7 cm) soft roller bandage or strip of material, clothing or a wide belt, firmly around the upper arm or leg as appropriate, avoiding the elbow or knee joints – the arterial pulse below the bandage should disappear completely.

If bleeding appears to increase rather than decrease, remove the arterial tourniquet and reapply because it has been applied incorrectly.

If the casualty complains of severe pain in the area, the tourniquet may be too narrow or too tight and will be damaging the tissues so it should be re-applied.

ARTERIAL TOURNIQUET APPLIED AT 4.30pm

2 Once the tourniquet is applied correctly do not release it. Record the time of application and mark this clearly on the casualty. Transfer the casualty to hospital promptly to avoid serious tissue damage.

Do Not cover the bandage with any clothing or covers.

NB Inform the ambulance officer, nurse or doctor that a tourniquet has been applied.

ACTION AT AN EMERGENCY

The basic principles of First Aid apply to all injuries or illnesses regardless of severity. Whatever the incident, it is the First Aider's responsibility to act quickly, calmly and correctly in order to preserve life, prevent deterioration in the casualty's condition and promote recovery. These objectives are best achieved by:

● A rapid but calm approach.

● A quick assessment of the situation and the casualty.
● A correct assessment of the condition based on the history of the incident, symptoms and signs.
● Immediate and appropriate treatment of any injury or condition.
● Appropriate referral of the casualty according to the injury or condition.

APPROACH

This should be speedy but calm and controlled. Ensure that you are not placing yourself in any danger when approaching the casualty. On arriving at the scene of any incident, introduce yourself and offer to help. If there is no ambulance officer, nurse, doctor or more experienced person present, take charge.

ASSESSING THE SITUATION

Immediately assess the situation and decide on the priorities of action. The conditions which affect these priorities are as follows: Safety, Getting others to help, Determining the Priorities and Calling for Assistance.

Safety

Minimise the risk of danger to yourself, the casualty and any bystanders, and guard against any further casualties arising in the case of:

● **Road Accidents** Request a bystander to control the traffic, keeping it well away from yourself and the casualty. Watch out for fire risks, especially from petrol spillage and switch off the ignition of the vehicles concerned. (See *Procedure at Major Incidents* p. 168).

● **Gas and poisonous fumes** If possible, cut off the source (see p. 48).

● **Electrical contact** Break the contact, if possible, and take the necessary precautions against further contact. Avoid any contact with fallen power lines (see p. 55).

● **Fire and collapsing buildings** Move the casualty to safety (see p. 49).

Getting Others to Help You

Some bystanders can be extremely useful and may be able to assist with treatment, for example, controlling severe bleeding or supporting a badly injured limb. Other bystanders may become nuisances so you must keep them occupied to prevent them interfering with your work. They can be asked to control traffic or crowds, or be sent to telephone for assistance (see p. 35). However, when sending bystanders to the telephone make sure that they understand the message that is to be sent. If possible, ask them to write it down but, in any case, ask them to repeat the message to you before actually sending it. Always make sure that they report back to you afterwards.

Determining the Priorities

In order to determine the condition of a casualty, perform the following checks.

Response
Check response to "Shake and shout". Place an unconscious casualty on his or her side promptly (see p. 16).

Airway and breathing
Quickly check that the airway is clear and open and that the casualty is breathing. If not, commence E.A.R. (see p. 18).

Circulation
Check the carotid pulse. If absent, commence C.P.R. (see p. 26).

Bleeding
Check the casualty for any severe bleeding and control it promptly (see p. 30–32).

Unconsciousness
An unconscious casualty who is breathing should be left in the Lateral Recovery Position (see p. 22). Keep a constant check on

the airway, breathing and circulation.

Shock

Keep the casualty warm, quiet and lying down until skilled help arrives (see p. 86).

Other needs

Unless there is immediate danger to life from the surroundings, treat serious injuries before moving a casualty. If you suspect spinal injury and the casualty is *conscious*, do not move him or her.

An unconscious casualty with suspected spine injury should be turned into the Lateral Recovery Position promptly to protect the airway. Where possible use one or more bystanders to help keep the casualty's spine straight (see p. 114).

Calling for Assistance

Once you decide that assistance is required from ambulance, police or fire brigade, gas or electricity authorities, send for it immediately. Go to the nearest telephone, or send a bystander, and in a metropolitan area dial 000, but in a country area, use listed emergency number. When the operator answers state the service required.

Whoever makes the call should ensure that the following information is passed on.

1 Your telephone number (if for any reason you are cut off the officer will then be able to contact you).

2 The exact location of the incident; if you can, point out nearby road junctions or other landmarks.

3 An indication of the type and seriousness of the incident, for example, "Road traffic accident, two cars involved, three people trapped".

4 The number, sex and approximate age of the casualties involved and, if possible, the nature of their injuries.

5 Request special aid if you suspect a heart attack, if the power lines are down or if a victim is trapped.

NB Each control officer has access to the other emergency switchboards and will pass on any messages.

Do Not replace the receiver before the control officer does so.

Multiple Casualties and Injuries

Where there is more than one casualty, you must decide by rapid assessment which one should receive priority of treatment. Any unconscious casualty should be placed in the Lateral Recovery Position immediately. Care for A.B.C. following the Basic Life Support Flow Chart (see p. 15). Temporary control of bleeding should be achieved with the assistance of the casualty or a bystander. Always remember that the noisiest casualty is rarely the most severely injured.

It should also be remembered that in First Aid common sense is almost as important as the actual knowledge of the subject. In real life serious accidents rarely produce only one injury. Frequently two or more injuries occur so that the correct treatment of one may interfere with the correct treatment of the other. You must decide which injury is the more serious, treat that one in the correct way, then deal with the second injury as correctly as possible under the circumstances.

Examination

Having dealt with the priorities (see p. 34), you should then attempt a fuller examination. This takes account of the casualty's *history* (and that of the incident), the *symptoms, signs* and *levels of responsiveness*.

HISTORY

This is the full story of how the incident occurred or the illness began, and should be taken directly from the casualty and a responsible bystander wherever possible. For example, a casualty may only say "I slipped and fell down" whereas a witness may say "I saw the old man fall and his head hit the wall". Pay full attention to the story which may provide clues to the likely injuries and especially if you suspect an existing illness such as diabetes or heart disease. Make a note of details of past similar occurrences and treatments for the examining doctor's benefit later.

Never hurry the casualty and remember to pass on all the information when skilled help arrives.

SYMPTOMS

These are sensations that the casualty feels and describes to you.

If the casualty is *conscious*, ask if there is any pain and, if so, where. Examine that part first, then run through the various sites at which pain is felt. Remember, however, that a severe pain in one area may mask a more serious injury, which produces less pain, in another. Other useful symptoms the casualty may disclose are nausea, giddiness, feelings of heat and cold, or loss of muscular control or sensation. All symptoms should then be investigated and confirmed by a physical examination.

If the casualty is *unconscious*, or unreliable because dazed or in shock, then treatment cannot be based on symptoms but has to be based on information from bystanders and signs.

SIGNS

These are details ascertained by you using your senses — sight, touch, hearing and smell. These may be: signs of injury such as bleeding, swelling, deformity or signs of illness such as a raised temperature and/or a rapid or an irregular pulse.

All these signs may be immediately obvious, noticed incidentally or deliberately discovered by *examination*.

Examination of a Conscious Casualty

A general examination should be carried out quickly to identify any imminent threats to life. Move the casualty as little as possible. Remember to look, feel, listen and smell; always compare both sides of the body.

If at any stage during the examination the casualty loses consciousness, turn him or her on the side promptly and care for airway, breathing and circulation following the Basic Life Support Flow Chart (see p. 15).

HEAD

Mouth Re-check *breathing*, noting the rate, depth, and nature (whether easy or difficult, noisy or quiet); note also any odour. Examine the *lips* for any signs of burning or discolouration that might indicate oxygen lack (see p. 12). Check the *teeth* for any damage or bleeding from the gums (see p. 72), and make sure that any teeth recently dislodged have not fallen down into the back of the throat. Make sure that dentures are firm fitting (essential for resuscitation); if they are not they should be removed.

Nose Check for signs of blood, clear fluid or a mixture of both which might come from inside the skull.

Eyes Examine both together to compare the pupils (the black circular centres) and note whether they are equal in size. The white globe of the eye should be examined for bloodshot appearance.

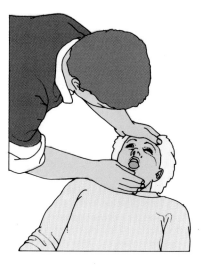

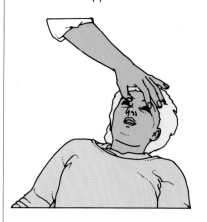

Pin-pointed pupils

Dilated pupils

Different sized pupils (possible compression)

Face Look at the *colour*, it may be pale or flushed, or even bluish if breathing is affected. At the same time, feel the *temperature* of the face to check whether it is particularly hot or cold and note the state of the *skin* – whether it is dry or clammy or even sweating profusely.

Ears These should be checked for foreign bodies and traces of blood and/or clear cerebro-spinal fluid that might indicate skull fracture. Speak into the casualty's ears to test hearing.

Skull Gently run your hands over the scalp searching for bleeding, swelling or indentation that might indicate a fracture.

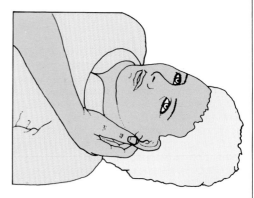

NECK AND SPINE

Injury to the spinal cord is relatively easy to assess in a conscious casualty. It is necessary to ask the casualty to move her toes, knees and hips in that order. In the upper region, ask the casualty to move her fingers, wrists and elbows in that order.

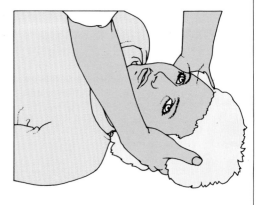

To assess whether normal sensation is present, progressively check response to touch from below upwards. The casualty may be unaware of any paralysis or loss of sensation immediately following injury. Sometimes a casualty may complain of pain or altered sensation. If the examination suggests that a spinal injury may be present, treat as for spine fracture (see p. 114) and avoid any further movement until the arrival of medical aid.

If there is no evidence of any spinal injury, examine the hollows under the shoulders and back for dampness or any abnormality. Take care to avoid accidental injury from sharp objects under the casualty's trunk or in pockets.

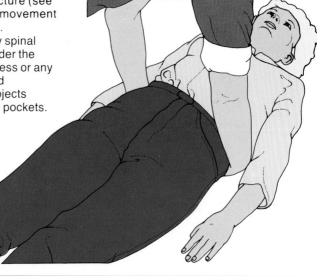

TRUNK

Gently check the chest for evenness of rib movement on breathing and examine for any wounds that might be "sucking" air. Check the *ribs* for irregularity or depression that might indicate a fracture and also feel along the line of the *breastbone*.

Check both *collar-bones* for irregularity and the *shoulders* for signs of deformity. Carefully feel either side of the *pelvis* looking for signs of fracture and note any indication of *incontinence*.

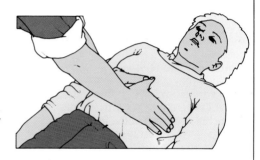

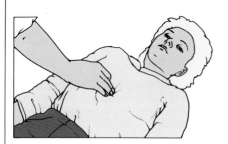

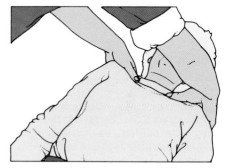

ARMS

The *upper-arm bones*, then the bones in the *forearm*, *wrists*, *hands* and *fingers* should be thoroughly examined. Check carefully for any deformity and swelling which might indicate fractures. The forearms should be checked to see if a casualty is wearing a medical warning bracelet and for injection marks.

LEGS

Check the *hips*, *thighs*, *knee-caps*, both bones of the *lower legs*, the *ankles*, *feet*, and *toes* in the same way as the arms. **NB** Use two hands so that both sides of the body can be examined and compared at the same time.

NB In an unconscious casualty the care of airway, breathing and circulation always takes precedence over the assessment of the levels of responsiveness or the treatment of specific injuries.

Levels of Responsiveness

There are various stages through which a casualty may pass during progression from consciousness to unconsciousness. These are dealt with in detail on p. 95, but basically, if the casualty responds well to stimuli then unconsciousness is only light (as in a faint, for example). But if the level of responsiveness is low or totally absent then the casualty should be turned into the Lateral Recovery Position promptly (see p. 22). Every 10 minutes you should re-check and note the casualty's response to the stimuli of *noise* (speak loudly into the ear), *touch* (try to arouse by shaking the shoulders gently). In addition, a similar check should be kept on the casualty's breathing (see p. 14), pulse (see p. 85) and skin temperature, and the findings should be recorded.

Aids to Assessment

Your assessment is based on information from various sources. By taking the history of the incident, asking the casualty for symptoms and examining the casualty for signs, it should be possible to make an accurate diagnosis. The following chart is a summary of how to achieve this.

HISTORY obtained from surroundings, casualty and bystanders

SYMPTOMS
These are the sensations experienced by the casualty obtained by asking tactful questions.

Pain
Tenderness
Loss of normal movement
Loss of sensation
Cold
Heat
Thirst
Nausea
Weakness
Dizziness
Faintness
Temporary loss of
    consciousness
Loss of memory

SIGNS
Noted by the First Aider's senses

Sight	**Touch**	**Smell**	**Hearing**
Respiration	Dampness	Breath	Breathing
Bleeding	(bleeding,	Burning	Groans
(type and	inconti-	Gas	
volume)	nence)	Alcohol	
Wounds	Temperature		
Foreign	Pulse		
bodies	Swelling		
Colour	Deformity		
Swelling	Irregularity		
Deformity	Tenderness		
Bruising			
Responses			
to touch			
and sound			
Incontinence			
Vomit			
Containers			
e.g., bowls,			
tablets,			
volatile			
fluids, etc.			

External Clues

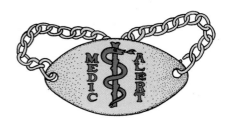

If a casualty is unconscious, the *pockets*, *handbag* or *briefcase*, may have to be checked for possible clues. These may be *appointment cards* for hospital/clinic or *information cards* that might show that the casualty is on steroids or insulin or is liable to epileptic fits. Any lumps of sugar or glucose present might indicate that the casualty is a diabetic. If possible, check this in the presence of a witness.

There are a number of *medical warning items* which can be worn by persons with

a medical condition. They may take the form of an inscribed medallion or bracelet (e.g., "Medic-alert"), or a locket for wrist or neck containing a strip of paper describing the condition (e.g., "S.O.S. Talisman" or "Identicare").

General Management

You should carry out the appropriate treatment for each condition found, gently and quickly. It is most important that you reassure and encourage the casualty constantly. Work calmly and efficiently, pay attention to any remarks or requests that the casualty makes and do not pester with questions. This is annoying for the casualty and is a sign of nervousness on your part. After giving the necessary treatment, place the casualty in the appropriate position and keep a watchful eye until help arrives.

Bear in mind your aim is to preserve life, prevent the condition worsening and promote recovery.

To prevent the condition worsening:
● Dress wounds.
● Immobilise any large wounds and fractures.
● Place the casualty in the most comfortable position consistent with the requirements of treatment.

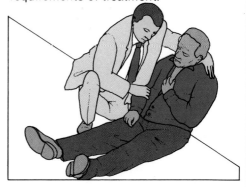

To preserve life:
● Maintain an open airway by positioning the casualty correctly.
● Begin resuscitation if necessary and continue until skilled medical aid is available.
● Control bleeding promptly.

To promote recovery:
● Relieve the casualty of anxiety and encourage confidence.
● Attempt to relieve the casualty of pain and discomfort.
● Handle the casualty gently.
● Protect the casualty from extremes of temperature such as heat or cold, wind and/or rain.

Follow-up Care

After you have carried out your treatment the casualty should normally receive attention from a qualified person (doctor or nurse) without undue delay. Depending on the severity of the condition and the availability of skilled help you should:

1 Arrange transport to hospital by ambulance, or by car for minor injuries.

2 Hand over the casualty to the care of an ambulance officer, nurse or doctor, when available.

3 Take the casualty to a nearby house or shelter to await the arrival of the ambulance or doctor.

4 Allow the casualty to go home and advise to seek medical advice, if necessary.

NB Never *send anyone home* who has been unconscious, even for a short time, or who is in shock; seek medical aid.

REPORTING ON THE CASUALTY

The casualty should always be accompanied by a brief written report when he or she leaves your care. If necessary, you should accompany the casualty yourself and make a personal report.

The need to supply complete information cannot be emphasised enough, and it should include the following:
- History of the accident or illness.
- Brief description of injury.
- The level of responsiveness and any changes.
- Any other associated injuries.
- The pulse and any changes.
- The skin colour and any changes.
- Blood loss sustained.

- Any unusual behaviour by the casualty.
- Any treatment given and when.

Property
Take care of any property belonging to the casualty and hand it over to the police or ambulance personnel.

DEALING WITH CLOTHES AND HELMETS

Sometimes it is necessary to remove clothing in order to expose injuries, make an accurate assessment or conduct a proper treatment. This should be done with the minimum of disturbance to the casualty and clothing and only remove as much as is actually necessary. Clothing should not be damaged unnecessarily. If very tight clothing has to be cut, do this along the seams, if it is possible.

If you need to remove the casualty's clothing ensure that sufficient privacy is maintained.

Removing Protective Helmets

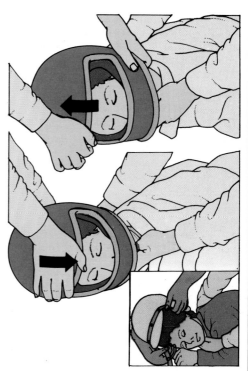

Whether or not you remove a protective helmet, such as a motor-cycle crash-helmet, depends on the situation and condition of the casualty. It is best left on and should only be removed if the casualty's condition warrants it. If possible, the helmet should be removed by the casualty. A full-face helmet that encloses the head and face should *only* be removed if the casualty is unconscious, vomiting or has severe head injuries. In most cases however, the removal of a helmet will depend entirely on the injuries and your ability to remove it.

To remove a helmet that covers the head only, unfasten or cut through the chinstrap, if necessary. Take pressure off the head by forcing the sides apart, then lift the helmet upwards and backwards.

A full-face helmet needs two persons to remove it safely, one to support the casualty's head and neck, while the other lifts the helmet. First, tilt the helmet back and lift until it is clear of the chin; second, tilt it forward to pass over the base of the skull, then lift it straight off.

Removing Clothing

REMOVING A COAT OR JACKET

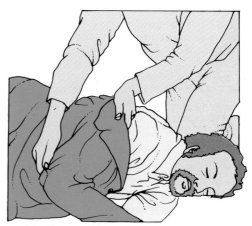

1 Raise the casualty and slip the garment over the shoulders. Bend the arm on the sound side and remove the coat from that side first. Then, slip the injured arm out of its sleeve, keeping the arm straight if possible.

2 If necessary, slit up the seam on the injured side.

REMOVING A SHIRT

Remove as for a coat. If necessary, slit it down the front or side.

REMOVING TROUSERS

1 Pull them down from the waist to reveal the thigh or raise the trouser leg to expose a calf or knee injury.

2 If necessary, slit up the inside seam.

REMOVING BOOTS OR SHOES

1 Support the ankle, undo or cut any laces and carefully remove the shoe.

2 If the casualty is wearing long boots that will not unfasten, carefully slit them down the back seam with a knife.

REMOVING SOCKS

1 If these are difficult to remove, insert your first two fingers between the sock and the leg.

2 Raise the sock and cut it between your fingers.

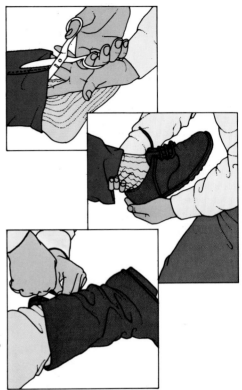

SUMMARY

- Ensure that there is no further danger to the casualty or yourself.
- Act quickly, quietly and methodically, giving priority to the urgent conditions.
- If unconscious, turn casualty on his or her side promptly and care for airway, breathing and circulation following the Basic Life Support Flow Chart (see p. 15).
- Control bleeding promptly.
- Determine the level of responsiveness.
- Reassure the casualty and bystanders to lessen anxiety.
- Minimise shock.
- Position the casualty correctly and comfortably but do not move more than is absolutely necessary.

- Consider the possibility of internal bleeding and poisoning.
- Treat large wounds and fractures before moving the casualty.
- If necessary, arrange for transfer of the casualty to a hospital or to the care of a doctor.
- Watch and record any changes.
- Do not attempt too much.
- Do not allow people to crowd round; this hinders First Aid and may cause the casualty anxiety or embarrassment.
- Do not remove clothing unnecessarily.
- Do not give anything by mouth to a casualty who is unconscious, who has a suspected internal injury or who may shortly need an anaesthetic.

EMERGENCIES WHICH CAUSE LACK OF OXYGEN

All body tissues and organs require an adequate supply of oxygen (see p. 11). If this supply is interrupted even for a short time, there is a risk of death or serious brain damage. Interruption of the oxygen supply to the tissues can occur for several reasons.

● *When there is insufficient oxygen in the air being breathed*. For example: in gas- or smoke-filled buildings, tunnels or mine shafts (see p. 48–9); at high altitudes, in depressurised aircraft; or when deep-sea diving.

● *When the breathing control centre in the brain is depressed by*: head injury (see p. 98); drug overdose (see p. 152); disease; or oxygen lack (see p. 12).

● *If the muscles involved in breathing are weak or paralysed, or breathing is impaired as a result of*: injury to the spinal cord (see p. 112); electric shock (see p. 54); compression of the chest wall, as in falls of earth or sand (see p. 46); inter-ference with the stability of the rib-cage, as in stove-in-chest (see p. 117).

● *If the airway is blocked or not open.* Airway obstruction can be due to: the tongue, food, vomit or other foreign material (see p. 15); suffocation by pillows or plastic bags (see p. 46); compression of the windpipe as in strangulation (see p. 47); swelling of the throat after a bee sting (see p. 156).

● *When there is compression of the lung by blood or air* (see pp. 76–8 and 116–7).

● *When there is blood or fluid in the air sacs* preventing the passage of oxygen into the blood (see p. 50).

● *Following some cases of poisoning* when the oxygen available cannot be taken up by the blood cells, or cannot be used efficiently by the tissue cells such as following carbon monoxide poisoning (see p. 48) and cyanide poisoning (see p. 153).

General Symptoms and Signs

The symptoms and signs of oxygen lack and the rapidity of onset will depend on whether the interruption of oxygen is complete (e.g., suffocation by a plastic bag), or partial (e.g., a slow leak of exhaust fumes or gas). It will also depend on whether the process is an acute episode (e.g., strangulation), or a chronic condition (e.g., people living at high altitudes whose blood cells adapt to the lowered oxygen content in the air).

The symptoms and signs may include:

● Alteration in the state of consciousness with lack of concentration, restlessness, confusion and later, unconsciousness.

● Signs of airway obstruction (see p. 16).

● Cessation of breathing.

● Blueness (cyanosis).

NB The only reliable places to look for cyanosis are the tongue and the inside of the mouth which are at the body temperature (see p. 12).

Aim

To maintain or restore the oxygen supply to the brain and the heart as well as ensur-ing safety for yourself and the casualty.

General treatment

1 Remove the casualty from the cause (e.g., from a gas-filled room) or remove the cause from the casualty (e.g., cut through a rope around the casualty's neck).

2 Overcome any airway obstruction by turning the casualty on to his or her side and care for the airway, breathing and circulation according to the Basic Life Support Flow Chart (see p. 15).

3 Manage specific problems as appro-priate.

Suffocation

Suffocation is when air is prevented from reaching the air passages by an external obstruction. Accidental suffocation may result when: a small child's head is covered with a plastic bag; an infant lies face down on a pillow; a child is locked in a refrigerator; or a casualty is covered by a fall of sand or earth.

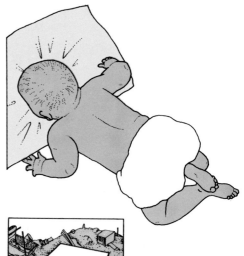

Symptoms and Signs
● General symptoms and signs of oxygen lack.
● Obvious air-tight seal over the mouth and nose or presence of "stale" air in a confined space.

Aim
Restore supply of air to the casualty. Resuscitate, if necessary and seek medical aid.

A baby may be suffocated through lying face-down on a pillow. However, being locked in an abandoned refrigerator can also result in suffocation

Treatment

1 Immediately remove any obstruction or remove the casualty to fresh air.

2 If the casualty is conscious and breathing normally, reassure and observe.

3 If the casualty is unconscious, turn him into the Lateral Recovery Position and care for the airway, breathing and circulation according to the Basic Life Support Flow Chart (see p. 15).

4 Seek medical aid. If in doubt about the casualty's condition, arrange transfer to hospital by ambulance.

Hanging, Strangulation and Throttling

Pressure on the outside of the neck by hanging, strangling or throttling, squeezes the airway shut and blocks off the flow of air to the lungs.

Strangulation involves accidental or deliberate compression of the windpipe; *hanging* involves accidental or deliberate suspension of the body by the neck from a noose; and *throttling* involves the intentional loss of air supply by squeezing a person's throat.

Aim

Remove the cause of the constriction immediately even if there are no signs of life and, if necessary, commence resuscitation. Arrange transfer to hospital.

NB Seek medical aid even if recovery seems complete.

Treatment

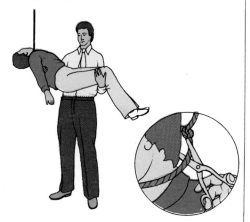

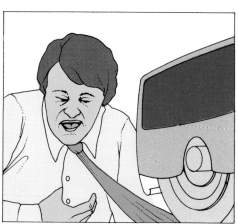

Symptoms and Signs
● General symptoms and signs of oxygen lack.
● Congestion of the face and neck with the veins becoming prominent.
● Constriction may be visible around the neck (e.g., scarf or wire).
● There may be marks round the throat or neck where a constriction has been removed.
● Body may still be suspended.

1 Remove any constriction from around the casualty's neck and face immediately. If the casualty is hanging, support the body while the noose is cut.

2 If the casualty is unconscious, turn him into the Lateral Recovery Position and care for the airway, breathing and circulation according to the Basic Life Support Flow Chart (see p. 15).

3 Arrange ambulance transport to hospital immediately.

Inhalation of Fumes

Whenever oxygen in the air is used up by fire (e.g., smoke inhalation), or displaced by non-toxic gases (e.g., butane), the oxygen level in the air will be dangerously low. Also there are many poisonous substances, gases and vapours which may cause severe oxygen lack when inhaled. Apart from the acute oxygen lack, there may also be other side-effects.

SMOKE INHALATION

Smoke may cause spasm in the air passages, making breathing difficult. During smoke inhalation, the casualty may suffer burns not only to the skin but also in the actual air passages. Also modern furniture often contains synthetic materials which, when burning, may give off highly toxic fumes.

CARBON MONOXIDE

Carbon monoxide is a colourless, odourless gas which reduces the oxygen carrying power of the blood; and, because of this a casualty may require prolonged resuscitation even when he or she is removed from the contaminated environment. If staff and facilities are available, oxygen treatment should be commenced as soon as possible.

Casualties who have inhaled carbon monoxide do not show the classical "bright pink" colour until the blood level of carbon monoxide is very high; they may be pale. Now that household gas supplies have been converted from coal gas to natural gas, the most common source of carbon-monoxide poisoning is fumes from engine exhausts in a confined space.

SOLVENTS

Commercial solvents, paint removers, adhesives, lacquers, paint thinners, nail-polish removers and dry-cleaning fluids, all produce vapours which have been used as a stimulant. Death can occur from oxygen lack if a plastic bag is put over the head to enhance the concentration of the substance inhaled, or from an acute toxic effect on the heart, which causes cardiac arrest (see p. 23).

Inhalation of solvents should be suspected if a group of children are behaving as if they are drunk.

Symptoms and signs

● Symptoms and signs of oxygen lack (see p. 45).
● Casualty may be burned or scorched.
● Symptoms and signs of shock (see p. 86).
● Casualty may be confused and uncooperative.
Carbon-monoxide poisoning
● Skin colour may be normal at first but deepen to cherry pink.
Solvent inhalation
● Spots around the mouth and nose, together with unexplained listlessness, loss of appetite and moodiness.

Aim

Call the appropriate emergency service immediately. Only attempt to remove the casualty from fire and smoke if you can be sure that there are no toxic fumes present. Try to extinguish any fire and, once the casualty is clear, resuscitate if necessary. Obtain medical aid.

Treatment

1 Call the appropriate emergency service, for example, ambulance or fire brigade etc.

2 Enter the area to remove the casualty only if you can be sure that you are in no danger. If the casualty is trapped in a garage with a car engine running remove the danger by opening garage doors.

3 Rig up a life-line with a bystander and work out a system of signals so that you can be pulled to safety if necessary. The best method is to tie a rope around your waist and keep tension on the rope. If the tension is released, the back-up person will know that you need to be pulled out.

4 Feel the temperature of the door with the back of your hand and check the temperature of the air coming from under the door. *If either is hot do not enter.*

NB Keep one foot near the door so that you can close it quickly if necessary.

5 If it is safe to enter the room, take several deep breaths so that your blood is fully oxygenated. Then, with your shoulder at right angles to the door, open the door slightly averting your face as you do so. The room may be filled with "super-heated" air under pressure which could explode.

NB In smoke-filled rooms, tying a wet handkerchief across the mouth will not protect you against toxic fumes from upholstery or vinyl coverings.

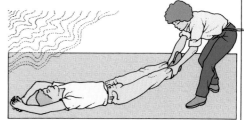

6 If the smoke is dense, keep your face close to the floor where there should be some clean air, and find the casualty. Turn the casualty so that his arms are extended above his head and drag him free (see p. 193).

7 Extinguish any clothing that is on fire or smouldering (see p. 134).

8 If unconscious, turn the casualty on his side and treat following the Basic Life Support Flow Chart (see p. 15).

9 Treat any burns (see Burns and Scalds, pp. 135–137).

10 Arrange transfer to hospital.

Drowning

The most important single consequence of drowning is interruption of the oxygen supply to the brain. The availability of early rescue and resuscitation are major factors in survival.

Vomiting and regurgitation frequently occur following immersion and because of the risk of inhalation, the casualty should be placed on his or her side for initial assessment. Turn the casualty on to the side again immediately if vomiting occurs during resuscitation.

Most immersion victims are cold and the carotid pulse may be difficult to feel, especially if the pulse rate is slow. So, during resuscitation it is important to protect the casualty from any further fall in body temperature.

Many immersion victims deteriorate after an apparently successful rescue, with loss of consciousness, cessation of breathing and circulation. Therefore, continuous observation is essential. Because lung complications may also occur, all immersion victims should be warned that if they develop a cough, breathlessness or fever, they should seek medical advice promptly. **NB** Hospital admission is necessary for any casualty who has been unconscious, even for a short while, and any casualty who has required resuscitation.

Aim

To get air into the casualty's lungs as quickly as possible. Arrange transfer to hospital.

Treatment

1 Commence Expired Air Resuscitation (see p. 18) as soon as possible. This will depend on your safety and that of the casualty. The Mouth-to-Nose method should be used when E.A.R. is carried out in the water.

NB Even for experienced swimmers, resuscitation in *deep water* requires training, and the use of a flotation device.

2 Once the casualty is brought to the shore, place him on the side to clear the upper airway of foreign material and check breathing. If the casualty is breathing, leave him in the Lateral Recovery Position (see p. 22).

3 If the casualty is not breathing, turn him on to the back and begin the appropriate treatment according to the Basic Life Support Flow Chart (see p. 15).

Do Not attempt to remove fluid from the lungs or apply pressure to relieve distension of the stomach during resuscitation.

If vomiting or regurgitation occurs during resuscitation, turn the casualty on to his side and clear the airway before you recommence resuscitation.

4 If the casualty is conscious, keep him warm with a blanket or similar covering, and observe for at least 15 minutes. The casualty may be discharged if he remains fully conscious and alert; has no cough; has a normal pulse, breathing rate and colour; is not shivering; and has been advised to seek medical advice promptly if a cough, fever or breathlessness develops.

5 Arrange transfer to hospital if necessary.

Choking

This normally occurs when the airway is partially or totally obstructed by a foreign object, or when something goes down the windpipe instead of the gullet (see p. 11).

Adults may choke on pieces of food which have been inadequately chewed and hurriedly swallowed; the frail, elderly person is at risk because the reflexes can be weakened by age or disease; the alcoholic, or a person affected by alcohol, may choke because of poor co-ordination and reduced protective reflexes (see p. 11). Young children are at risk because they like putting small objects into their mouths, and peanuts are a particular hazard to children less than 6 years old. All children should be discouraged from running about or laughing and giggling when they have food in their mouth.

It is important to relieve any obstruction as soon as possible. However, if the casualty is still able to breathe, speak, cry or cough, he or she is not in any immediate danger and should be encouraged to cough freely to expel the obstruction and, at this stage, active first aid can be harmful. If the casualty is wheezing or breathing noisily, it indicates that a small foreign body has been inhaled and is causing partial blockage of an air passage. In such cases, back slaps may lead to total airway obstruction.

If the casualty is unable to breathe, speak, cry or cough, prompt first aid is essential. If the casualty becomes unconscious, care of airway and breathing following the Basic Life Support Flow Chart (see p. 15) will be needed. Expired Air Resuscitation may be used to try to blow air past the obstruction and into the lungs. In fact, in an unconscious casualty, the initial airway spasm may relax enough to allow some air past the obstruction. If efforts to inflate the lungs with Expired Air Resuscitation fail, a combination of Expired Air Resuscitation, back blows and Lateral Chest Thrusts may have to be used. In the majority of cases, a combination of the steps on the following pages will be enough to overcome the obstruction.

Symptoms and signs

● General symptoms and signs of oxygen lack (see pages 12 and 45).
● Casualty is unable to breathe, speak, cry or cough, and may be gripping his or her throat.
● Congestion of the face and neck with prominent veins.
● Collapse and unconsciousness.

Normal passage of food

Food inhaled down windpipe

Aim

Try to relieve the obstruction. If unsuccessful, clear the airway and begin Expired Air Resuscitation. Arrange urgent medical aid.

Treatment

1 Encourage the casualty to keep coughing to expel the obstruction. Reassure the casualty frequently, but avoid the temptation to use back slaps.

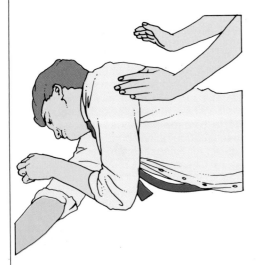

If the casualty is an infant or child, sit or kneel down with him face downwards across your lap with the head low and administer two back slaps in the same way.

2 If the casualty is unable to breathe, speak, cry or cough, and is turning blue as he makes frantic efforts to breathe, quickly place the casualty on the floor on the side. Give two back blows between the shoulder blades using the heel of your hand.

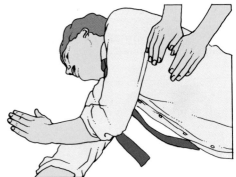

3 If the casualty is still conscious and making frantic efforts to breathe, give two Lateral Chest Thrusts; these increase the pressure of air in the chest and help expel the obstruction. With the casualty lying on the side, place the palm of one hand against the lower fold of the armpit. Place the other hand beside it and give two quick, downward thrusts in an attempt to dislodge the obstruction.

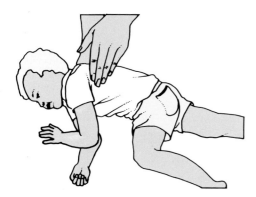

If the casualty is an infant or child, place your hands on either side of the rib-cage against the fold of the armpits. Give two quick squeezing thrusts from each side simultaneously.

NB In either case, avoid applying any pressure below the rib-cage or over the abdomen because this can cause serious internal injuries.

4 If the casualty becomes unconscious, turn him on the side promptly and clear the airway. Check the mouth and throat for any visible foreign body which can be removed with your fingers (see p. 16). Maintain head tilt and jaw support with the face pointing slightly downwards and check breathing. In particular, listen for any wheezing and look for signs of laboured breathing. This may indicate that an obstruction is still present.

5 If the casualty is breathing watch him closely and leave in the Lateral Recovery Position until he regains full consciousness and tries to sit up.

6 If the casualty is not breathing, turn him onto the back and begin E.A.R. (see p. 18). If an obstruction is present, you will be aware that there is resistance to inflation and the chest will not rise. Ensure that the head is correctly positioned with head tilt and jaw support to avoid tongue obstruction. Continue Expired Air Resuscitation to try and blow air past the obstruction and overcome any spasm in the airway. When successful, you will be aware of the lack of resistance and the casualty's chest will be seen to rise. If this occurs, continue to give care of airway and breathing following the Basic Life Support Flow Chart (see p. 15) until the casualty regains full consciousness.

7 If efforts to inflate the lungs with Expired Air Resuscitation are unsuccessful, roll the casualty on his side again and give two back blows and two Lateral Chest Thrusts as above. Continue vigorous efforts to relieve the obstruction by alternating E.A.R. with back blows and Lateral Chest Thrusts.

8 When the obstruction has been overcome and the casualty is breathing normally again, arrange transfer to hospital for a medical check.

NB Sometimes the foreign object will be blown down into the lung with Expired Air Resuscitation and medical treatment will be needed to remove it and prevent later complications.

Electrical Injuries

The passage of electrical current through the body may result in cessation of breathing and/or heartbeat, and burns. The current can come from a high or low voltage supply or from lightning. The electric shock can cause a quivering of the heart muscle (fibrillation) which causes the circulation to fail, or it may cause the heart to stop completely (cardiac arrest), which will also result in cessation of breathing. However, the First Aider has no way of telling whether the heart has stopped completely or is in fibrillation, because the carotid pulse will be absent in both conditions. Therefore resuscitation should always be begun promptly according to the Basic Life Support Flow Chart (see p. 15).

The casualty may also have severe burns where the electricity enters the body as well as where it leaves the body to "earth". The higher the voltage which passes through the body, the more extensive the burns.

Low-voltage appliances and cables in workshops, homes, offices and shops can cause electrical injuries. Most appliances and cables are insulated by non-conducting materials such as plastic or rubber to provide protection from the current. Many injuries result from faulty switches, frayed cables or defects within the appliances themselves. Young children are at risk because they may try to play with switches, wires and plugs.

Water is an excellent conductor of electricity so that handling an otherwise safe appliance with wet hands or when standing on a wet floor, increases the risk of electrical injury.

Lightning is a natural source of electricity which occurs during a thunderstorm. It seeks contact with the ground through the nearest tall feature in the landscape. A person may be hit if in contact with, or standing near, isolated features such as trees, towers or pylons or simply by being the tallest feature in a flat area.

The current produced by lightning is of extremely short duration but, whilst it may only stun the casualty, it can also cause instant death; clothing may be set on fire. A casualty should always be removed from a dangerous area as soon as possible.

Aim

Break the current or remove the casualty from the source if it is safe to do so. Arrange transfer to hospital.

Treatment

1 If the casualty is unconscious, turn him or her on to the side and give care for the airway, breathing and circulation following the Basic Life Support Flow Chart (see p. 15).

2 If the casualty is conscious, treat any burns (see pp. 135 – 7). Examine them carefully; they may be deeper than they appear at first.

3 To minimise shock, treat as on p. 86.

4 Transfer to hospital in all cases where a casualty required resuscitation, was unconscious, sustained burns or developed any of the symptoms and signs of shock.

NB Pass on any information you have about duration of electrical contact.

INJURIES FROM A LOW-VOLTAGE CURRENT

Break the contact by switching off the current at the mains or meter if it can be quickly reached; if not, switch off at the power point and remove the plug or wrench the cable free.

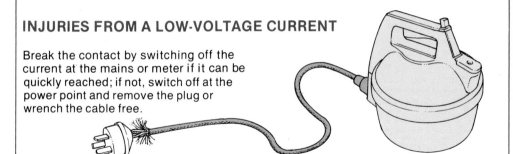

INJURIES FROM HIGH-VOLTAGE ELECTRICITY

Contact with high-voltage currents found in power lines and overhead cables is usually immediately fatal. Severe burns always result and the force of sudden muscular spasm caused by the electricity may throw the casualty some distance from the point of contact.

If a casualty remains in contact with, or is still within 6m (20 ft) of a high-voltage current, never attempt to rescue or even approach until the power has been cut off by the authorities. This is because the electricity may "arc" and jump considerable distances. Insulating material (e.g., dry wood or clothing) will *not* protect you.

If overhead cables have been brought down and are in contact with a car, the driver should be advised to stay inside the car until the electricity supply authorities make the area safe. Remain at a safe distance of at least 6 metres and shout re-assurance to the casualty. Any attempt at rescue could be fatal for both the casualty and First Aider.

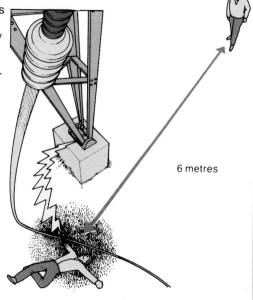

6 metres

NB Whatever the cause of the electrical injury, *never* touch the casualty with bare hands until you are sure that there is no further danger to yourself and that the casualty is no longer in contact with the source. In the case of injury from high-voltage electricity do not approach the casualty until you are informed by the police or similar authority that it is safe to do so.

Asthma

Asthma is a distressing condition in which the muscles in the air passages go into spasm with swelling of the mucous membrane lining. There are excessive secretions of mucus and the airway becomes constricted making breathing, particularly breathing out, very difficult. Asthma attacks can be triggered off by upper respiratory tract infection, allergy, exercise or nervous tension, or a change in the weather conditions, although in many cases there is no obvious cause. Sudden attacks of difficult breathing sometimes occur at night. Regular asthma sufferers usually carry their own medication in the form of an aerosol to ease breathing in which case they will generally know how to cope with an attack.

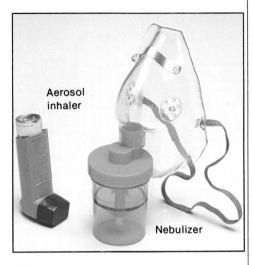

Aerosol inhaler

Nebulizer

Symptoms and Signs
- Wheezing.
- Difficulty in breathing and talking.
- Anxiety.
- Fatigue.

Aim
Reassure and calm the casualty. If possible, provide a source of fresh air and place casualty in a position which will ease breathing. Reduce airway obstruction with prescribed treatment. If the asthma attack persists or is severe, seek prompt medical advice.

Treatment

1 Reassure the casualty and stay calm.

2 Advise the casualty to sit down and lean forward resting on a support such as a table.

3 If the casualty has some prescribed medication, help him take it.
Always note the time at which medication was taken.

4 If the asthma attack persists, the casualty looks tired, or if you are in doubt about the severity of the condition, seek medical advice promptly — asthmatics can collapse suddenly.

NB Do not allow the casualty to exceed the prescribed dose of medication, or repeat the treatment in less than the recommended time.

Winding

A blow to the solar plexus (the upper part of the abdomen just below the rib-cage) can cause great difficulty in breathing for a short time.

Symptoms and Signs
- Difficulty in breathing-in.
- Casualty may be unable to speak.
- Casualty will be clutching the upper abdomen and is bent double.
- Possible nausea and vomiting.

Aim
Assist the casualty into a position where breathing is eased. Seek medical aid only if the casualty does not make a full recovery quite quickly.

Treatment

1 If the casualty is conscious help him to find the most comfortable and relaxed position for breathing.

2 If the casualty is unconscious, turn him on the side promptly and care for airway, breathing and circulation following the Basic Life Support Flow Chart (see p. 15).

Do Not massage the upper abdomen or pump the legs.

Hiccups

Repeated, noisy intakes of air, called "hiccups" are caused by involuntary contractions of the diaphragm. Hiccuping attacks generally do not last more than a few minutes and are usually only a minor irritation to the sufferer.

Aim
Break the sequence of these involuntary contractions and seek medical aid if attack is prolonged or severe.

Treatment

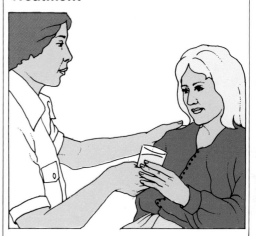

1 Ask the casualty to sit quietly and hold her breath. Give long drinks.

2 If hiccups persist for more than a few hours, seek medical advice.

WOUNDS AND BLEEDING

To operate efficiently the body has to have enough blood circulating at sufficient pressure to reach all the body's tissues all the time. Severe blood loss interferes with the circulation and this can damage the tissues, especially those of the major organs; this may result in the death of the casualty (see *Dangers of Blood Loss*, p. 29).

A wound is an abnormal break in the skin or other tissues which allows blood to escape. External wounds are complicated by the fact that germs (bacteria) can enter the tissues and cause infection.

Types of Wound

Wounds are classified as open or closed. Open wounds allow blood to escape from the body. There are several types: incised wounds, lacerated wounds, puncture wounds, grazes and gunshot wounds.

Closed wounds allow blood to escape from the circulatory system, but not the body. They may be seen as bruises or collections of blood under the skin or there may be no external evidence.

Incised Wound
A knife, razor or sharp edge of paper may cause an incised wound. This type of wound may bleed profusely.

Lacerated Wound
The skin may be torn irregularly by contact with barbed wire, machinery or the claws of an animal. These wounds are sometimes contaminated.

Puncture Wound
Nails, needles, garden forks, railings, even teeth, can cause wounds which may result in serious internal injury. If the wound is deep, the risk of infection is high because bacteria and dirt may have been carried into it.
NB Tetanus spores can multiply inside a deep puncture wound, leading to a severe illness, or even death (see p. 65).

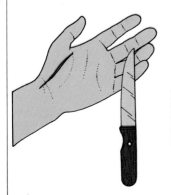

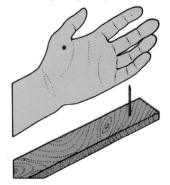

Graze (abrasion)
A graze normally results from a sliding fall. Superficial layers of skin are scraped off leaving a tender, raw area. These wounds often contain dirt or grit which has become embedded during the injury and may easily become infected.

Certain friction burns (see p. 132) where the skin has been broken are treated as grazes.

Firearm injury
Firearm injuries can result in serious internal injury. There will be a wound where a bullet enters the body and often a much larger exit wound. Internal organs, tissues and blood vessels may be damaged during the bullet's passage through the body. In addition to external bleeding, there may be internal bleeding.

Contused Wound
This can be caused by a fall or a blow with a blunt object which splits the skin and bruises the surrounding tissues. In a contused wound the risk of damage to underlying structures (e.g., fracture), should be considered.

With a bruise, damaged blood vessels leak blood into the tissues although the skin remains unbroken (see p. 83).

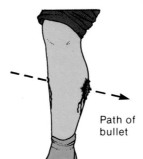

Path of bullet

Types of Bleeding

There are three different types of bleeding: arterial, venous and capillary. Each is named after the type of blood vessel damaged (see *Blood and the Circulation*, p. 28). Major arterial bleeding is the most serious and *must* always be treated first (see *Dangers of Blood Loss*, p. 29). Capillary bleeding is always present, however, in some wounds both arterial and venous bleeding will also be evident.

Arterial Bleeding
Blood carried in the arteries is normally fully oxygenated and is bright red. It has just come from the heart so it is under pressure and often spurts from a wound in time with the heartbeat.
NB Blood in the artery which takes blood from the heart to the lungs is not fully oxygenated.

Venous Bleeding
Normally darker red because it contains less oxygen, venous blood flows at a lower pressure than arterial blood and will not spurt. It may, however, gush profusely if a major vein is ruptured.

Capillary Bleeding
The capillaries contain both arterial and venous blood and capillary bleeding is the most common type. It is present in any wound and it may be the only type in minor wounds where blood oozes from the wound.

How the Body Responds to Injury

The natural response of the body is to restrict blood flow which minimises blood loss. Almost immediately, the ends of the damaged blood vessels contract to stem the leakage of blood. If bleeding is severe, the blood pressure drops so that less blood is pushed out. If the wound is large, the outer (peripheral) blood vessels which carry blood to the skin and muscles, constrict allowing the major blood vessels to carry sufficient blood to the vital organs.

When the blood leaves the damaged vessels it solidifies to form a clot. This clot plugs the blood vessels and seals the wound.

The body then begins to repair the damage. It brings a defence mechanism into play in order to combat local infection (see p. 64). The repair procedures will result initially in a swelling of the tissues.

Cross-section of Skin Showing Damaged Area

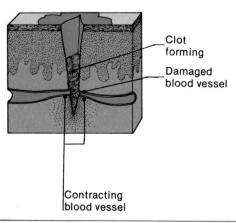

Clot forming

Damaged blood vessel

Contracting blood vessel

Major External Bleeding

This occurs most often after a deep incision or laceration in the skin. It is dramatic and may distract you from the priorities of treatment (see p. 34).

Always remember that if a casualty is unconscious, he or she should be turned on the side promptly for care of airway, breathing and circulation following the Basic Life Support Flow Chart (see p. 15). Otherwise, treat the casualty in the position which is most effective.

Major bleeding must be treated as soon as possible. In some cases you may find that it is only possible to reduce, not actually stop, the flow of blood but this may be enough to preserve life.

Follow the order of treatment laid out opposite. Apply direct pressure to a wound first and only if this is not possible or effective and you suspect arterial bleeding, apply indirect pressure (see p. 32). Finally, position the casualty to control blood flow.

Symptoms and Signs
● Evidence of major external blood loss.
● Symptoms and signs of shock:
Casualty complains of thirst.
Vision may be blurred and casualty feels faint and giddy.
Face and lips become pale.
Skin feels cold and clammy.
Pulse becomes faster but weaker.
Casualty becomes restless and talkative.
Breathing becomes shallower, sometimes accompanied by yawning and sighing (air hunger).
Possible unconsciousness.

Aim
Control bleeding as soon as possible. Keep the wound clean and dress it to minimise blood loss and prevent infection. Arrange urgent transfer to hospital.

Treatment

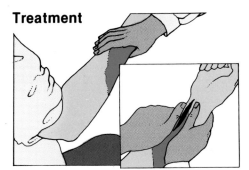

1 Expose the wound and check for the presence of foreign bodies (see p. 62). Apply direct pressure to control bleeding by pressing with fingers or palm of hand (see p. 30). If the wound is large, squeeze the edges together.

2 Assist the casualty to lie down. If the wound is on a limb and you do not suspect a fracture, raise and support it.

3 If the injury is on a limb and direct pressure is ineffective, apply indirect pressure to the main artery which supplies the limb (see p. 32).

4 Place a sterile bulky, unmedicated dressing over the wound, making sure that it extends well beyond the edges of the wound. Press it down firmly and secure with a bandage. Tie bandage firmly enough to control bleeding but not so tight as to cut off circulation (see p. 178). Immobilise the injured part (see *Fractures* pp. 104–125).

If no suitable dressing is available, place a thick bulky pad over the wound and bandage it firmly. An improvised dressing can be made from any suitable material (see p. 175).

If bleeding continues, check that the pad and bandage are correctly applied. Relocate or replace the dressing as necessary. Use direct pressure with hand or fingers if bleeding is severe.

5 To minimise shock, treat as p. 86.

6 Transfer to hospital immediately.

AMPUTATIONS

Recent advances in surgery have made it possible to rejoin amputated limbs, fingers and toes. The chances of a good result are greater when the casualty and severed part are transferred to hospital promptly. Always place the severed part in a suitable container to protect it, and ensure that the tissues are kept cool during transport. Inform the ambulance service of an amputation injury immediately so that the hospital can be warned.

Aim
Control bleeding and transfer casualty to hospital as soon as possible with the severed part.

Treatment
1 Control bleeding using direct pressure and elevation; take great care to avoid further damage to the tissues of the stump.

2 Place the severed part in a clean plastic bag to keep the tissues from drying out. Inflate the bag with air from your mouth and seal it. If possible, float the bag in a container of water with added ice cubes. Avoid direct contact with ice to prevent freezing the damaged tissues. Mark the package clearly with the casualty's name and the time the amputation occurred.

3 Transfer the casualty to hospital immediately, carrying the severed part discreetly.

NB An arterial tourniquet is generally unnecessary and may lessen the chances of successful reattachment.

Do Not apply excessive pressure to the stump or freeze the severed part.

FOREIGN BODIES

Small foreign bodies may be removed from the surface of a wound if they can be wiped off easily with a swab or rinsed off with cold water.

If the casualty has a large foreign body embedded in the skin, *never* attempt to remove it. It may be plugging the wound therefore restricting bleeding. Moreover, the surrounding tissues may be injured further if it is pulled out.

Treatment

1 To control bleeding, apply direct pressure by squeezing the edges of the wound together alongside the foreign body (see p. 30).

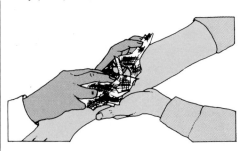

2 Gently place a piece of gauze around the foreign body.

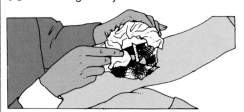

3 Build up dressings and padding around the wound until they are high enough to prevent pressure on the object.

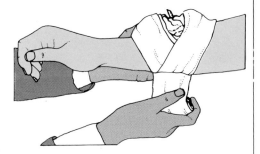

4 Secure with a diagonally applied bandage (see p. 187). Make sure bandage is not over the foreign body.

5 Elevate the injured part and immobilise as far as possible (see *Fractures*, pp. 104–125).

6 Transfer to hospital immediately.

If severe bleeding persists use indirect pressure (see p. 32).

If the casualty is impaled on railings or other spikes, do not attempt to lift the casualty off, but try to support the weight of the limbs and trunk. Call an ambulance immediately and state that cutting tools may be required (see Calling for Assistance, p. 35).

Minor External Bleeding

Many wounds are relatively trivial and involve only slight bleeding. Although blood may ooze from all parts of the wound, it will soon stop of its own accord. A small adhesive dressing is normally all that is necessary, and medical aid need only be sought if there is a serious risk of infection (see p. 64).

Symptoms and Signs
● Pain at the site of the wound.
● Steady trickle of mixed blood.

Aim
Clean and dress the wound as soon as possible to minimise infection.

Treatment

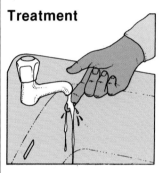

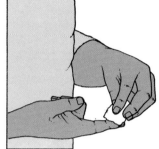

1 If possible wash your hands before dealing with the wound. Then, if the wound is dirty, lightly rinse it with running water, If available, until it is clean.

2 Temporarily protect the wound with a sterile swab. Carefully clean the surrounding skin with water and soap if available. Gently wipe away from the wound using each swab once only and taking care not to wipe off any blood clots. Dab gently to dry.

3 If bleeding persists apply direct pressure (see p. 30).

5 Raise and support the injured part unless you suspect an underlying fracture.

6 If in any doubt about the injury, seek medical aid.

If the wound is large, apply a sterile unmedicated dressing or gauze and clean pad and bandage firmly in position (see p. 61). Seek medical advice for all large wounds.

4 Dress a small wound with an adhesive dressing (see p. 173).

Infected Wounds

All open wounds will be contaminated by bacteria which either come from the cause of the injury, from the air or from the First Aider's breath or fingers. Some particles of dirt may be carried away from the damaged tissue by bleeding. Any harmful bacteria which remain are usually destroyed by the white cells in the blood and the wound then stays clean and healthy (see below).

Normal First Aid treatment for wounds includes prevention of infection. However, any wound which has not begun to heal properly after about 48 hours may be infected because either dirt, dead tissue, foreign bodies and/or bacteria may still be present. If infection develops, it can have serious consequences. It may enter the blood system and subsequently spread to other parts of the body perma-nently destroying tissue and occasionally leading to death.

Symptoms and Signs

- Increasing pain and soreness in the wound.
- Increased swelling and redness of the wound and surrounding parts with a feeling of heat.
- Pus may ooze from the wound.
- Fever, sweating, thirst, shivering and lethargy if the infection is severe.
- Swelling and tenderness in glands.
- Faint red trails (infected lymph vessels) may be seen on the surface of the inside of the arms or legs leading towards the lymph glands.

Aim

Seek medical advice as soon as possible.

The Lymphatic System

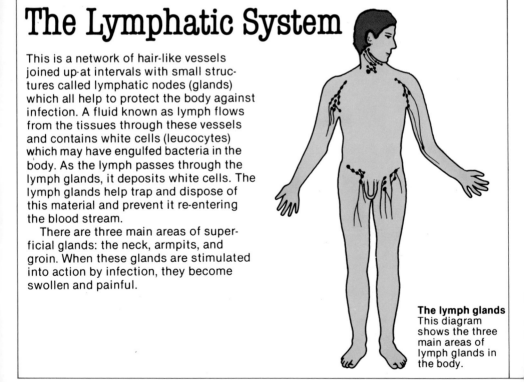

This is a network of hair-like vessels joined up at intervals with small structures called lymphatic nodes (glands) which all help to protect the body against infection. A fluid known as lymph flows from the tissues through these vessels and contains white cells (leucocytes) which may have engulfed bacteria in the body. As the lymph passes through the lymph glands, it deposits white cells. The lymph glands help trap and dispose of this material and prevent it re-entering the blood stream.

There are three main areas of superficial glands: the neck, armpits, and groin. When these glands are stimulated into action by infection, they become swollen and painful.

The lymph glands
This diagram shows the three main areas of lymph glands in the body.

Treatment

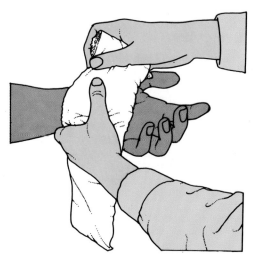

1 Dress wound with prepared sterile unmedicated dressing or similar clean, preferably sterile, material and secure with a bandage.

2 Elevate the injured part and immobilise especially if swollen.

3 Transfer to hospital.

TETANUS INFECTION (LOCKJAW)

This particularly dangerous infection results from a toxic substance produced by tetanus spores in a wound spreading into the body's nerves and causing severe muscular spasm, particularly in the jaw, hence the name "Lockjaw". It is a difficult condition to treat which, if it is not treated at an early stage, can lead to the death of a casualty.

Every wound carries the risk of infection. However, the risk of tetanus infection is greater in a dirty wound, especially wounds containing dead tissue; in a puncture wound, dog bite or crush injury; also in wounds where there is, or has been, a foreign body (e.g., treading on a rusty nail).

Everyone should be immunised against tetanus regularly and you should always ask a wounded casualty how recently an anti-tetanus injection was given. Any casualty who has never had an anti-tetanus injection or who has not kept the protection up to date, should be referred to medical aid.

Internal Bleeding

This may occur following an injury such as a fracture or crush injury or because of a medical condition such as a bleeding stomach ulcer. Internal organs, the spleen and liver for example, can be damaged by blows to the body although there may be no external evidence.

Internal bleeding is as serious as external bleeding. Although the blood is not actually lost from the body, it is lost from the circulatory system and the vital organs become starved of oxygen (see *Dangers of Blood Loss*, p. 29). Blood collecting internally may also cause problems if it presses on vital structures. For example, blood inside the skull can compress the brain causing loss of consciousness; bleeding inside the chest may prevent the lungs expanding.

Blood from internal injuries may collect in one of the body's cavities and remain concealed. Alternatively, it may be revealed by a flow of blood from one or more of the various openings (orifices) of the body such as the mouth or rectum (see chart overleaf) or by the appearance of discoloration and bruising.

Always suspect internal bleeding after a violent injury, if there are symptoms and signs of shock without any visible blood loss or if there is any "patterned" bruising corresponding to the seams and/or texture of the casualty's clothing.

Symptoms and Signs

These will vary according to the amount, the rate at which blood is lost and the site of bleeding.
● History of sufficient injury to cause internal bleeding.
● History of a medical condition which may cause internal bleeding (e.g., ulcer).
● Pain and tenderness around the affected area; swelling and tension may be felt.
● Symptoms and signs of shock (see p. 86).
Breathing becomes shallow, sometimes accompanied by yawning and sighing (air hunger).
Casualty becomes restless and talkative.
Casualty complains of thirst.
● Blood may appear from one of the body's orifices (see p. 68).

Aim

Arrange transfer to hospital.

Treatment

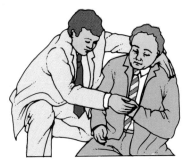

1 Place the casualty at rest lying down to ensure an adequate flow of blood to the brain. Advise the casualty to keep still.

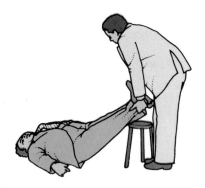

2 If the casualty's injuries allow, raise the legs to aid the return of blood flow to the vital organs.

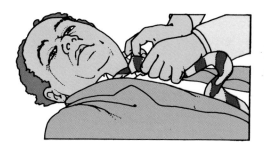

8 If the casualty becomes unconscious, turn him on to the side and give care of airway, breathing and circulation following the Basic Life Support Flow Chart (see p. 15).

3 Loosen any constricting clothing around the neck, chest and waist.

4 Reassure the casualty and explain the necessity to relax.

9 If breathing and heartbeat stop, begin resuscitation immediately. (see pp. 18 – 21).

10 Keep casualty covered and place a blanket underneath, if possible.

11 Arrange for transfer to hospital immediately; transport as a stretcher case, maintaining the treatment position.

5 To minimise shock, treat as on p. 86.

6 Check breathing rate (see p. 12), pulse (see p. 85) and levels of responsiveness (see p. 95) at frequent intervals. Record all observations and pass them on to the ambulance crew or doctor (see p. 42).

Do Not give the casualty anything by mouth. If medical care is likely to be delayed, moisten the casualty's lips at frequent intervals.

7 Examine the casualty for other injuries (see pp. 36 – 39) and treat as necessary.

Forms of revealed internal bleeding and their source

Orifice	How revealed	Description	Possible cause
Nose	Profuse flow	Fresh (bright red) blood	Damage to nasal passages and possible fractured nose.
	Trickle	Straw-coloured fluid (blood mixed with clear cerebro-spinal fluid).	Fractured skull
Ear	Steady bleeding	Fresh (bright-red) blood	Perforated eardrum
	Small trickle of blood	Straw-coloured fluid (blood mixed with clear cerebro-spinal fluid)	Fractured skull
Mouth	Spat out (sputum)	Small amounts of fresh blood	Jaw fracture
	Vomited	Dark-red-brown resembling coffee grounds	Injury to digestive tract, probably bleeding ulcer
	Coughed-up	Fresh (bright-red) blood	Upper airway injury
		Bright-red frothy blood	Injury to lungs caused by rib fracture
Rectum	Steady bleeding	Fresh (bright-red) blood	Piles (haemorrhoids)
	Stool (faeces)	Black tarry consistency	Bleeding from upper intestine
Urethra	Urine	Blood-stained	Bleeding from kidneys or bladder
		Clotted or diluted blood	Injury to urinary tract or bladder (possibly the result of fractured pelvis)
Vagina	Gradual steady bleeding	May be fair to heavy or moderate flow with abdominal cramps.	Severe menstrual bleeding
	Sudden flow	Severe loss, shock and possible history of pregnancy.	Miscarriage or result of abortion

Special Forms of Bleeding

There are a number of wounds and special forms of bleeding where the treatment does not follow the general rules of pressure and/or position of the injured part. Treatment for these wounds is described on the following pages.

Scalp Wounds

Injuries to the scalp most often occur during falls and are particularly common amongst the elderly, ill or intoxicated. Other causes include road traffic accidents, fights, sporting accidents, and falling debris.

Scalp wounds can bleed profusely due to the rich supply of blood to the scalp and because the skin covering the skull is normally tightly stretched. When damaged the skin splits open leaving a gaping wound. This bleeding may appear more alarming than it really is, but there may also be a skull fracture.

Symptoms and Signs
● Pain, tenderness and bleeding of the scalp. Possible lifted flap of scalp.
● Swelling around the wound.
● Possible symptoms and signs of skull fracture (see p. 109).
● Signs of brain damage may be evident (see *Concussion* and *Compression*, p. 98).
● Unconsciousness may develop.

Aim
Arrange transfer to hospital as *all* head injuries should be examined by a doctor. Control bleeding promptly.

Treatment

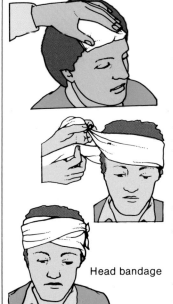

Head bandage

1 Control bleeding using gentle pressure (see p. 30). Place a dressing or pad of material over the wound and bandage lightly.

NB The triangular scalp bandage is not intended to apply direct pressure for control of bleeding − use a narrow fold cravat bandage.

If the wound is bleeding severely, apply direct pressure over the pad with your hand or fingers.

2 If the casualty is conscious, help him to lie down with the head and shoulders raised.

3 Check breathing rate (see p. 12), pulse (see p. 85), and levels of responsiveness (see p. 95) at frequent intervals.

4 If the casualty becomes unconscious, turn him on to the side promptly with the injured side *downwards* (see overleaf). Give care of airway, breathing and circulation following the Basic Life Support Flow Chart (see p. 15).

5 Arrange transfer to hospital; transport as a stretcher case maintaining the treatment position.

Bleeding from the Ear

Bleeding from inside the ear canal differs from that found in external ear wounds. It generally occurs when an eardrum ruptures or when a skull fracture is present (see p. 68). A perforated eardrum can result from pushing an object into the ear (see p. 161), falling while water-skiing, diving, or being too near an explosion.

Skull fractures are more serious and should be suspected if blood and/or a clear, watery fluid (cerebro-spinal fluid) is issuing from the ear.

Symptoms and signs

If from the eardrum
- Severe pain inside the ear.
- Deafness.
- Moderate flow of blood from the ear.

If from within the skull
- History indicating possible skull fracture (see p. 109) or other head injury (see p. 98).
- Casualty complains of a headache.
- Small amounts of blood mixed with clear, watery cerebro-spinal fluid may be coming from the ear.
- Possible unconsciousness.

Aim

Arrange transfer to hospital. If skull fracture is suspected pay particular attention to the levels of responsiveness (see p. 95).

Treatment

1 Help the casualty into the most comfortable position − generally sitting − and tilt the head towards the injured side so that blood and fluid can drain freely.

2 Cover the ear with a sterile, unmedicated dressing or similar clean, preferably sterile, material. Secure it very lightly with a bandage or adhesive strapping.

Do Not plug the ear or try to stop the flow from the ear; pressure may build up inside the middle ear.

3 Check breathing rate (see p. 12), pulse (see p. 85) and levels of responsiveness (see p. 95) at 10-minute intervals.

4 To minimise shock, treat as on p. 86.

5 If the casualty becomes unconscious, turn him on to the side immediately so that he is lying *on the injured side*. Give care of the airway, breathing and circulation according to the Basic Life Support Flow Chart (see p. 15).

6 Arrange urgent transfer to hospital, transport as a stretcher case maintaining the treatment position.

Nose-bleeds

This is a common condition usually due to bleeding from the blood vessels inside the nostrils. It may occur after a blow to the nose or be the result of sneezing, picking or blowing the nose. However, blood-stained fluid issuing from the nose may be a sign of a fractured skull (see p. 109).

Nose-bleeds can not only involve considerable loss of blood but may also cause the casualty to swallow or inhale a great deal of blood. This may cause vomiting or affect the airway and breathing.

Symptoms and Signs
● Moderate flow of blood from nose.
● If skull fracture is present there may be a mixture of blood and clear, watery cerebro-spinal fluid.

Aim
Safeguard the airway by preventing inhalation of blood and control bleeding.

Treatment

1 Sit the casualty down with the head well forward and loosen any tight clothing around the neck and chest.

2 Advise the casualty to breathe through the mouth and to pinch the soft part of the nose. (Be prepared to take over if it is tiring for the casualty.)

3 Tell the casualty to spit out any blood in the mouth; swallowed blood may cause nausea and vomiting.

4 Release the pressure after 10 minutes. If the bleeding has not stopped, continue treatment for a further 10 minutes, or as necessary.

Do Not let the casualty raise the head.

5 While the head is still forward, gently clean around the nose and mouth using a swab or clean dressing soaked in luke-warm water. Do not plug the nose.

6 When the bleeding stops tell the casualty to avoid exertion. Advise the casualty not to blow the nose for several hours to avoid disturbing the clot.

7 If after 30 minutes the bleeding persists or recurs seek medical aid.

Bleeding Gums/Displaced Teeth

Bleeding from a tooth socket can occur some time after a dental extraction, immediately after accidental loss of a tooth or be associated with jaw fracture (see p. 110). The tearing or knocking out of a tooth generally produces a lacerated mouth wound. If a tooth has been dislodged, seek dental aid promptly; a tooth replaced in the socket within minutes of the accident has a 90% chance of successful re-implantation.

Symptoms and Signs
● Bleeding from a tooth socket and possible lacerations around the socket.

Aim
Safeguard breathing by preventing inhalation of blood and control bleeding. If a tooth has been dislodged, replace it and seek dental aid.

Treatment

1 Ask the casualty to sit down with the head inclined toward the injured side to allow blood to drain.

2 Place a thick pad of gauze or a clean cloth on, but *not* into, the bleeding socket. This pad must be thick enough to prevent teeth meeting when the casualty bites on it.

3 Ask the casualty to hold the pad in position with the fingers and then to bite on it for 10 – 20 minutes, supporting the chin on the hand.

4 Tell the casualty to spit out any blood in the mouth while keeping the pad in position; swallowed blood can cause vomiting.

5 After 10 – 20 minutes carefully remove the pad, disturbing the clot as little as possible, and inspect the socket. If it is still bleeding, change the pad and ask the casualty to continue the pressure for a further 10 minutes.

6 Do not wash out the mouth as this may disturb the clot. Advise the casualty to avoid all hot drinks for the next 12 hours.

7 If the bleeding persists or recurs, seek dental or medical aid.

If you suspect jaw fracture treat the casualty as on p. 110.

8 If the casualty has lost a tooth and it can be found, cleanse and replace it promptly. Ask the casualty to suck the tooth clean but, if this is not possible, rinse it in milk *not water*.

9 When clean replace it in the socket. Hold the tooth in position with finger pressure for a couple of minutes, then splint it with a piece of cooking foil moulded over the displaced tooth and one or two teeth on either side. Ask the casualty to bite firmly on the splint.

If the tooth cannot be replaced the casualty should carry it in his mouth to keep it moist. If this is impossible, store the tooth in the casualty's saliva or a small amount of milk — both are less harmful than water.

10 Seek prompt dental advice for all injuries to teeth or gums.

Mouth Wounds

Cuts in the tongue, lips or lining of the mouth range from trivial injuries to larger wounds. They are usually caused by the casualty's teeth during falls on, or blows to, the face. Bleeding may be severe because the blood supply to this area is rich and the skin covering the blood vessels is very thin.

Symptoms and Signs
● Bleeding in or around the mouth.
● Pain in the affected area.

Aim
Safeguard breathing by preventing the inhalation of blood and control bleeding.

Treatment

1 Ask the casualty to sit down with the head forward and inclined towards the injured side.

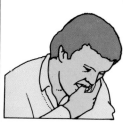

2 To control bleeding, place a clean dressing over the wound and apply direct pressure by squeezing it between thumb and fingers.

3 Tell the casualty to spit out any blood in the mouth; swallowed blood may cause vomiting.

4 If the bleeding persists after 10-20 minutes or the wound is large and gaping, transfer to hospital.

5 Do not wash out the mouth as this may disturb the clot. Advise the casualty to avoid hot drinks for 12 hours.

Eye Wounds

All eye injuries are potentially serious. Even superficial grazes can lead to scarring of the surface of the eye (cornea) or infection, with possible deterioration of eyesight and even blindness.

The eye can be cut or bruised by direct blows, broken spectacles, or sharp, chipped fragments of metal, grit or glass which fly into it. A blow to the face around the eye may fracture the eye socket and cause loss of vision. All "black eyes" should be examined promptly by a doctor.

Symptoms and Signs
● Partial or total loss of vision of the affected eye, even with no visible injury.
● Pain, eyelid spasm and watering of the eye.
● Loss of blood or clear fluid from the eye wound, possibly with flattening of the normal round contour of the eyeball as the contents leak.

Aim
Protect the eye and seek medical aid.

Treatment

1 Help the casualty into the most comfortable position. Support the head and advise the casualty to keep as still as possible.

Do Not attempt to remove embedded foreign bodies.

2 Ask the casualty to close the injured eye and gently cover it with an eyepad or a sterile unmedicated dressing. Secure the pad lightly in position with bandage or adhesive tape.

3 Advise the casualty to keep the sound eye still because movement will cause the injured eye to move.

4 Transfer to hospital by ambulance maintaining the treatment position.

Wounds to the Palm of the Hand

Wounds in the palm can occur when a person handles broken glass or sharp tools or falls on to sharp objects. Such wounds may bleed profusely and can be accompanied by fractures. If the wound is deep, the nerves and tendons in the hand may be damaged.

Symptoms and Signs
- Pain at the site of the wound.
- Profuse bleeding.
- Loss of sensation and movement in the fingers and hand if the underlying nerves and tendons are severed.

Aim
Control bleeding and arrange transfer hospital immediately *without* attempting to remove any embedded foreign bodies.

Treatment

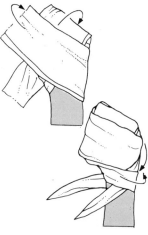

1 To control bleeding, place sterile dressing or gauze and a clean pad over the wound and apply direct pressure (see p. 30). If no dressing or pad is available, use any clean cloth or tissue.

2 Ask casualty to maintain pressure by clenching the fist over the dressing or pad.

If this is not possible, the casualty should grasp the fist of the injured hand with the other hand.

3 Elevate the injured limb with the elbow resting on a firm surface.

4 Take one end of the bandage up and across the front of the clenched fist, over the back of the fist and down to the wrist again. Take the other end of the bandage up and across the front of the fist to cross the first bandage. Bring both ends of the bandage across the front of the wrist, cross them over and tie off firmly on the outside of the wrist to maintain pressure.

5 Support the arm in an elevation sling (see p. 182).

IF FOREIGN BODY IS PRESENT

1 Control the bleeding. Apply direct pressure by squeezing the edges of the wound together alongside the foreign body. Treat as on p. 62.

2 Secure dressing with a bandage applied diagonally (see p. 187).

3 Support the arm in an elevation sling (see p. 182).

Abdominal Wounds

A deep wound of the abdominal wall is serious not only because it will involve external bleeding but also because the underlying organs may have been punctured or lacerated. Either can result in severe internal bleeding and possible infection. Part of the intestine may also be protruding from the wound.

Symptoms and Signs
● General abdominal pain.

● Bleeding and associated wounds in the abdominal area.
● Part of the intestine may be visible in, or protruding from, the wound.
● Casualty may be vomiting.
● Symptoms and signs of shock (see p. 86).

Aim
Control bleeding and minimise infection while preventing protrusion of the intestines. Arrange urgent removal to hospital.

Treatment

1 Control any bleeding by carefully squeezing the edges of the wound together.

2 Place the casualty in a half-sitting position with the knees bent up to prevent the wound gaping and reduce strain on the injured area. Support the shoulders and the knees.

3 Apply a bulky dressing to the wound and secure with a bandage or adhesive strapping.

4 If the casualty loses consciousness, support the abdomen and turn the casualty on to the side. Give care of the airway, breathing and circulation following the Basic Life Support Flow Chart (see p. 15).

5 To minimise shock, treat as on p. 86.

Do Not give the casualty anything by mouth. If help will be delayed, moisten the lips with water.

6 Check breathing rate (see p. 12), and pulse (see p. 85) at frequent intervals. Look for evidence of internal bleeding (see p. 68).

7 If the casualty coughs or vomits support the abdomen by pressing gently on the cloth or dressing to prevent protrusion of the intestines.

8 Arrange ambulance transport to hospital; transport as a stretcher case maintaining the treatment position.

IF PART OF THE INTESTINE PROTRUDES FROM THE WOUND

1 Control bleeding (see p.30) but avoid heavy direct pressure.

Do Not touch the protruding intestines.

2 Cover with a *damp* sterile dressing or clean cloth secured with a loose bandage.

If the casualty coughs or vomits, support the wound as in step 7.

3 Position and treat the casualty as steps 2–8, left.

Penetrating Chest and Back Wounds

Chest and back injuries caused by a sharp knife or gunshot penetrating the body or ribs being forced outwards through the skin allow air directly into the chest cavity. These wounds can become complicated and may develop into "sucking wounds".

In these injuries, the lung on the affected side deflates, even if it is not punctured, and is unable to take in air. In addition, as the ribs rise when the casualty breathes in, air is sucked in through the wound filling the chest cavity and impairing the action of the sound lung. The amount of oxygen reaching the bloodstream may be insufficient and collapse may result (see p. 45).

Symptoms and Signs
- Casualty has pain in the chest.
- Difficulty in breathing; breaths are shallow due to air in the chest cavity.
- Blueness of the mouth or tongue indicating insufficient oxygenation of the tissues.
- Coughed-up, bright-red, frothy blood if lung is injured.
- The sound of air being sucked into the chest may be heard when the casualty is breathing in.
- Blood-stained liquid bubbling from the chest wound during breathing out.
- Symptoms and signs of shock (see p. 86).

Aim
Ease breathing by immediately covering and sealing the wound. Arrange urgent ambulance transport to hospital.

Treatment

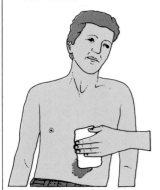

1 Gently cover the wound with a sterile dressing as soon as possible.

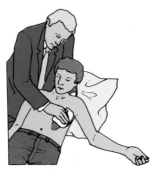

2 Assist the casualty to lie down in the position which he finds most comfortable. The casualty will generally wish to sit up with support. If possible, incline the body towards the injured side.

3 Fix the dressing in place over the wound using adhesive tape, ensuring that the lower edge remains unsealed to permit air under pressure to escape.

If possible form a seal over the wound by covering the dressing with a sheet of plastic or kitchen foil and fixing it into position with adhesive tape on three sides as in step 3.

NB A totally airtight seal over the wound can allow a dangerous increase of pressure inside the chest.

4 If the casualty becomes unconscious, turn him on to the side with the *sound lung uppermost*. Give care of airway, breathing and circulation following the Basic Life Support Flow Chart (see p. 15).

5 To minimise shock, treat as on p. 86.

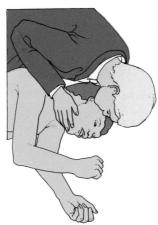

6 Check breathing rate (see p. 12), pulse (see p. 85), and levels of responsiveness (see p. 95) at frequent intervals. Look for evidence of internal bleeding (see p. 68).

7 Arrange for transfer to hospital immediately; transport as a stretcher case maintaining treatment position.

IF A FOREIGN BODY IS PRESENT

1 Seal the wound, by squeezing the edges of the wound alongside the foreign body.

2 Place a dressing around the foreign body, not over it, and build up padding as necessary (see p. 62).

3 Position and treat the casualty as steps 3–7, left.

Blast Injuries

Explosions can result from a bomb or if a flame or electrostatic discharge, from a doorbell or telephone for example, is introduced into an area where a combustible gas has been accumulating. The waves of high pressure from the blast may damage the lungs and other organs of the body.

The casualty may also be suffering from extensive burns, fractures, damaged eardrums and other injuries due to flying glass or other debris.

Symptoms and Signs
● General symptoms and signs of oxygen lack.
● Casualty may cough up frothy, blood-stained sputum.
● Casualty may be anxious.
● Probability of multiple injuries.
● Bleeding from the ear if the eardrum is damaged (see p. 70).
● Symptoms and signs of shock (see p. 86).

Aim
Reassure the casualty and treat where found unless the possibility of further explosions exists. Arrange urgent ambulance transport to hospital.

Treatment

1 Reassure the casualty and move as little as possible until a full examination reveals the extent of the injuries (see *Examination* pp. 36 – 39).

2 If the casualty's general condition and injuries allow, assist him into the most comfortable position — generally half-sitting with support for the head and shoulders.

3 Loosen any constricting clothing around the neck, chest and waist.

4 Control bleeding and treat any wounds (see pp. 60–3) or burns (see pp. 135–7). Immobilise fractures (see pp. 104–25).

5 Check breathing rate (see p. 12), pulse (see p. 85) and levels of responsiveness (see p. 95) at frequent intervals.

6 If the casualty becomes unconscious but is breathing normally, turn him on to the side and give care of the airway, breathing and circulation according to the Basic Life Support Flow Chart (see p. 15).

7 Arrange for urgent ambulance transport to hospital. Transport as a stretcher case maintaining the treatment position.

Animal Bites

Bacteria and viruses are harboured in the mouths of all animals. Animals have sharp, pointed teeth. Because of this, their bites often leave deep puncture wounds and bacteria and viruses may be injected deep into the tissues. Human bites are also potentially dangerous.

Any bite causing a break in the skin needs prompt attention to prevent infection. It may be complicated by tetanus (see p. 65) and in some countries rabies; (see below). Savaging by a dog may also result in multiple lacerations.

Symptoms and Signs
● One or more small puncture wounds in the pattern of the teeth.
● A number of lacerations indicating a tearing bite.
● Bleeding can be severe or may be slight, depending on the extent of injury.

Aim
Treat the wound and seek medical aid: arrange urgent transfer to hospital if wound is serious. Dog bites should be reported to the police.

Treatment
FOR SUPERFICIAL BITES

1 Wash wound thoroughly with soapy water for 5 minutes.

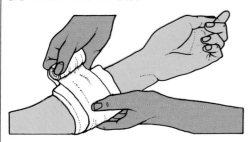

2 Dry the wound and cover it with a sterile unmedicated dressing.

3 Seek medical aid.

FOR SERIOUS WOUNDS

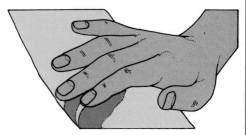

1 Control any serious bleeding with direct pressure and elevation and dress the wound.

2 Cover with a sterile unmedicated dressing and bandage securely.

3 Transfer to hospital

RABIES

Rabies is a potentially fatal condition spread by the saliva of infected animals. Although not currently found in Australia, rabies is endemic in many countries. Therefore, if an animal bite is sustained in a foreign country or if you suspect an infected animal may have been smuggled into the country, you *must* make sure that the casualty has a course of injections.

To confirm or exclude a rabies infection, the animal must be examined medically. If possible, attempt to isolate the animal, *without* endangering yourself. If the animal escapes, notify the police immediately.

Vaginal Bleeding

This can be severe menstrual bleeding or the result of a miscarriage or internal injury; the history of the condition is essential to the diagnosis of the emergency. If you suspect a miscarriage treat as described on p. 208. Heavy menstrual bleeding or miscarriage may also be accompanied by severe cramps. These normally occur at the beginning of the period but may last for several days.

Symptoms and Signs
● Moderate to severe bleeding from the vagina.
● Symptoms and signs of shock may be present (see p. 86).
● Cramp-like pains in the lower abdomen or pelvic area.

Aim
Reassure casualty and if in doubt about the severity of the bleeding, arrange transfer to hospital.

Treatment
1 If possible, remove the woman to a place which has some privacy or arrange for screening. Give her a sanitary dressing, if available, or a clean towel to place over the entrance of the vagina.

2 Lay the woman down with the head and shoulders slightly raised and the knees bent, supported on a blanket. (This will relax the abdominal muscles.)

3 If the pains are severe, and obviously due to menstruation, the casualty may be allowed to take one or two of her own pain-killing tablets or those made specifically for the relief of menstrual cramps.

4 If bleeding continues and is severe, minimise shock by treating as on p. 86. Arrange transfer to hospital immediately; maintain the treatment position.

Bleeding Varicose Veins

Certain veins in the legs contain numerous cup-like non-return valves to keep the blood flowing back to the heart. When these valves deteriorate, the blood tends to pool and the veins become swollen and protruding or "varicosed". Because the leg veins are large and contain a large volume of blood when varicosed, a sudden massive blood loss can occur when they are injured or burst. If such bleeding is not controlled immediately the condition can be fatal.

Symptoms and Signs
● Severe external bleeding; blood will be dark red.
● Symptoms and signs of shock (see p. 86).
● Unconsciousness may develop.

Aim
Control bleeding by using direct pressure and arrange transport to hospital immediately.

Treatment

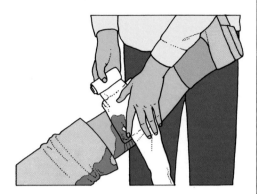

1 Immediately expose wound and apply direct pressure by pressing with fingers or palm of the hand (see p. 30).

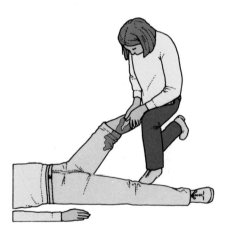

2 Place the casualty on the back and raise the injured leg as high as possible to encourage the blood to return to the heart.

3 Remove any constricting clothing such as elastic-topped or support stockings, garters or tights which may be impeding blood flow back to heart.

4 Place a sterile, unmedicated dressing over the wound. It should be large enough to cover the whole area around the bleeding varicose vein. Tie bandage firmly enough to control bleeding but not so tight as to cut off circulation (see p. 178).

If no suitable dressing is available, place a piece of gauze over the wound, cover it with a pad of cotton wool and bandage firmly. Alternatively make an improvised dressing (see p. 175).

If bleeding does not stop and bandages are soaked with blood, check that the pad and bandage are applied correctly. Relocate and reapply if necessary. Use fingers or hands to control persistent bleeding.

5 Keep both legs raised and supported.

6 To minimise shock, treat as on p. 86.

7 Arrange transfer to hospital maintaining the treatment position.

Crush Injuries

These injuries often involve damage to a great deal of skin, muscle and bone and medical aid should always be sought. There may be serious external and internal bleeding. In particular, there may be damage to the blood vessels supplying a limb, therefore, if release and rescue are delayed, the part may be lost due to a prolonged lack of oxygenated blood. In some cases where the part remains crushed for more than an hour, serum will pour into the injured tissues causing them to become swollen and hard, blood pressure will fall and shock may develop. There will also be an accumulation of toxic chemicals within the body because of substances released by damaged muscle. On release from crushing, these substances can flood back to the rest of the body causing kidney failure which can be fatal.

Therefore, although a casualty may show little sign of injury when released, except redness and swelling, a serious condition may be present.

Symptoms and Signs
- Crushed limb may be tingling or numb.
- Swollen and hard tissue around injured part because serum from the blood has poured into the area.
- Bruising and formation of blisters at the site of injury.
- General symptoms and signs of fracture (see p. 106).
- Crushed or trapped limb will be cool, pale and pulseless if arteries are compressed.
- Symptoms and signs of shock (see p. 86).

Aim
Control bleeding, immobilise fractures and prevent damage to the kidneys.
Where a casualty has been trapped with a crushed limb for longer than 60 minutes call the emergency services *before* attempting release.

Treatment

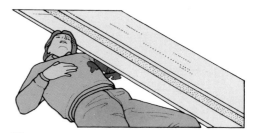

1 Control serious bleeding and treat any wounds; immobilise fractures as far as possible (see pp. 104–25).

2 If the trapped limb can be released without delay, remove the weight. Keep casualty lying down with the head level with the heart and, where possible, raise the legs. Advise the casualty not to move.

NB Record time of release and duration of crushing.

If the casualty can be released from crushing weight, observe closely for sudden onset of shock or collapse.

3 Immobilise the affected limb using pillows and rolled-up clothing or blankets, and if injuries allow, elevate limb. Cover the injured area lightly with a sterile or clean dressing because severe swelling can occur — avoid undue pressure.

4 To minimise shock, treat as on p. 86.

5 Check breathing rate (see p. 12), pulse (see p. 85) and levels of responsiveness (see p. 95) at 10-minute intervals.

6 If the casualty becomes unconscious, give care of airway, breathing and circulation according to the Basic Life Support Flow Chart (see p. 15).

7 Arrange transfer to hospital immediately. Transport as a stretcher case maintaining treatment position; notify ambulance crew of duration of crushing.

If removal to hospital will be delayed by more than 30 minutes and internal injury is *not* suspected, give the casualty sips of cold water.

NB If the crush injury is short-lived and only involves the fingers, hand or foot, place the injured part under cold running water or apply a cold compress (see p. 176). Seek medical aid.

Bruises

A bruise consists of internal bleeding from damaged blood vessels which seeps through the tissues, and appears as a discoloration under the skin. A heavy fall on fleshy parts of the body such as the hip and buttocks, can result in considerable internal bleeding.

Symptoms and Signs
● Pain and swelling in the affected area.
● Bluish-purple discoloration at site of injury.
● Pattern bruising, in which outlines of clothing worn is seen in bruise. This should be regarded as a potentially dangerous sign as it may indicate damage to internal organs.

Aim
Minimise bleeding and swelling with ice, compression and elevation.

Treatment
1 Raise and support the injured part in the position the casualty finds most comfortable.

2 Apply a cold compress to the injured area (see p. 176) to restrict bleeding and reduce swelling.

NB Cold compresses should be applied for up to 10 minutes then removed until the skin returns to normal temperature. Never apply ice directly to the skin.

3 Apply a supportive roller bandage to minimise swelling (see p. 186).

4 If in doubt about the severity of the injury, seek medical aid.

CIRCULATORY DISORDERS

Blood is circulated around the body by the heart through blood vessels to the tissues and cells of the body, before returning via the heart to the lungs where it is reoxygenated. (See *Blood and the Circulation*, pp. 28–9.)

There are several factors which can affect circulation: the volume and quality of the blood in the system, the pressure at which it is circulated, and the condition of the heart and the vessels through which the blood flows.

The average adult has 6 litres (10 pints) of blood circulating in the body. The composition of the blood is vital to the health of the tissues. Normal blood consists of a transparent yellow fluid called plasma in which red cells, white cells and blood platelets are suspended. The coloured pigment in the red cells (haemoglobin) carries oxygen to the tissues. The white cells engulf and remove any harmful bodies in the tissues, such as germs and dead cells, and the platelets assist the blood to clot.

The pressure at which blood flows is determined by the force required to make sure all the blood reaches the tissues. If it is too low, due to severe loss of blood volume for example, then the vital organs receive a reduced supply of blood and cannot function properly and shock may develop.

Blood will continue to flow around the body and will only clot if it escapes from damaged blood vessels (see *Wounds and Bleeding*, p. 60). However in one form of circulatory condition, thrombosis, clotting may occur within a blood vessel – this can block the vessel concerned and so cut off vital supplies of oxygenated blood. Clots may lodge where they form, or be carried around the body until they block an important artery.

Hardened arteries are another cause of circulatory disorder. Continually raised blood pressure (which is more common as age increases) can cause arteries to rupture resulting in internal bleeding. The most common example of this is a cerebral haemorrhage (a form of stroke) and it occurs when a cerebral artery which supplies the brain, ruptures and blood leaks into brain tissue.

Poor blood circulation, possibly aggravated by the slowing-down process of old age, can contribute to thrombosis

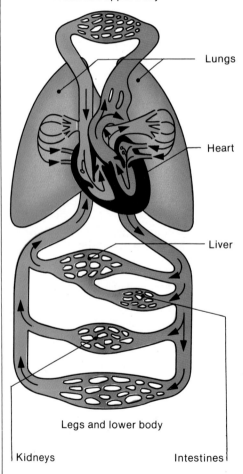

Head and upper body

Lungs

Heart

Liver

Legs and lower body

Kidneys

Intestines

as can the presence of narrowed blood vessels which may also have "fatty" deposits on their walls. Clots carried up into the arteries of the brain can cause a stroke (cerebral thrombosis); clots in the lungs may interrupt the normal blood flow and therefore the oxygenation process (pulmonary embolism); clots which form in the coronary arteries of the heart itself cause heart attacks (coronary thrombosis/coronary occlusion).

The heart muscle contracts and relaxes in the same way as other muscles and has its own separate blood supply, the coronary arteries. Unlike other muscles, however, it must function continuously in order to sustain all the other organs of the body – even if its own oxygen supply is reduced.

The coronary arteries can, like all other arteries, become narrowed with age so that the amount of blood able to pass through them to the heart is reduced. The more heart muscle that is affected by this lack of blood, the less efficient the heart becomes; the beat will become weak and/or irregular and eventually it may stop altogether (cardiac arrest).

The Pulse

This is the wave of pressure which passes along the arteries indicating the pumping action of the heart. It can be felt at any place where an artery is close to the surface of the body and can be pressed against a bone.

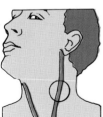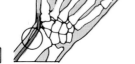

Carotid pulse   Radial pulse

The most useful pulse, the carotid pulse, can be felt just below the angle of the jaw in the hollow between the voice box and the adjoining muscle (see p. 23). However, unless cardiac arrest is suspected, the pulse is usually taken at the wrist on the thumb and palm side just above the crease where the artery runs along the inner side of the forearm bone (radial pulse). Slip your fingers into the hollow just above the bottom end of the bone and press your finger-tips lightly over the artery (do not use your thumb because it has a pulse of its own). To take the pulse, use a watch with a second hand and count the number of beats in a minute.

The three things to check and record are: the rate, strength and rhythm. Note whether it is fast or slow, strong or feeble, or regular or irregular. The average pulse rate in an adult is 72 beats per minute but it can vary between 60 and 80. It increases during stress, exercise, some illnesses, while taking alcohol, or as a result of injury. The pulse rate in elderly persons and some athletes may be slower (between 50 and 60 beats per minute), and it is faster in young babies (about 120 beats per minute).

A normal pulse is regular and strong. An abnormality such as a weak or bounding pulse may indicate an abnormal state in a casualty. For example, a fast, weak pulse in an apparently uninjured person could indicate that there is concealed internal loss of blood or fluid and that the heart is having to work much faster to circulate a lower volume of blood.

Shock

Shock is the term used to describe the condition of a casualty when the oxygen supply to the tissues is inadequate to meet the needs of the body. It implies a sense of urgency – that the casualty is ill and in need of immediate treatment.

Shock may result from several factors including: a reduction in the volume of blood circulating due to bleeding; from plasma loss in burns; or loss of fluids due to vomiting or dehydration. Shock also occurs following a reduction in the pumping ability of the heart or when blood pools in the peripheral vessels (e.g., in the abdomen), as in a faint.

Symptoms and Signs

The body reacts to shock by directing more blood to the arteries supplying the vital organs (e.g., brain, heart and kidneys) at the expense of those supplying the less important tissues (e.g., muscle and skin). As the casualty's condition deteriorates the symptoms and signs will become more pronounced.

● Casualty may have a pain which relates to the cause of shock.
● Casualty feels weak, faint and giddy; he or she may lose consciousness.
● Casualty may feel nauseated and may vomit.
● Casualty's skin will feel cold and clammy and he or she will look pale.
● Breathing will be increasingly shallow and rapid; the casualty may be yawning and sighing, a pattern known as "air hunger".
● The pulse rate will increase and become weaker as shock develops.

Aim

Ensure an adequate blood supply to the heart, lungs and brain. Determine the cause of the shock, treat it and arrange transfer to hospital.

Treatment

1 If the casualty is unconscious, turn him on to the side and give care of airway, breathing and circulation according to the Basic Life Support Flow Chart (see p. 15).

2 Control any obvious bleeding.

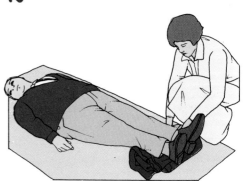

3 If the casualty is conscious, help him to lie down. If possible, raise the casualty's legs but keep the head level with the heart.

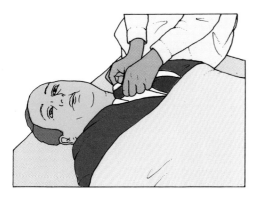

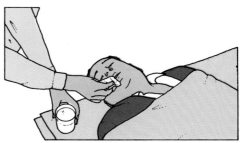

4 Loosen any tight clothing at the neck, chest and waist.

5 Give the appropriate First Aid treatment for the condition causing shock.

7 If the casualty complains of thirst, moisten the lips with water but *do not* give anything to eat or drink.

8 If the casualty becomes unconscious, turn him on to the side promptly and give care of airway, breathing and circulation according to the Basic Life Support Flow Chart (see p. 15).

9 Check breathing rate (see p. 12), pulse (see p. 85) and levels of responsiveness at frequent intervals.

10 Arrange for transfer to hospital. Transport casualty as a stretcher case maintaining treatment position.

6 Protect the casualty from any extremes of temperature. If possible, place a blanket or coat underneath the casualty and place a light cover over him to maintain body heat.

Do Not give the casualty anything by mouth including alcohol. Food or fluids will prevent or delay the subsequent administration of an anaesthetic.

Do Not move the casualty unnecessarily — this will increase shock.

Do Not let the casualty smoke.

Do Not overheat the casualty as this will increase blood flow to the skin and take it away from vital organs.

Fainting

Fainting is a very common emergency in which there is a brief loss of consciousness or "passing out". It may be associated with bleeding, fear, pain, emotional shock, prolonged standing (e.g., soldiers on parade), hunger or fatigue. A person who is bedridden may feel faint when he or she is allowed up. In this case any change in posture should be gradual and they should be given assistance and support.

More serious emergencies may present an appearance similar to fainting so if a casualty does not recover rapidly when you lie him or her down, appropriate treatment following the Basic Life Support Flow Chart (see p. 15) should be given.

Symptoms and Signs

- Restlessness.
- Pallor.
- Cold, moist skin.
- Sighing.
- Vomiting.
- A SLOW pulse.

Aim

Position the casualty so that gravity helps increase the flow of blood to the brain.

If the casualty does not respond to 'Shake and Shout', turn him or her into a Lateral Recovery Position (see p. 22) and give care of airway, breathing and circulation according to the Basic Life Support Flow Chart (see p. 15).

Treatment

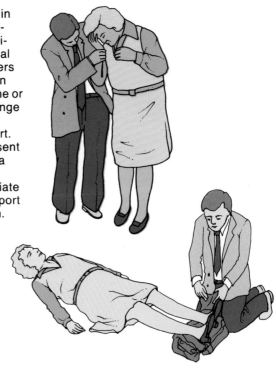

1 Help the casualty to lie down keeping the head level with the heart and raise the legs.

Do Not put the casualty's head between the knees.

NB The casualty will usually recover quickly when horizontal. As she regains consciousness, colour will return to the face, normal breathing will return, and the pulse rate will increase to normal rate.

If the casualty does not lie down, she will lose consciousness, breathing will slow down and there may be a brief seizure. In this case a fall may cause injury. If there is any delay in placing the casualty in a horizontal position cessation of breathing and heartbeat may occur.

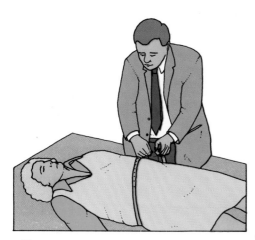

6 Reassure the casualty whilst she regains full consciousness; when conscious gently raise to a sitting position.

If in doubt about the condition of the casualty, seek medical advice.

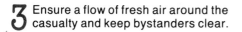

2 Loosen any tight clothing at neck, chest and waist to assist breathing and circulation.

3 Ensure a flow of fresh air around the casualty and keep bystanders clear.

4 Check for and treat any injury that the casualty has sustained on falling.

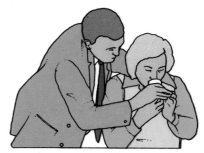

Do Not give the casualty any food or fluid by mouth until she is fully conscious, and then only give sips of water. Avoid giving any alcohol.

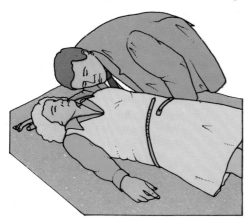

5 Once full consciousness returns, do not move the casualty for 10–15 minutes.

Heart Disease

Sudden interference with the normal action of the heart will have serious consequences. This can occur if a blood clot blocks a coronary artery preventing blood reaching the heart muscle (*coronary occlusion/thrombosis*).

Angina is a condition which occurs when the coronary arteries become seriously narrowed by disease and the supply of oxygenated blood to the heart becomes insufficient for the increased oxygen need during exercise or activity.

Sometimes heart disease can disturb the heart rhythm and the heartbeat may become slow, rapid or irregular. Some irregularities of rhythm may be serious, for example, quivering of the heart muscle (ventricular fibrillation) which causes *cardiac arrest*. If the heart rate frequently becomes too slow, an artificial pacemaker may be fitted to maintain a more satisfactory rate. The pacemaker takes the form of a fine wire inserted into the heart which is connected to a small external battery.

Sometimes an elderly person, or someone who has a long history of heart problems, can suffer from chronic heart failure (congestive cardiac failure). In this condition, the heart is unable to circulate the blood returning from the lungs adequately and there is a build-up of "back pressure" in the lungs which reduces the effective oxygenation of the blood and therefore the tissues, leading to breathlessness and congestion.

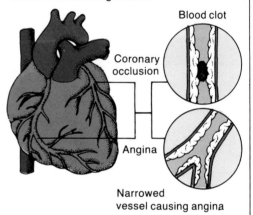

Blood clot

Coronary occlusion

Angina

Narrowed vessel causing angina

CORONARY OCCLUSION
Symptoms and Signs
● Sudden, crushing, vice-like pain in the centre of the chest (sometimes described as severe indigestion) which may spread to the arms, throat, jaw or back. Although the pain may resemble indigestion, it should be considered serious if it lasts longer than 10 minutes despite rest.

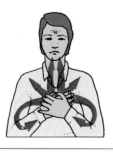

● Sudden dizziness or giddiness causing the casualty to sit down or lean against a wall for support.
● Casualty's skin may be pale, cold and clammy.
● Profuse sweating may occur.
● Casualty may feel nauseated.
● Casualty may be breathless.
● Pulse may be rapid, weak or irregular.
● Casualty may collapse followed by cessation of breathing and heartbeat.

Aim
Minimise the work of the heart by helping the casualty into an appropriate resting position. Arrange urgent transfer to hospital. Be prepared to give resuscitation if necessary.

Treatment

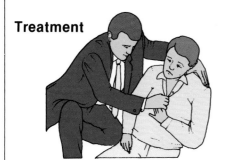

1 If the casualty is conscious, gently support and assist him into the position of greatest comfort, usually a half-sitting position with support.

Do Not allow the casualty to move unnecessarily as this will put extra strain on the heart.

2 Loosen any constricting clothing around neck, chest and waist.

3 If the casualty collapses, turn him on to the side and give care of airway, breathing and circulation according to the Basic Life Support Flow Chart (see p. 15).

4 To minimise shock, treat as on p. 86.

5 Check breathing rate (see p. 12), pulse (see p. 85) and levels of responsiveness (see p. 95) at 10-minute intervals and record your observations.

6 Arrange for urgent ambulance transport to hospital; transport on a stretcher maintaining the treatment position.

ANGINA PECTORIS

This is a condition where the casualty experiences severe pain in the chest which usually occurs following exertion or emotional stress. Normally these attacks will only last a few minutes and the pain will stop if the casualty rests. Many people who suffer from angina have medication for use in preventing or treating an attack.

Symptoms and Signs
● Pain in chest often spreading down the left shoulder to arm and fingers. (It may also spread to the casualty's throat and jaw and across to the other arm.)

● Skin may be pale, cold and clammy.
● General weakness, faintness and nausea may be present.
● Symptoms and signs of shock (see p. 86).

Aim
Help the casualty into the most appropriate resting position in which the heart is able to work most effectively.

Treatment
1 Help the casualty to sit down. Support in this position by placing a blanket or jacket behind the casualty.

2 Reassure the casualty and advise to rest. Loosen clothing around neck, chest and waist.

NB Many people who suffer from Angina Pectoris carry special medicine with them for the prevention or treatment of an attack. Glyceryl trinitrate is commonly prescribed in the form of a tablet or a paste. A tablet should be placed under the tongue for rapid absorption. The paste is applied to the skin over the chest, abdomen or thighs through a special applicator. The First Aider should avoid direct contact with the paste.

3 If symptoms persist, arrange ambulance transport to hospital.

CHRONIC HEART FAILURE

This condition occurs when the heart is weakened by old age or long-term heart disease. There is an excess of fluid which builds up in the lungs and circulatory system causing noisy, gurgling breathing, and swelling of the body tissues. It develops over a long period of time and when it occurs it requires close medical supervision.

Symptoms and Signs
● Severe fatigue.
● Skin colour will be poor and casualty may be sweating profusely.
● Severe breathlessness with noisy, gurgling breathing.
● Swelling of feet, ankles and area around base of spine.

Aim
Minimise the work of the heart and assist breathing by placing the casualty in the most comfortable position. Arrange ambulance transport to hospital. Be prepared to resuscitate.

Treatment

1 Help the casualty into a supported sitting position.

2 Reassure the casualty and loosen any tight clothing around the neck, chest and waist.

NB The casualty must be allowed to rest without any unnecessary movement to avoid additional strain on the heart.

3 Check breathing (see p. 12), pulse (see p. 85), and levels of responsiveness at frequent intervals (see p. 95) and record your observations for the ambulance officer or doctor.

4 If the casualty becomes unconscious, turn her on to the side and give care of airway, breathing and circulation following the Basic Life Support Flow Chart (see p. 15).

5 Arrange ambulance transport to hospital maintaining treatment position.

Stroke

This term is used to describe a condition in which the blood supply to a part of the brain is impaired. Strokes are also called cerebro-vascular accidents (C.V.A.). Strokes are more likely to occur in a person over 50 who has a history of high blood pressure, but an important exception is the young woman who is a smoker and who takes oral contraceptives.

Strokes may be brief and reversible: these are called little strokes or transient ischaemic attacks (T.I.A.). These may last from a few seconds to a few hours, but they usually do not last for more than 30 seconds. Little strokes are usually the result of a spasm in an artery causing a narrowing of the vessel. These attacks can be followed by a full stroke.

Major strokes result from interference with the blood flow to the brain either by a blood clot in an artery or bleeding into the tissues of the brain following a rupture of an artery. The symptoms and signs of a major stroke will depend on the location and the amount of brain tissue damaged.

Symptoms and Signs

These may include one or several of the following:
● Casualty may be confused.
● Casualty may be in a coma.
● Casualty may have difficulty with speech.
● Weakness (hemiparesis) or paralysis (hemiplegia) of one or both sides of the body.
● Paralysis of the mouth causing saliva to dribble.
● Casualty may have a headache.
● There may be loss of bladder or bowel control.
● Sudden death.

NB If an elderly person suddenly becomes confused, a stroke should be suspected and you should seek medical advice promptly.

Aim

In general, First Aid for a stroke is supportive. Be prepared for unconsciousness to develop and/or deepen at any time. Keep the airway open and begin resuscitation, if necessary. Arrange transfer to hospital as soon as possible.

Treatment

1 If the casualty is conscious help him into a resting position. If he complains of a headache, he may prefer to have the head and shoulders slightly raised and supported. Position the head on the side to allow saliva to drain.

If a conscious casualty loses speech he may be distressed at losing the ability to communicate. Reassure the casualty and let him know that help is on the way.

2 Loosen any constricting clothing around the neck, chest and waist to assist circulation and breathing.

3 To minimise shock, treat as on p. 86.

Do Not give casualty anything by mouth.

4 If the casualty becomes unconscious, turn him on to the side and give care of airway, breathing and circulation according to the Basic Life Support Flow Chart (see p. 15).

5 Arrange ambulance transport to hospital; transport as a stretcher case maintaining treatment position.

UNCONSCIOUSNESS

The movements and functions of the body and the levels of responsiveness are governed by the nervous system.

Any change in the state of the casualty's consciousness indicates that there is an interruption of the normal activity of the brain which can be dangerous. There are many causes of unconsciousness, the most common of which are: fainting, head injury, epilepsy, stroke, poisoning, diabetes and conditions associated with oxygen lack.

THE NERVOUS SYSTEM

This system comprises the brain, spinal cord and nerves.

The brain is an extremely delicate structure made up of a mass of nerve cells. It is here that sensations are analysed and orders are given to the muscles. The brain is encased in the skull and suspended in clear (cerebro-spinal) fluid, which acts as a partial shock absorber. Nonetheless, since it is free to move within the skull, the brain is sensitive to violent movement or pressure.

The spinal cord is a mass of nerve fibres extending from the brain through an opening in the base of the skull. The cord runs down through the neck and the spinal column (see p. 112).

The peripheral nerves emerge in pairs, each containing motor and sensory nerves, from the brain and spinal cord. Sensory nerves transport impressions received by the senses (sight, hearing, touch, etc.) to the brain and motor nerves then transport the "orders" given by the brain to the voluntary muscles (those under the control of the will, see p. 126), and the muscles of the autonomic nervous system. When a nerve is cut, there is loss of feeling, power and movement, and of autonomic functions in the part of the body controlled by the damaged nerve.

If the body is subjected to a harmful stimulus, such as when touching a hot object, a "reflex action" will attempt to remove the affected part of the body from the stimulus quickly by by-passing the normal pathway to and from the brain.

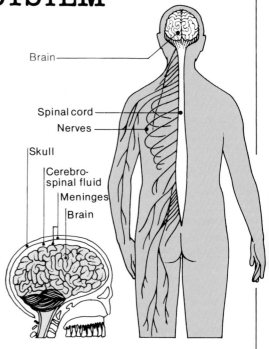

Brain

Spinal cord

Nerves

Skull

Cerebro-spinal fluid

Meninges

Brain

THE AUTONOMIC SYSTEM

This is the network of nerves which controls the involuntary muscles — the muscles which regulate the vital functions of the body such as circulation, respiration and digestion. This system is not controlled by the will, and acts continuously whether a person is awake or asleep.

The Unconscious Casualty

Unconsciousness is the result of an interference with the functions of the brain. The seriousness of the condition can be gauged by testing the casualty's response to stimuli such as sound or touch.

It is important to take note of any change in the casualty's condition because it will govern the treatment eventually given. A casualty may progress through any of the stages outlined below – either improving or deteriorating.

If possible a written report of the levels of responsiveness and the times at which they are noted, should be given to the ambulance crew, nurse or doctor. If you are on your own, this report will have to wait until you have treated the casualty or casualties and are waiting for skilled help

to arrive. If there are any bystanders, they can be asked to keep a record while you treat any casualties.

NB In an unconscious casualty the care of airway, breathing and circulation always takes precedence over the assessment of the levels of responsiveness or treatment of specific injuries.

Aim

To protect the unconscious casualty from danger, care for airway, breathing and circulation following the Basic Life Support Flow Chart (see p. 15). Arrange ambulance transport to hospital as soon as possible for accurate diagnosis and medical management.

LEVELS OF RESPONSIVENESS

These are the stages through which a casualty may pass during the progression from consciousness to unconsciousness, or vice versa. Progress through each level of responsiveness is gradual and continuous rather than in clear stages.

1 *Fully conscious state*: The casualty responds normally to commands or questions.

2 *Semi-conscious state*: The casualty only responds to questions very sluggishly or vaguely; commands may need to be shouted to provoke any response.

3 *Unconscious state*: Casualty does not respond to touch or a shouted command.

Do Not check response to pain because the casualty may be able to feel the pain yet be unable to respond to it. Use only the "Shake and Shout" tests for reponse.

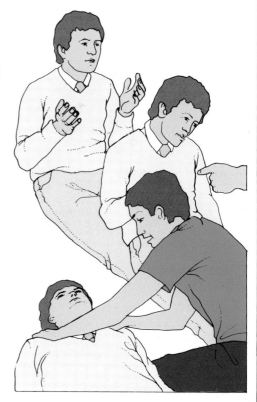

General Management of the Unconscious Casualty

1 If there is no response to "Shake and Shout", turn the casualty into the Lateral Recovery Position (see p. 22), and care for airway, breathing and circulation according to the Basic Life Support Flow Chart (see p. 15).

NB If you suspect spine injury, turn the casualty on to the side supporting the head and neck and keeping the spine straight during the turn — ask bystanders to help if available. Remember that the airway takes precedence over any fracture.

2 If any obvious bleeding is present, control it promptly (see p. 30). Cover any serious wound and give adequate support to a fracture (see p. 107).

3 Loosen any tight clothing at neck, chest and waist, noting the presence of any warning bracelets, pendants or medallions (see p. 41).

4 Rapidly check the casualty for other injuries, and give appropriate First Aid.

5 Protect the casualty from any extremes of heat or cold. If lying on a hot surface or if it is cold and/or wet, ease a blanket or groundsheet under the casualty with minimal disturbance to the position in which he is lying. Cover the casualty with a light covering to maintain body heat.

6 While waiting for the ambulance, continue to systematically check and recheck the casualty's level of consciousness, breathing and circulation at frequent intervals, note any spontaneous movements or noises. Note time and results of every check and pass everything on to the ambulance officer, nurse or doctor.

Do Not allow anyone to give food or fluids to an unconscious casualty.

Do Not leave an unconscious casualty unattended.

If the casualty regains consciousness, he must still be examined by a doctor to determine the cause of collapse.

Emergencies in Diabetes

Diabetes (diabetes mellitus) is a condition which arises when there is a disturbance in the way the body regulates the sugar concentrations in the blood. This can result in two conditions: too much sugar in the blood (hyperglycaemia) or too little sugar in the blood (hypoglycaemia). If prolonged, both conditions can result in unconsciousness and eventually, the death of a casualty. However, hyperglycaemia normally develops very gradually so it is rare for a First Aider to find a casualty in this condition.

Diabetics need to control their blood sugar levels carefully by balancing the amount of sugar in their diets with insulin injections or tablets. Most diabetics, including children, give their own treatments two or three times a day, and eat an appropriate amount of the correct types of food. As a result many carry hypodermic needles, insulin bottles or other medication on them all the time. Most diabetics will also carry a card or wear a bracelet (see p. 41) indicating that they have diabetes.

LOW BLOOD SUGAR (HYPOGLYCAEMIA)

If a diabetic has taken too much insulin by mistake, has eaten too little food or missed a meal or if exercise has burned up the sugar, the concentration of sugar in the blood falls. Low blood sugar will affect the brain and if prolonged or very low it will result in unconsciousness and the possible death of the casualty.

Symptoms and Signs
- A diabetic may feel faint, dizzy and light-headed and may be aware that sugar-level is low.
- Casualty might be confused and disorientated and may appear to be drunk and possibly aggressive.
- Skin becomes pale with profuse sweating.
- Pulse becomes rapid.
- Breathing becomes shallow and breath will be odourless.
- Limbs may begin to tremble.
- Casualty's level of responsiveness may deteriorate rapidly.

NB The longer a diabetic has been on insulin the less evident the early warning symptoms may become.

Aim
Give sugar as soon as possible. If the casualty is unconscious, arrange transfer to hospital immediately.

Treatment

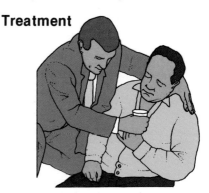

1 If the casualty is conscious and capable of swallowing, immediately give sugar lumps, a sugary drink, chocolate or other source of sugar or carbohydrate in order to raise the level of sugar in the blood.

2 If the casualty becomes unconscious, turn him on to the side and care for airway, breathing and circulation according to the Basic Life Support Flow Chart (p. 15).

3 Arrange for urgent ambulance transport to hospital.

Head Injuries

Head injuries can result in damage to, or disturbance of, the brain. If this occurs, then consciousness may be clouded or lost, concussion or compression may result and other associated injuries or conditions may be masked. A thorough examination of the casualty is, therefore, essential (see pp. 36–40).

Direct blows to the head, heavy enough to cause scalp wounds or bruising, may be accompanied by skull fractures. This type of injury must, therefore, receive urgent medical attention (see *Skull Fracture*, p. 109 and *Scalp wound* p. 69). With thin skulls, a fracture may be present with little evidence of external damage. If any casualty has received a blow to the head, the state of consciousness must be checked. If unconscious, turn him or her on to the side immediately and give care of airway, breathing and circulation according to the Basic Life Support Flow Chart (see p. 15).

These injuries are common results of: falls, particularly in the elderly, ill or intoxicated; road accidents; sporting activities; or day-to-day work in high-risk occupations such as construction work or mining.

CONCUSSION

This is a condition of widespread but temporary disturbance of the brain sometimes described as "brain-shaking". It can result from a blow to the head, a fall from a height on to the feet or buttocks or a blow on the point of the jaw.

This condition can occur *without* apparent unconsciousness. In some cases unconsciousness may have been so brief that the casualty may be unaware of, or have forgotten, the initial incident. However, because concussion can precede compression (see below), it is important to observe the casualty closely after any incident involving to the head. If symptoms persist or the casualty's condition deteriorates, refer to a doctor without delay.

Symptoms and Signs
● Brief or partial loss of consciousness.
● Casualty may not be able to remember any events immediately preceding the injury clearly (amnesia).
● Casualty may complain of a headache.
● Irritability.
● Casualty may feel nauseated or already be vomiting.

CEREBRAL COMPRESSION

This is a very serious condition in which pressure rises within the skull due to either tearing of brain tissue, or a blood clot developing within the brain or between the meninges which cover the brain (see p. 94). There may be continuing bleeding which rapidly leads to death, or severe brain swelling associated with lack of oxygen or carbon-dioxide retention. At first, compression distorts the brain in the area of the injury, but later, as it increases, the distortion extends to the centres which control respiration and circulation.

Compression can follow concussion and it may develop up to 48 hours after the casualty has apparently recovered.

Slight bleeding

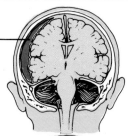

Severe compression

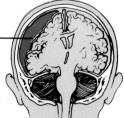

- Loss of fine coordination, particularly in manual skills.
- Numbness, tingling and loss of power in limbs.
- Casualty may complain of blurred or double vision.

NB If unconsciousness persists, suspect compression.

Aim
To assess the casualty to determine state of consciousness and give First Aid as necessary. To seek medical advice for any signs or symptoms of concussion.

Treatment
1 If the casualty is unconscious, turn him or her on to the side immediately and give care of airway, breathing and circulation according to the Basic Life Support Flow Chart (see p. 15).

2 If fully conscious, assess the casualty for any warning symptoms and signs. If they are present, seek medical advice promptly. If none are present, place the casualty in the care of a responsible adult and advise him or her to see a doctor.

3 If the casualty was unconscious for a brief period of time, or you are in any doubt about his or her condition, arrange transport to a doctor or hospital.

4 If there is any scalp wound apply a light dressing (see p. 69).

5 Check for any discharge from the ear or nose; if clear fluid or blood-stained discharge can be seen, treat as for a skull fracture (see p. 109).

NB Any person who has received a blow to the head during sport or recreational activity, should be assessed by a doctor and obtain a medical clearance before continuing or returning to the activity. Repeated head injuries increase the risk of permanent brain damage. Seek urgent medical advice if any of the following symptoms and signs appear: headache, vomiting, altered conscious state, weakness of limbs, fits or undue slowing down of the pulse.

Symptoms and Signs
These will vary according to the rate at which expansion and compression occurs.
- Breathing becomes noisy.
- Body temperature may rise; face becomes flushed but remains dry.
- Pulse is full and bounding but slow.
- Pupils may be different sizes.

- There may be weakness or paralysis of one side of the body.

NB As compression develops the casualty's level of responsiveness falls.

Aim
Arrange transfer to hospital immediately. This condition requires urgent medical treatment.

Treatment
1 If the casualty becomes unconscious turn him or her on to the side promptly with injured side *downwards* (see p. 70). Give care of airway, breathing and circulation following the Basic Life Support Flow Chart (see p. 15).

2 If the casualty is conscious, arrange for urgent transfer to hospital, preferably by ambulance.

Epilepsy and Seizures

Epilepsy is a condition which results from a tendency towards brief disruptions in the normal electrical activity of the brain. Epileptic seizures (fits) may vary from momentary loss of consciousness (Minor Epilepsy) to muscular spasms and convulsions (Major Epilepsy). People who are liable to epileptic seizures often carry an identification card or wear a warning bracelet.

Seizures may occur in the following people:

- Known epileptics.
- Casualties who have suffered a head injury, have been in contact with a certain poison, or who have been in any other situation where the blood and oxygen supply are *severely* impaired (e.g., shock).
- Children under the age of four years suffering from any illness which results in a high temperature. This is referred to as an "infantile convulsion" or "febrile (feverish) convulsion".

MINOR EPILEPSY

This may start in childhood and may persist into adulthood. This type of seizure can pass unnoticed because the casualty often only appears to be daydreaming.

Symptoms and Signs
- Casualty may appear to be in a daydream and be staring ahead blankly.
- Casualty might start behaving strangely; these "automatisms" include chewing or smacking lips, saying odd things, or fiddling with clothing.
- Casualty may have lost memory.

Aim
Keep calm and protect the casualty while consciousness is impaired. For example, prevent the casualty wandering on to a busy road.

Treatment

1 Do nothing except:

- Protect the person from any dangers such as busy roads.
- Keep other people away.
- Talk to the casualty quietly.

2 Stay with the casualty until you are certain that the person has recovered and can get home.

NB It is not unusual for a major seizure to follow a minor one.

3 Advise the casualty to see a doctor.

MAJOR EPILEPTIC SEIZURES

A major epileptic seizure is often referred to as a "Grand Mal" seizure. Most epileptic seizures occur without any warning. However, sometimes a person experiences an "aura" which is an indication of an impending fit. This aura may differ from one person to another. For example, for one person it may take the form of a strange feeling in the body, for another it may be a particular smell or taste. During an aura, a person's normal mood may be altered, although this may not last for long.

Symptoms and Signs

Major epileptic seizures follow a two-stage pattern of rigidity and loss of consciousness, followed by jerking spasms. Usually the progression is as follows:

● Casualty suddenly loses consciousness and falls to the ground, sometimes letting out a strange cry.

● The casualty becomes rigid for a few seconds and normal breathing may cease. There will be signs of congestion around face and neck with poor skin colour.

● The muscles then begin convulsive movements. These consist of contraction and relaxation of alternate groups of muscles, and the jerking movements will be quite vigorous. During this stage, the breathing may be laboured or noisy through clenched jaws; frothy saliva may appear around the mouth − it will be blood-stained if the lips or tongue have been bitten. There may be loss of bladder and bowel control, resulting in soiling of clothes.

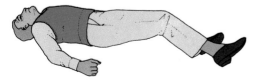

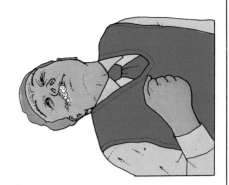

● Finally, the muscles relax although the casualty will remain unconscious for a few more minutes.

After the seizure is over, usually within five minutes at the most, breathing will return to normal and the casualty will regain consciousness. The casualty may feel dazed and confused and act strangely while going through a stage of "automatism" in which he or she may be physically active but be unaware of actions. The recovery stage may last from a few minutes to an hour or more and the person may want to rest quietly. Discourage the casualty from driving a car or undertaking any other activity which requires a high level of coordination.

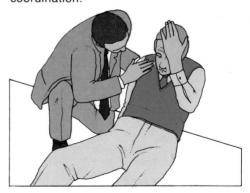

Aim

Protect the casualty from injury during the seizure and provide care once the casualty has regained consciousness.

Treatment

See Treatment for Seizures, overleaf.

INFANT CONVULSIONS

Convulsions in infants or small children under four years normally result from a high temperature caused by the onset of an infectious disease, or an ear or throat infection; they are rarely dangerous if correct First Aid is given promptly.

Symptoms and Signs

● Child is obviously unwell with a high fever, the skin is hot, flushed and sweating.

● The muscles of the face and limbs are twitching with occasional squinting or up-turning of the eyes.

● There may be a generalised stiffness or rigidity of the body, with the head thrown back and spine arched.

● Child may be holding his or her breath, resulting in congestion of the face and neck.

● Saliva may appear as froth around the mouth.

Aim

Protect the child from injury and cool the body to reduce the severity of the convulsion.

General Treatment for Seizures

1 Protect the casualty from any danger by removing any hard objects or electrical appliances in the area immediately surrounding him.

2 If the casualty is in any immediate danger from a busy road, fire or surf for example, move him using the clothing drag method to avoid restraining any joints (see p. 193).

NB If an epileptic has a seizure during a swimming lesson with a qualified instructor, he may be allowed to continue in the water if the instructor can support the head and shoulders above water to avoid water entering the airway. However, if the water is deep, or if the casualty vomits or suffers a prolonged fit, he must be removed from the water.

3 Turn the casualty into the Lateral Recovery Position (see p. 22) as soon as it is possible to do so without injury.

4 Loosen any tight clothing especially at the neck and chest.

Do Not attempt to prise the casualty's mouth open with any hard object as this may cause more damage than accidental biting of the tongue.

Do Not try to restrain the convulsive movements of

Hysteria

the body because this may lead to further injury. Direct contact with the casualty should be limited to protecting him from injury.

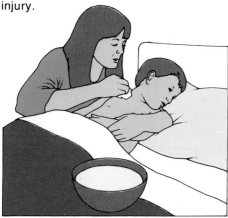

5 If the convulsion is due to a fever, remove the child's clothes and cool the skin by sponging. Always begin at the head and work down and using water which is at body temperature.

Do Not allow the child to become too chilled.

NB Although frightening for the parents, feverish convulsions in children are resolved quickly once the temperature is reduced. High-speed journeys to a doctor or hospital are never necessary and may increase the risks for the family.

6 Even if the casualty makes a full, rapid recovery, advise him to inform the doctor about the latest attack.

Do Not give the casualty anything to eat or drink until recovery is complete.

7 Seek medical advice for any seizure which lasts longer than 5–10 minutes, if one seizure follows another, or where there is no established history of epilepsy.

This is usually caused by an over-reaction to an emotional upset or nervous stress and is likely to be heightened by the presence of onlookers.

Symptoms and Signs
● Temporary loss of behavioural control with dramatic shouting, screaming, crying, wild beating of limbs. Casualty may be rolling around on the ground and/or tearing at hair and clothes.
● Hysterical over-breathing (hyperventilation) may follow causing spasm and tingling of fingers.
● Casualty may be unable to move or be walking strangely for no apparent reason.

Aim
Isolate the casualty from any onlookers and gently but firmly help casualty to calm down enough to regain control.

Treatment
1 Reassure the casualty, refrain from showing any sympathy and, gently but firmly, escort to a quiet place.

Do Not physically restrain or slap the casualty; this may make the casualty more violent.

2 Stay with the casualty and keep under observation until fully recovered.

NB In severe cases of hysterical over-breathing, the casualty can be helped by rebreathing his or her expired air from a paper bag; this keeps more carbon dioxide in the circulation and relieves discomfort.

3 Advise the casualty to see a doctor.

4 In a psychiatric emergency where a casualty needs restraint for his or her own protection as well as others, seek the help of police or ambulance officers.

FRACTURES

A fracture is a broken or cracked bone. Although the outside of a bone is hard, it may crack or break if struck, twisted or overstressed. Generally, considerable force is required to break a bone. However, the elderly often have brittle bones and only slight force is needed to produce a break. Conversely, the long bones of infants can bend slightly.

All fractures must be handled very carefully; mishandling by the unskilled may result in further damage to the surrounding tissues.

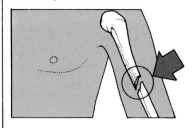

A bone can be fractured directly at the point where the force of a blow is applied. For example, if someone is struck by a moving vehicle the lower leg may be broken at the point where it was hit by the vehicle's bumper.

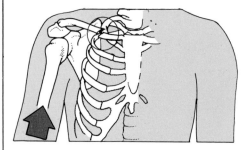

However, a bone can also be fractured indirectly at some distance from the spot where the force is applied. In this case, the bone is broken by the force being transmitted along it, or the adjacent bone, from the point of impact. For example, a fall on the outstretched hand may result in a fractured collar-bone.

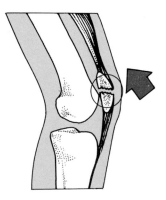

Another form of indirect force occurs when sudden, powerful, muscular contractions pull pieces of bone away from the point where the muscle is attached. For example, a footballer who tries to kick a ball but misses and hits the ground, can cause the knee-cap to snap in two because the powerful thigh muscles jerk suddenly at the anchorage points on that bone.

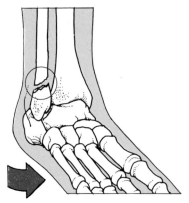

In the same way, the "wrenching" of a joint can cause its ligaments to pull so hard at the joint that they fracture one of the bones to which they are attached. For example, a person who turns the foot over by tripping or stumbling may fracture a lower leg bone at the ankle.

THE SKELETON

The body is built on a framework of bones called the skeleton. This skeleton supports the body, gives it its basic shape and provides protection for the internal organs of the body. For example, the skull surrounds and protects the brain and the rib-cage protects the lungs, heart and other vital organs. The bones are also important for movement. They provide anchorage points for the muscles, and many of them also act as levers for the muscles to pull against.

Bones have blood vessels running through and alongside them. A fracture can result in severe blood loss mainly because of the damage to the surrounding tissues caused by the broken bone ends.

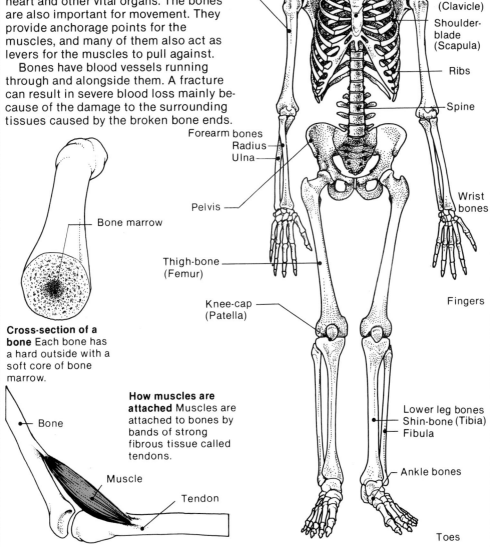

Upper arm bone (Humerus)

Skull

Jaw

Breastbone (Sternum)

Collar-bone (Clavicle)

Shoulder-blade (Scapula)

Ribs

Spine

Forearm bones
Radius
Ulna

Pelvis

Wrist bones

Thigh-bone (Femur)

Knee-cap (Patella)

Fingers

Lower leg bones
Shin-bone (Tibia)
Fibula

Ankle bones

Toes

Bone marrow

Cross-section of a bone Each bone has a hard outside with a soft core of bone marrow.

How muscles are attached Muscles are attached to bones by bands of strong fibrous tissue called tendons.

Bone

Muscle

Tendon

Types of Fracture

Fractures fall into two categories, closed or open, and both can be complicated.

Closed Fracture
This is a fracture where the skin surface around the damaged bone is not broken.

Open Fracture
When a wound leads from the surface of the skin to the fracture or a broken bone end penetrates the surface of the skin, the fracture is said to be "open".

Open fractures are serious not only because they can result in severe external blood loss but also because bacteria can gain access to the soft tissues and the broken bone. Such infection can be dangerous and difficult to cure.

Complicated Fracture
Closed or open fractures are said to be "complicated" when there is an associated injury. For example, if an important structure, nerve or organ is damaged by the broken bone end or when a fracture is associated with a dislocated joint.

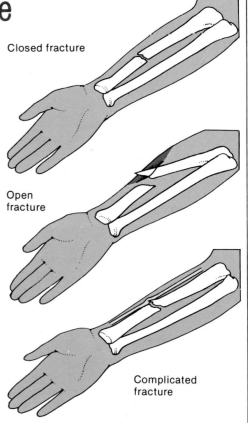

Closed fracture

Open fracture

Complicated fracture

General Symptoms and Signs
● The snap of the bone may have been felt or heard by the casualty.
● Pain at or near the site of injury increased by movement.
● Casualty may find it difficult or impossible to move the part normally.
● Tenderness at the site of the fracture when gentle pressure is applied over the affected area.
● Swelling and, later, bruising of the injured part. This may not be evident at first but will develop as blood leaks into the tissues; it may mask the true nature of the injury.
● Deformity at the site of the fracture. This may be irregularity of the bone; shortening, angulation or rotation of the

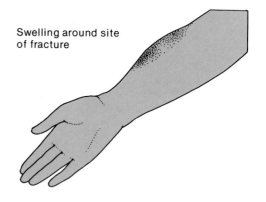

Swelling around site of fracture

limb (e.g., the limb has twisted further than is normally possible — a turned out foot is common with a fractured neck of thigh-bone), or depression of a flat bone.

● Coarse bony grating (crepitus) may be heard or felt upon examination — this should *never* be sought deliberately.

● Symptoms and signs of shock (see p. 86).The degree of shock will be particularly noticeable in those with a fractured thigh-bone or pelvis.

NB Not all the symptoms and signs will be present in every fracture. As many as possible should be noted by simple observation without moving any part unnecessarily. Compare the shape of the injured and uninjured limbs whenever possible. If you are in any doubt about the severity of an injury, treat as a fracture.

Aim
The keynote of First Aid treatment for any fracture is prevention of movement at the site of injury (immobilisation). Movement can not only make a fracture more painful but it frequently makes it worse. In all cases, arrange removal to hospital.

General Treatment
Casualties with fractures should *not* be moved unless it is absolutely necessary. For example, an unconscious casualty must be turned into the Lateral Recovery Position to protect the airway. Make the casualty comfortable, steady the injured part and await the arrival of skilled help. If you must move the casualty, do so carefully and gently to avoid further injury and increased pain.

Specific fractures are dealt with individually later in the chapter. However, the general rules for treatment of any fracture are as follows:

1 If the casualty is unconscious you must care for airway, breathing and circulation according to the Basic Life Support Flow Chart (see p. 15).

2 Always control severe bleeding before immobilising any fractures.

If time will allow, temporarily immobilise and support a fractured limb before moving the casualty to safety.

3 Protect the casualty from extremes of temperature (see p. 87).

Do Not move the injured part unnecessarily.

4 *When transfer to hospital is imminent,* gently support the injured part by hand. Place the casualty in the most comfortable position and support with rolled-up blankets or similar materials.

5 *When ambulance transportation to hospital will be delayed*, immobilise the injured part by securing it to a sound part of the body with padding and bandages.

NB Bandages should be firm enough to prevent movement but not so tight as to interfere with the circulation (see p. 178) or cause pain.

6 After immobilisation, support the injured part in a raised position, to minimise discomfort and swelling.

7 To minimise shock, treat as on p. 86.

NB A fractured limb may be so deformed that it will be impossible to apply bandages or splints without some realignment of the limb. In populated areas where ambulance transport or medical aid is readily available within a reasonable period of time, realignment of the injured limbs should NOT be attempted by the First Aider. In remote areas where ambulance transport or medical aid is likely to be delayed for many hours, it may be necessary to carefully and gently apply traction to the end of the limb: straighten the limb as far as the casualty will allow within the limits of pain.

Open Fractures

IF THE BONE IS PROTRUDING FROM THE WOUND

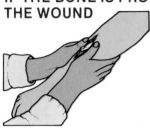

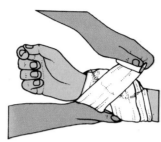

1 Control bleeding by applying pressure alongside the bone.

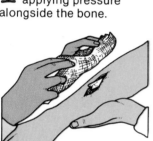

2 Gently place a piece of gauze over the protruding bone.

3 Build up padding around the bone until it is high enough to prevent pressure on the protruding bone.

4 Secure dressing with a bandage applied diagonally to avoid pressure on the under-side of the fracture.

5 Support the injured part if possible and immobilise it.

6 Transfer the casualty to hospital maintaining the treatment position. Transport as a stretcher case if necessary.

IF THERE IS NO BONE PROTRUDING FROM THE WOUND

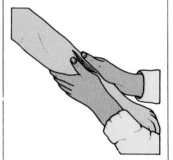

1 Control bleeding by squeezing the sides of the wound together gently but firmly.

Do Not apply firm downward pressure on the wound over the site of the fracture.

2 Place a dressing over the wound and build up padding of suitable material around the edge of the wound.

3 Treat as in steps 4 – 6, left.

Skull Fractures

The skull provides a strong, protective case for the brain. Although damage to the bone may not appear to be significant, a "depressed" fracture or leakage of blood from the site of fracture may exert pressure on the brain (see p. 99).

Skull fractures may result in damage or disturbance to the brain, consciousness may be clouded or lost (see p. 95) and symptoms of any other injury or condition may be masked. Therefore, all head injuries should be regarded as serious, even if there is no sign of a wound.

A fracture of the crown of the head (cranium) is usually caused by a direct blow to the skull or a fall on the head; the bone may be depressed. A fracture of the base of the skull is usually caused by an indirect force such as a fall on to the feet or a blow to the jaw.

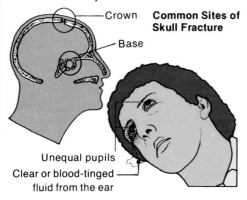

Crown — **Common Sites of Skull Fracture**

Base

Unequal pupils
Clear or blood-tinged fluid from the ear

Symptoms and Signs
● Obvious signs of head injury.
● Blood and/or clear, watery cerebrospinal fluid may issue from the ear or the nose.
● There may be a bloodshot and, later, a black eye.
● Pupils may be unequally dilated (see *Compression* p. 99).
● Brief or partial loss of consciousness.

Aim
Arrange urgent transfer to hospital.

Treatment
1 If the casualty is unconscious, turn him on to the side with *the injured side downwards*, and give care of airway, breathing and circulation according to the Basic Life Support Flow Chart (see p. 15).

2 If the casualty is conscious, place in a half-sitting position with the head and shoulders supported.

3 If any discharge issues from the ear, incline the head towards the injured side, cover the ear with a sterile dressing or similar pad and secure very lightly with bandage. *Do not* plug the ear.

4 Check the breathing rate (see p. 12), pulse (see p. 85), and levels of responsiveness (see p. 95), at 10-minute intervals. Record your observations for the ambulance officer, nurse or doctor.

5 To minimise shock, treat as on p. 86.

6 Transfer the casualty to hospital maintaining treatment position.

Jaw and Facial Fractures

Fractures and wounds to the jaw and face may be complicated by further damage to the brain, skull and/or bones in the neck. There are three serious risks associated with these injuries:

- The airway may be obstructed or blocked. This can be caused by: internal bleeding into the lungs and breathing passages (nose, mouth or throat); the tongue falling to the back of the throat if the casualty is unconscious; swollen, displaced or lacerated tissues in the throat; or broken or detached teeth.
- Inadequate or absent cough reflex which would allow secretions, blood and foreign matter to run unnoticed into the lungs, causing oxygen lack.
- Possibility of severe bleeding. This may be profuse and alarming initially,

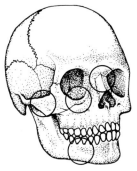

Common Fracture Sites of Face and Jaw

although it is not usually prolonged (see *Wounds and Bleeding*, pp. 71–3).

Injuries to the face may include fracture of the lower jaw, cheek-bone, orbit, upper jaw and nose.

LOWER JAW FRACTURE

This is usually the result of direct force, for example a heavy blow to the jaw. However, a blow to one side of the jaw can cause a fracture on the other side. Usually only one side of the jaw is affected but a fall on to the point of the chin can lead to a fracture of both sides of the jaw.

Symptoms and Signs

- Pain, increased by jaw movement or swallowing.
- Difficulty in speaking.
- The casualty feels nauseated.
- Casualty may dribble because of difficulty in swallowing. Saliva is normally stained by blood issuing from tooth sockets or other mouth wound.
- Wound inside the casualty's mouth.
- Swelling, tenderness and later bruising of the casualty's face and lower jaw.
- Irregularity may be felt along underside of jaw.
- Irregularity of the teeth may be seen.

Swelling on one side of the jaw

Irregularity may be felt along the jaw

Treatment

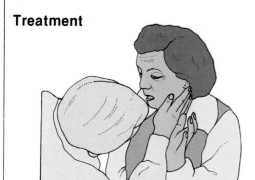

1 Maintain the casualty's breathing by ensuring a clear airway.

2 Control any bleeding and treat any wounds (see p. 71–3).

3 If conscious and not seriously injured, sit the casualty up with the head well-forward to allow any secretions to drain away.

4 Assist the casualty to support the injured part of the jaw, using both hands if necessary.

5 If vomiting occurs, support the casualty's jaw and head. Gently clean the casualty's mouth to remove any material still in the mouth.

NB If vomiting is severe, help the casualty into the Lateral Recovery Position (see p. 22) to help drainage and to protect the airway.

6 If the injury is severe, or if the casualty becomes unconscious, turn her into the Lateral Recovery Position and give care of airway, breathing and circulation according to the Basic Life Support Flow Chart (see p. 15). If necessary, use the casualty's free hand to support the injured jaw.

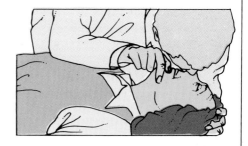

If resuscitation is required it may be necessary to use the Mouth-to-Nose method (see p. 18).

7 Arrange transfer to hospital immediately maintaining treatment position.

CHEEK-BONE AND UPPER JAW FRACTURE

Although there may not be any obvious signs of soft tissue wounds around the injury, there will probably be a significant amount of blood issuing from the nose. Severe swelling of the face and bruising may affect breathing. A blow to the cheek-bone may also cause swelling around and behind the eyes which can permanently impair vision. For this reason, all serious cheek-bone injuries should be transferred to the nearest doctor or hospital promptly.

Treatment

1 Place a cold compress (see p. 176) over the injured area to lessen swelling, bleeding and pain. Make sure you do not interfere with breathing and that bleeding from any mouth wound does not obstruct airway.

2 Treat any mouth wound (see p. 73).

3 Transfer to a hospital or doctor as soon as possible.

NASAL FRACTURE

Besides bleeding, the main problem associated with a nasal fracture is blockage of the airway so every effort must be made to ensure that the casualty has an open airway. A cold compress may provide some relief and assist in controlling the swelling (see p. 176).

Usually there is no pressing need to immobilise a nasal fracture. Treat any nose-bleed (see p. 71) and transfer the casualty to hospital.

THE SPINE

Made up of a series of small bones or "vertebrae", the spine forms a canal through which the spinal cord runs (see p. 94). Almost all vertebrae are separated by a pad of cartilage called an intervertebral disc. The vertebrae have limited movement upon these discs, which act as a form of "shock-absorber" in case the spinal column is jarred. The whole column of bones is supported by numerous strong ligaments and the muscles of the trunk.

The spinal cord consists of nerve fibres which run from the brain and control many of the functions of the body. It is very delicate, and damage to it can result in loss of power or sensation in all parts of the body *below* the injured area. Temporary damage can occur if the cord is pinched by dislocated discs or if the cord becomes swollen or bruised.

Spine Fractures

Australia has one of the highest incidences of spinal fracture in the world. A fractured spine is *always* classed as a serious injury, necessitating the greatest care in handling because it may be complicated by damage to the spinal cord.

Injury can result from both direct and indirect force. Impact from vehicle collisions and from heavy objects falling across the casualty's back, or severe jarring of the spine by falling on to the feet, buttocks or head can all result in serious spine injury. Many diving accidents have resulted in a fractured spine when a person has dived into shallow water or hit a submerged obstruction.

"Whiplash" results from the violent backward movement of a person's head which commonly occurs when a vehicle is run into from behind. With this type of injury there may be severe muscular damage or, occasionally, the neck may be broken.

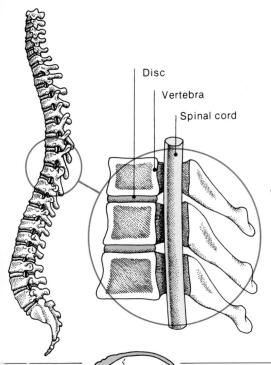

Disc

Vertebra

Spinal cord

Permanent damage will occur if the cord is partially or completely severed.

Possible injuries to the spine include fractures, displaced intervertebral discs, strains and sprains; fractures may involve nerve damage. Slipped discs, strains and sprains are dealt with in the chapter on *Injuries to Muscles, Ligaments and Joints* (see pp. 126—31). However, if you have any doubt about the nature of the injury it *must* be treated as a fracture. Always suspect a fracture if the general history of the incident suggests the possibility (see p. 38).

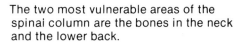

The two most vulnerable areas of the spinal column are the bones in the neck and the lower back.

Symptoms and Signs
- Casualty may complain of severe pain in the back and may feel "cut in half".
- Casualty may have no control over limbs; ask the casualty to move wrists, ankles, fingers and toes.
- Possible loss of sensation. Test this by gently touching limbs without the casualty's knowledge and ask if anything can be felt.

Direct impact

Jarring

Aim
Prevent any further damage by immobilising the spine. Avoid moving the casualty unless absolutely necessary and arrange ambulance transport to hospital as soon as possible.

Treatment for a Fractured Spine

1 If the casualty is unconscious, turn her on to the side immediately to protect the airway. If bystanders are available they can help keep the casualty's spine straight and support the head during the turn. Give care of airway, breathing and circulation according to the Basic Life Support Flow Chart (see p. 15).

NB Remember that maintaining an open airway takes precedence over all fractures including fractured spine.

2 If the casualty is conscious, reassure her and advise against trying to move.

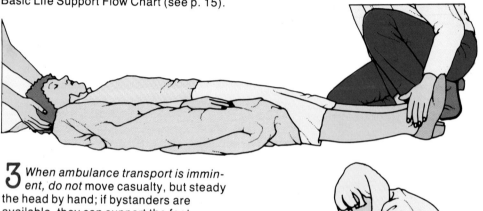

3 *When ambulance transport is imminent, do not* move casualty, but steady the head by hand; if bystanders are available, they can support the feet. Place rolled clothing alongside the trunk to support the casualty. Cover with a blanket and await arrival of medical aid.

4 *When ambulance transport will be delayed*, steady the casualty's shoulders and pelvis and carefully place soft padding between the lower limbs. Tie a figure-of-eight bandage around the ankles and feet and broad bandages around the thighs and knees.

5 *In a remote area when ambulance transport will be delayed*, and you suspect neck fracture, apply a neck collar to support the neck spine, see opposite.

If the casualty has suspected spine fracture following a diving accident, do not attempt to remove her from the water unless unconscious. Little effort is needed to keep her afloat with the neck and spine straight and when skilled help arrives, she can be immobilised before removal from the water.

6 Transfer the casualty to hospital by ambulance maintaining treatment position.

FITTING A NECK (CERVICAL) COLLAR

1 If a cervical collar is not available, fold a newspaper to a width of about 10 cm (4 in) or you may use a folded bandage, jumper or towel. Wrap this up in a triangular bandage or insert it into a stocking or leg of a pair of tights.

2 Place the centre of the collar at the front of the casualty's neck below the chin. Ensure that the casualty's head and neck are supported in a stable position.

3 Fold the collar around the casualty's neck and tie in position at the front of the neck.

4 Ensure there is no obstruction to breathing.

UPPER TRUNK AND LIMBS

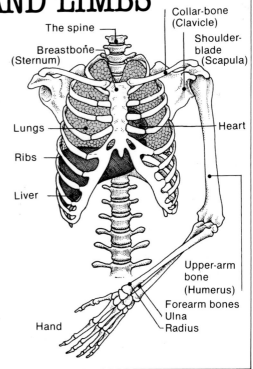

The *ribs* consist of 12 pairs of curved bones which extend from the vertebrae round to the front of the body.

The *chest cavity* is bounded in front by the breastbone, behind by the spine, below by the diaphragm, then encircled by the ribs. It contains the heart and major blood vessels, the lungs and the gullet.

The *shoulder girdle* and *upper limbs* consist of the collar-bone, the shoulder-blade (which is rarely broken) and the arm bones. The *collar-bone* is situated between the upper part of the breastbone and the shoulder, and forms a strut to hold the upper limbs away from the chest and support the neck and head. The *shoulder-blade* forms a joint with the collar-bone and the *upper-arm bone*.

Each upper limb consists of the upper-arm bone; the two bones in the forearm which allow for the turning action of the wrist; and the small bones at the wrist.

More bones form the framework of the palm of the hand and there are several small bones in the fingers and thumb.

The spine
Breastbone (Sternum)
Collar-bone (Clavicle)
Shoulder-blade (Scapula)
Lungs
Heart
Ribs
Liver
Upper-arm bone (Humerus)
Forearm bones
Ulna
Radius
Hand

Rib and Breastbone Fractures

These fractures normally result from direct force, such as a blow to, or heavy fall on to, the chest, or from indirect force as a result of being crushed. If the fracture is complicated by a "sucking wound" of the chest (see p. 76) or by "paradoxical breathing" due to a Stove-in-Chest, (see opposite) collapse may occur unless the injuries are treated immediately.

Symptoms and Signs
● General symptoms and signs of fracture.
● Casualty may feel a sharp pain at the site of the fracture, increased by anything more than shallow breathing or by coughing.
● Possible symptoms and signs of internal bleeding (see pp. 66—8). indicating damage to internal organs such as the lungs or liver.
● There may be an open wound of the chest wall over the fracture causing a "sucking wound" of the chest.
● Possible paradoxical breathing or flail chest if there are multiple fractures (see opposite).

Aim
Support the rib-cage, ease breathing and arrange transfer to hospital.

Treatment
1 Place padding between the upper arm and chest on the injured side, then apply a broad bandage around the body and bind the arm firmly to the chest wall supporting the rib-cage. Tie off with a reef knot in front of the chest on the uninjured side.

2 Support the arm on the injured side with an elevation sling (see p. 182).

3 Transfer the casualty to hospital.

FOR A COMPLICATED FRACTURE

1 Immediately treat any "sucking" wound (see p. 76).

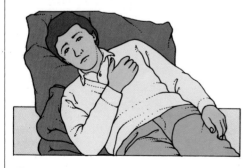

2 Help the casualty into the position in which he is most comfortable –

generally a half-sitting position with the head and shoulders supported and the body inclined *towards* the injured side. Support the casualty by placing a folded blanket lengthwise along the back.

3 Apply a broad bandage and elevation sling as in steps 1–2 above.

4 If the casualty is unconscious, turn him on to the side with the injured side *downwards*. Give care of airway, breathing and circulation according to the Basic Life Support Flow Chart (see p.15).

5 Transfer to hospital by ambulance maintaining the treatment position.

Stove-in-Chest

Multiple fractures of the chest wall result in the area losing its rigidity and prevent it following the normal movements of the rib cage during breathing (see p. 12). Instead, the fractured ribs are sucked in during breathing-in and pushed out during breathing-out (flail chest). This is a reversal of normal movement of the rib-cage and the opposite of what is happening on the sound side. This condition is known as *paradoxical breathing* and it may also inhibit the lung action on the uninjured side. In addition to this, the broken bones may damage other internal organs or penetrate the skin causing a "sucking" wound (see p. 76).

Common causes of this type of injury are road traffic accidents in which the driver of a vehicle is thrown against the steering column or the steering column is pushed back into the driver's chest.

The same effect can result if the chest is crushed by heavy objects.

Symptoms and Signs
- General symptoms and signs of oxygen lack (see p. 45).
- Casualty finds it difficult and painful to breathe.
- Casualty may be very distressed.
- Unusual movement in the rib cage. Injured part of the chest wall will be seen to have lost its rigidity.
- Possibility of frothy blood-stained sputum indicating lung damage (see *Penetrating Wound of the Chest*, p. 76).

Aim
Stabilise the chest wall in order to ease breathing. Arrange urgent transfer to hospital.

Treatment

1 Support the affected part of the casualty's rib cage with your hand.

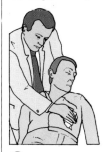

2 Help the casualty into the position in which he is most comfortable; generally half-sitting and inclined towards the injured side. Support the head and shoulders.

3 If there is a "sucking" wound, treat as on p. 77.

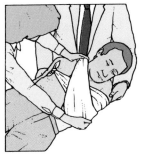

4 Immobilise the chest wall. Place a thick pad of soft material over the injured area and place the arm on the injured side across the pad. Apply a broad bandage around the body to bind the arm to the chest wall and support the rib-cage. Apply an elevation sling as described on p. 182.

5 Loosen any constricting clothing around the neck and waist.

6 Check for any signs of other injury.

7 If the casualty becomes unconscious, turn him on to the side with the injured side *downwards* and give care of airway, breathing and circulation according to the Basic Life Support Flow Chart (see p. 15).

8 Arrange for urgent ambulance transport to hospital; transport as a stretcher case maintaining treatment position.

Collar-bone Fractures

A collar-bone fracture is commonly caused by indirect force resulting from a fall on to an outstretched hand (see p. 104) or the point of a shoulder. Collar-bone fractures due to direct force are rare.

Symptoms and Signs
● General symptoms and signs of fracture.
● Pain and tenderness at the site of injury increased by movement.
● Casualty is reluctant to move the limb on the injured side.
● Casualty may support the arm on the injured side at the elbow and may keep the head inclined towards the injured side to relieve pain.
● Swelling or deformity may be seen or felt over the site of fracture.
● Injured shoulder may droop slightly or appear lower than the sound side.

Aim
Immobilise fracture and transfer casualty to hospital.

Treatment
1 Gently place the lower arm on the injured side across the casualty's chest in the position of greatest comfort.

2 Place padding between the limb and chest on the *injured* side.

3 Support the limb on the injured side in an arm sling (see p. 181). Tie knot on injured side, avoiding any pressure on the injury site. Pad under knot if necessary.

4 Gently apply a narrow or broad bandage around the body to support the limb against the chest wall on the injured side.

5 Transfer to hospital as a sitting or walking casualty unless there are complications.

Arm Fractures

Fractures can occur anywhere along the length of the upper-arm bone (humerus) or the two forearm bones (radius and ulna) and may involve the elbow joint. The bones most frequently broken, however, are those at the wrist (Colles Fracture).

Fractures involving the upper arm or elbow joint may also cause extensive damage to surrounding blood vessels and nerves.

Symptoms and Signs
● General symptoms and signs of fracture (see p. 106).

Aim

Immobilise the fracture and transport casualty to doctor or hospital.

Treatment
UPPER ARM FRACTURE
1 Ask the casualty to support the injured arm across the chest with fingertips close to the opposite shoulder.

2 Apply a collar-and-cuff sling (see p. 183) and secure the arm to the chest with a broad- or narrow-fold triangular bandage but avoid pressure on the fracture site. If the injury site permits, apply a second broad- or narrow-fold bandage above or below the fracture.

NB Check the casualty's pulse at the wrist after completing immobilisation and again at 10-minute intervals (see p. 178) to ensure bandages are not too tight.

3 Arrange transfer to hospital as a sitting or walking casualty.

FOREARM FRACTURE

1 Make a splint with rolled-up newspaper, magazine or card that is long enough to support the forearm from the elbow to the fingers. Roll it around the arm so that it fits closely at the elbow and over the hand or use it as a "gutter" splint. Secure it with one or two bandages or adhesive tape.

2 Apply an arm sling (see p. 181). Check the pulse at the wrist after immobilisation and again every 10-minutes thereafter (see p. 178) to ensure bandages are not too tight.

3 Arrange transfer to hospital or doctor as a sitting or walking casualty.

NB Fractures involving the arm or elbow joint must be treated gently and without moving the limb from the position which the casualty has adopted.

IF THE ELBOW CANNOT BE BENT

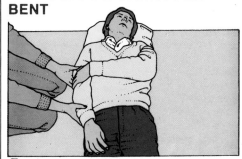

1 Help the casualty to lie down and place the injured limb beside the casualty's trunk. *Do not* attempt to bend the elbow forcibly. Ask the casualty to support the arm with the other hand if possible. Place soft padding between the injured arm and the body.

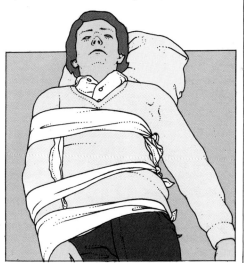

2 Secure the injured limb to the body by three broad bandages: around the wrist and thighs, around the upper arm and trunk, around the forearm and trunk.

3 Check the pulse at the wrist after immobilisation and again at 10-minute intervals thereafter (see p. 178).

4 Transfer the casualty to hospital by ambulance.

Hand and Finger Fractures

Fractures of the hand are usually due to direct force. They are sometimes the result of crush injuries and may involve severe bleeding.

Symptoms and Signs
- General symptoms and signs of fracture.
- Casualty is unable to use fingers.
- Extensive swelling and bruising at the site of injury.

Aim
Immobilise the injured hand and transfer the casualty to hospital or doctor.

Treatment
1 Control any bleeding (see p. 30) and treat any wounds.

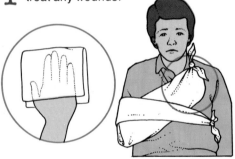

2 Protect the injured hand by placing in a fold of soft padding.

3 Gently support the affected limb in an elevation sling (see p. 182).

4 For additional support, secure the limb to the chest by applying a broad bandage over the sling; tie the knot in front on the *uninjured* side. Check the pulse after immobilisation to ensure that the circulation is satisfactory (see p. 178).

5 Transfer to hospital as a sitting or walking casualty.

LOWER TRUNK AND LIMBS

The *pelvis* is a basin-shaped structure of bone attached to the lower part of the spine. It supports and protects the contents of the lower abdominal cavity and contains sockets for the hip joints.

Each *lower limb* consists of: the thigh-bone; the two bones of the lower leg, the shin-bone (tibia) and the fibula; and a number of smaller bones in the foot and ankle. The thigh-bone reaches from the hip to the knee and is the longest and strongest bone in the body. At its lower end it forms part of the knee-joint, at its upper end its head fits into the pelvis. The knee-cap (patella) is a small, flattish bone which lies in front of the knee-joint. The two bones in the lower leg extend from the knee to the ankle, the long thin bone (fibula) lies on the outer side of the thicker shin-bone (tibia).

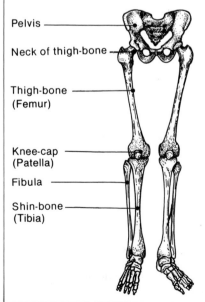

Pelvis

Neck of thigh-bone

Thigh-bone (Femur)

Knee-cap (Patella)

Fibula

Shin-bone (Tibia)

Pelvic Fractures

These are usually caused by a direct crush injury or by indirect force such as might occur during vehicle collisions. For example, the impact of a knee on a car's dashboard can force the head of the femur through the socket of the hip-joint.

One or both sides of the pelvic girdle may be fractured and pelvic injuries can be complicated by injury to the bladder and urinary passages.

Symptoms and Signs
● General symptoms and signs of fracture.
● Pain and tenderness in the region of the hips and groin which is increased by movement.
● Casualty is unable to walk or even stand although the legs appear sound.
● Casualty may express a great desire to pass water if the bladder or urinary passages are damaged. If the casualty does pass water it may be bloodstained.

Aim
Make the casualty comfortable and arrange urgent transfer to hospital.

Treatment

1 Assist the casualty to lie down with the legs straight or, if it is more comfortable for the casualty, bend the knees slightly and place a rolled blanket underneath them.

2 If the casualty expresses a desire to pass water, advise against it; urine may escape into the tissues.

3 *If removal to hospital is imminent,* cover the casualty with a blanket and await the arrival of the ambulance.

4 *When ambulance transport to hospital is likely to be delayed*, gently apply two broad bandages around the pelvis, the lower one first. Overlap them by half with the centres lined up with the hip-joint on the injured side. Tie off on the un-injured side. (If both sides of the pelvis are injured, tie off in the centre.)

5 Place adequate soft padding between the knees and ankles.

6 Apply a figure-of-eight bandage around the ankles and feet and a broad bandage around the knees. Tie knots on the uninjured side.

7 To minimise shock, treat as on p. 86.

8 Transfer to hospital by ambulance as a stretcher case maintaining treatment position.

Lower Limb Fractures

A fracture can occur anywhere along the length of the thigh-bone. It is the longest and strongest bone in the body and has a rich blood supply. All incidents where the thigh-bone is fractured should be regarded as serious because, in most cases, a large volume of blood is lost into the tissues with extensive soft tissue injuries which result in severe shock (see p. 86).

This type of fracture often results from falls and road traffic accidents. In the aged a fracture may result from a minor fall; in most adults, however, considerable force is required to break the femur.

Fractures of the hip joint involving the neck or upper portion of the thigh-bone are often mistaken for a badly bruised hip. Any elderly person who complains of pain in the hip after a fall or other minor accident should be considered as having a possible neck of femur fracture and be transferred to hospital.

Either or both of the two bones in the lower leg, the shin-bone, tibia and the fibula, may be broken. Fractures of the upper end of the shin-bone commonly occur when pedestrians are hit by car bumpers and are known as "bumper" fractures. Shin-bone fractures are often open because only a thin layer of skin and tissue covers the bone.

The fibula is most commonly broken by "wrenching" of the ankle joint. However, because this is not a weight-bearing bone, a simple fracture is often mistaken for a severe sprain, especially if a crack fracture occurs a few inches above the ankle. As a result, the casualty may not seek medical advice until a few days after the injury.

Common Sites of Leg Fracture

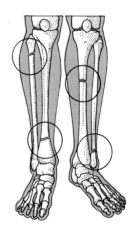

Symptoms and Signs
● General symptoms and signs of fracture.
● Symptoms and signs of shock (see p. 86).
Hip and thigh-bone fracture:
● Visible deformity of lower limb: if fracture of shaft, the limb may be shortened by contraction of the muscles around the fractured bone; if fracture of the neck, the foot may be turned out.
Lower leg fracture:
● Swelling and bruising apparent.
● Angulation and rotation will be seen only if both bones are broken.
● Deformity may be seen or felt along one or both bones.
● Possible "open" wound if shin-bone is fractured.

Aim
Make casualty comfortable and arrange transfer to hospital by ambulance.

Treatment for Lower Limb Fracture

1 *When ambulance transport is imminent,* help the casualty to lie down and carefully steady and support the limb by hand. Await the arrival of skilled help.

BASIC IMMOBILISATION

If the casualty is in severe pain, or ambulance transport is likely to be delayed, use the following method of immobilisation.

2 Place plenty of padding between the knees and ankles.

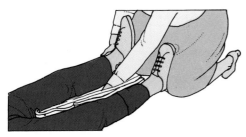

3 Gently bring the sound limb alongside the injured limb using gentle traction with support.

4 Tie a figure-of-eight bandage around the feet and ankles and a broad bandage around the knees; tie all knots on the uninjured side.

REMOTE AREA IMMOBILISATION TECHNIQUE

In a remote area, additional immobilisation will be needed for the casualty's comfort and to prevent complications. However, at least two people are needed to adequately immobilise a lower limb fracture and a third person would be useful. Follow steps 5–9.

5 Place a padded splint between the legs extending from the crotch to the feet. Gently bring the sound limb alongside the injured limb. Apply gentle traction to the injured limb while supporting the foot under the heel and around the toes. Maintain the traction until the second First Aider has applied a figure-of-eight bandage around the feet and ankles and secured it with a knot. The third person should support the injured limb while traction is applied.

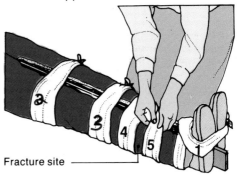

Fracture site

6 Apply a broad bandage around the knees and a third bandage around the thighs. Apply a fourth bandage around the lower legs and finally apply a bandage below the fracture site. Secure all bandages with a reef knot on the outside of the sound limb.

NB Make sure that all bandages avoid pressure on the actual fracture site.

7 When the limbs are immobilised, raise them slightly to minimise discomfort and swelling.

8 To minimise shock, treat as on p. 86.

9 Transfer to hospital as a stretcher case maintaining treatment position.

Knee Joint Injuries

The knee forms a hinge joint, which swings to and fro in one plane only. The lower end of the thigh-bone (femur) rests on the upper end of the shin-bone (tibia), the bones being connected by strong ligaments. Attached around the rim of the upper surface of the shin-bone are two thick, half-moon shaped cushions of cartilage. The knee-joint is supported by strong muscles and in front of the joint lies the kneecap (patella).

Any of these structures may be damaged by violent twists or strains. If the knee-joint is forced sideways or backwards, ligaments may rupture. A rotational strain, whilst the weight of the body is on the same foot, often results in rupture and displacement of a cartilage. A direct blow or violent contraction of the attached muscle may dislocate or fracture the kneecap.

Distinction between these injuries may be difficult, but the treatment is the same for them all.

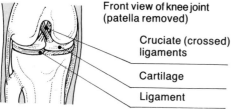

Front view of knee joint (patella removed)

Cruciate (crossed) ligaments

Cartilage

Ligament

Symptoms and Signs
- Pain, which may be localized at first to the site of injury, but quickly becomes deep seated in the joint. All attempted movement of the joint is painful.
- Possible local tenderness.
- Rapid swelling of the joint due to internal bleeding.
- Possible "locking" of the knee in a bent position.
- Possible deformity.

Aim
Protect the knee in the most comfortable position, whilst transporting the casualty to hospital.

Treatment

Do Not attempt to force the knee straight. There may be a displaced cartilage or internal bleeding from a ruptured ligament or a fractured kneecap, which makes the knee joint tense and impossible to straighten.

1 If he is standing, do not allow the casualty to walk. Help him to lie down on his back and support his leg in the most comfortable position.

2 Bandaging is not essential but for comfort and protection, place soft padding around the joint. Bandage carefully, allowing for swelling.

3 Support the knee by placing a small pillow, folded blanket or coat underneath. Give nothing by mouth.

4 Transfer to hospital by ambulance as a stretcher case, maintaining the treatment position.

Foot and Ankle Fractures

Fractures of the foot and ankle often result from injuries such as being run over, or hit or crushed by heavy objects. However, injury can also result from twisting falls or jumps. It may be hard to distinguish a sprained ankle from a fractured ankle; if in doubt always treat as a fracture.

Symptoms and Signs
- General symptoms and signs of fracture.
- Pain in foot increased by movement.
- Tenderness at fracture site.
- Loss of movement of foot; casualty unable to walk properly on foot.
- Swelling and bruising may be present at site of injury.
- Deformity, such as irregularity of the bony arch may be present.

Treatment

1 Assist the casualty to lie down and raise and support the injured foot.

Do Not remove the casualty's shoe and sock unless an open wound is suspected or excessive swelling is present.

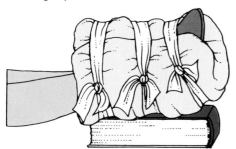

2 Immobilise injured area with a pillow or blanket splint secured with three bandages; tie off on the outside of the limb.

3 Arrange transfer to doctor or hospital.

IF OPEN WOUND OR SEVERE SWELLING IS PRESENT

1 Assist the casualty to lie down, raise the injured foot and gently remove casualty's shoe and sock (see p. 44).

2 Control any external bleeding using direct pressure and cover wounds with dressings and bandages (see p. 30).

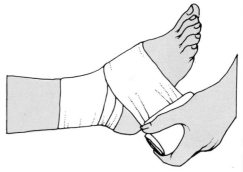

3 Minimise swelling by applying a crepe roller bandage around the foot and ankle. Check pulse and circulation to the toes after bandaging and again at 10-minute intervals thereafter (see p. 178) — adjust bandage as necessary.

4 If possible apply an ice pack or cold compress (see p. 176), to minimise swelling and reduce pain.

5 Arrange transfer to hospital or doctor.

INJURIES TO MUSCLES, LIGAMENTS AND JOINTS

Injuries which involve damage to the muscles, joints or ligaments which strengthen the joints are common and they can be painful. Use of *Ice, Compression and Elevation* (I.C.E.), will reduce pain and swelling for soft tissue injuries.

A dislocated joint in particular may also be mistaken for, or accompanied by, a fracture. In all cases where you are in doubt about the injury, treat it as a fracture and arrange transfer to hospital.

THE MUSCLES

These cause the various parts of the body to move and are of two types: voluntary and involuntary; both produce movement by contracting and relaxing.

Voluntary muscles are so-called because they are under the control of the will. Their movement is co-ordinated through the motor nerves which pass directly from the brain or via the spinal cord (see p. 94). The bones of the skeleton act as a framework for these muscles to pull against and the muscles are attached to the bones by bands of strong, fibrous tissue called *tendons*. Voluntary muscles operate in pairs: one muscle or group of muscles contracts in order to move a bone at the same time as its paired muscle or group of muscles relaxes so that movement can take place.

Involuntary muscles operate the vital organs, such as the heart and intestines, and work all the time, even when we sleep. Most of these muscles cannot be controlled by the will but only by the nerves in the autonomic nervous system (see p. 94).

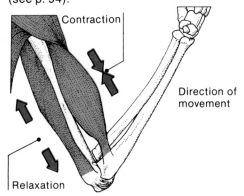

Contraction

Direction of movement

Relaxation

THE JOINTS

Joints are formed by the junction of two or more bones and there are two types: immovable and movable.

Immovable joints are those where the bone edges fit firmly into each other or are fused together so that no movement can take place. The best example of this type of joint is in the skull.

Movable joints can either allow free movement in all directions (ball-and-socket joints), movement in one plane only (hinge joints) or only limited movement (slightly movable joints).

The ends of any bones forming a joint are covered in a smooth cartilage to minimise friction and the joint is strengthened by bands of strong tissue called *ligaments*. The joint itself is enclosed in a capsule filled with a lubricant called synovial fluid.

BALL-AND-SOCKET JOINTS

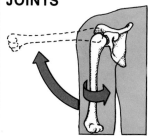

Formed by the round head of one bone fitting into the cup-shaped cavity of another, ball-and-socket joints allow movement in all directions. Examples are the shoulder and hip joints.

HINGE JOINTS

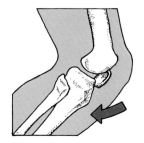

When the surfaces of the bones are moulded together they only allow movement in one direction — bending (flexion) and straightening (extension). Examples are the elbow and knee joints.

SLIGHTLY MOVABLE JOINTS

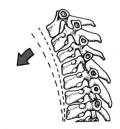

With this type of joint only limited movement is possible. Examples are the joints between the vertebrae and those between the ribs and the spine.

Strain

A strain occurs when a muscle or group of muscles is over-stretched and possibly torn, by violent or sudden movement. This might occur when a person is lifting heavy weights incorrectly or participating in sports.

Symptoms and Signs
- Sudden, sharp pain at the site of the injury which may radiate outwards with subsequent stiffness and/or cramp.
- Swelling at the site of injury.

Aim
Minimise swelling, relieve spasm and pain, and seek medical aid.

Treatment

1 Place the casualty in the most comfortable position.

2 Steady and support the injured part; elevate an injured limb.

3 Apply an ice pack for a maximum of 10 minutes (see p. 176). Repeat every hour if necessary, allowing tissues to regain normal temperature after each application. Apply a firm bandage after the ice pack has been removed, and maintain elevation if possible.

4 If you are in any doubt about the casualty's condition, treat as a fracture (see p. 104–25).

5 Transfer to a doctor or hospital.

NB I.C.E. treatment should be continued regularly while the skin around the injury feels warm to the touch. This may last for several days. DO NOT APPLY HEAT in any form until the skin temperature is normal to touch because heat may cause increased bleeding and swelling of the injured part.

FOR BACK STRAIN

If the casualty is in extreme pain, assist him to lie down on a firm surface, place a cold compress on the back (see p. 176) and seek medical aid.

If you are in any doubt about the severity of the injury treat as a fractured spine (see p. 114).

Sprain

This is an injury which occurs at a joint when the ligaments and tissues around that particular joint are suddenly "wrenched" or torn. For example, a sprained ankle may result if your foot turns over unexpectedly while walking or running. Some sprains are minor, others are associated with extensive damage to the tissues and are difficult to distinguish from fractures. In all doubtful cases, treat the injury as a fracture.

Symptoms and Signs
● Pain and tenderness around the joint increased by movement.
● Swelling around the joint followed later by bruising.

Aim
Minimise swelling, relieve pain and seek medical advice.

Treatment

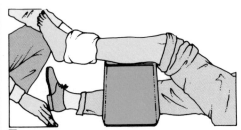

1 Rest and support the injured part in the most comfortable position for the casualty; elevate an injured limb.

2 Carefully expose the joint and apply an ice pack for 10 minutes (see p. 176) to reduce swelling and pain.

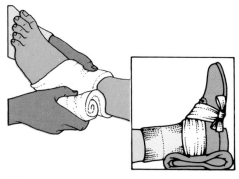

3 When the ice pack is removed, provide some support by bandaging firmly but not tightly.

Do Not apply heat in any form until the skin temperature is normal to touch (see p. 127).

If an ankle is sprained where skilled help is not available *do not* remove the shoe or sock but apply a figure-of-eight bandage over the boot or shoe.

4 If the symptoms persist, seek medical aid.

If you are in doubt about the injury, treat as fracture (see pp. 104–125).

Dislocation

This is the displacement of one or more bones at a joint. It occurs when a strong force acts directly or indirectly on a joint wrenching a bone into an abnormal position. Alternatively, it can be the result of a sudden muscular contraction.

Joints which are most frequently dislocated are the shoulder, elbow, thumb, finger and jaw. In some cases it is diffi-

cult or even impossible to distinguish between a dislocation and a fracture and both may be present. If in doubt, *always* treat as a fracture.

Symptoms and Signs
● Casualty complains of severe (often sickening) pain at or near the joint.
● Casualty is unable to move affected

part: joint "fixed" in position.
- Injured joint appears deformed.
- Swelling and later bruising at the site of injury.

Aim

Immobilise the joint, minimise swelling and arrange transfer to hospital.

Treatment

1 Support the injured part in the most comfortable position for the casualty using pillows or cushions. Immobilise with bandages or slings if available.

2 Apply an ice pack or cold compress for up to 10 minutes at a time (see p. 176).

3 Transfer to hospital immediately.

Do Not attempt to replace bones in their normal positions as further damage may result.

Displaced Cartilage of the Knee (Locked Knee)

The knee-joint contains two separate semi-lunar cartilages one of which may become displaced or torn. This can be caused by a sporting incident, such as a missed kick, by slipping off a step or by twisting the body whilst the weight is balanced on one leg.

Aim

Make the casualty as comfortable as possible and arrange transfer to hospital.

Symptoms and Signs

- Casualty complains of severe sickening pain around the knee, more commonly on the inner side.
- The injured knee is held in a bent position. Although it may be further flexed, it cannot be straightened.
- Swelling may occur due to fluid collecting in the joint.

Treatment

1 Support the injured leg in the most comfortable position for the casualty.

Do Not change the bent position of the knee or attempt to straighten it.

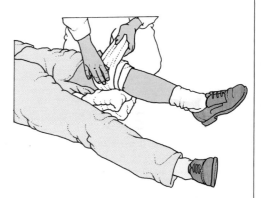

2 Bandaging is not essential but for comfort and protection, place soft padding around the joint. Bandage carefully, allowing for swelling.

3 Support the knee by placing a small pillow, folded blanket or coat underneath. Give nothing by mouth.

4 Transfer to hospital by ambulance as a stretcher case, maintaining the treatment position.

Displaced Intervertebral Disc

Commonly known as a "slipped disc", this occurs when the disc between two vertebrae ruptures and its centre presses against the adjacent nerve root. It can be a very painful condition although the onset of pain may be sudden or gradual.

Symptoms and Signs

● Severe, sharp pain in the back which may radiate towards the legs and may be increased by movement.
● Casualty may be unable or reluctant to move the neck or back.

Aim

Make casualty comfortable and seek medical aid.

Treatment

1 Assist the casualty to lie down on a firm surface in the most comfortable position.

2 Seek medical aid.

Cramp

A cramp is a sudden, involuntary and painful contraction of a muscle or group of muscles. It can occur if there is poor muscular co-ordination during exercise; if chilling occurs following or during exercise such as swimming; if the body loses excessive amounts of salt and body fluids through severe sweating, diarrhoea or persistent vomiting; or during sleep. Cramps due to salt and water loss may also be associated with heat exhaustion (see p. 146).

This condition is normally relieved by stretching the contracted muscle with a gentle, sustained stretch. Gentle massage of the cramped muscle also may help to relax the spasm.

Symptoms and Signs

● Pain in the affected area.
● Feeling of tightness or spasm in the affected muscles.
● Casualty is unable to relax contracted muscles.

Treatment
FOR CRAMP IN HAND

Gently, but firmly, straighten out the fingers and gently massage the area.

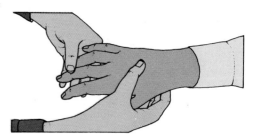

FOR CRAMP IN THIGH MUSCLES

Straighten the knee and raise the leg with one hand under the heel; with the other hand, press down the knee. Gently massage the affected muscles.

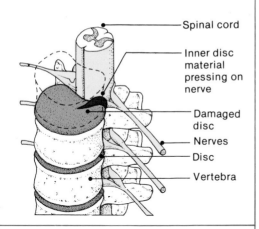

- Spinal cord
- Inner disc material pressing on nerve
- Damaged disc
- Nerves
- Disc
- Vertebra

FOR CRAMP IN CALF MUSCLES

Straighten the knee and gently draw the casualty's foot upwards towards the shin. Gently massage the affected muscles.

FOR CRAMP IN FOOT MUSCLES

Straighten out the casualty's toes and help the casualty to stand on the ball of the foot. Gently massage the foot.

Hernia

An abdominal hernia or rupture is a protrusion caused by a part of the contents of the abdomen protruding through the muscular wall under the skin.

A hernia occurs most frequently in the groin (1) but it is not uncommon at the navel (2) or through the scar of an abdominal operation (3). It may happen after exercise, while lifting heavy objects or when coughing.

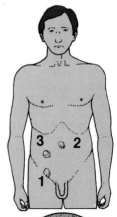

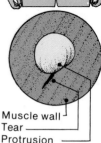

Muscle wall
Tear
Protrusion

Symptoms and Signs

- Painless swelling which may persist or worsen or there may be sudden, painful swelling with possible vomiting. (The latter may indicate a "strangulated" hernia which is a serious condition requiring urgent medical attention.)

Treatment

1 Reassure the casualty.

2 Assist the casualty to lie down in a half-sitting position, support the head and shoulders. Bend the knees and support in this position.

3 If vomiting occurs; or seems likely, turn the casualty into the Lateral Recovery Position promptly (see p. 22).

4 Seek medical aid.

Do Not attempt to reduce the swelling.

BURNS AND SCALDS

These are injuries to body tissues caused by heat, chemicals or radiation. Burns caused by "wet" heat such as steam or hot liquids, are called scalds. Burns vary in depth, size and severity and may damage the underlying parts of the body as well as the skin. Most burns will require medical attention.

Heat is the most common cause of burns. Other causes include contact with dry or liquid corrosive chemicals whether acid or alkali, and over-exposure to radiation and sun rays.

There is considerable risk of infection with burns because, in damaging the skin, burns reduce the skin's protection against bacteria. There is also a danger of shock developing, because serum leaks out of the circulatory system into the burnt area (see p. 86).

Types of Burns

Dry Burns
Flames, lighted cigarettes and hot electrical equipment such as irons are all common causes of dry burns.

Fast-moving objects rubbed against the skin produce dry friction burns. Alternatively, they may be caused by the skin rubbing against an object. The most common example of this is a "rope burn".

Scalds
Wet heat such as steam, hot water or fat produces scalds.

Cold (Cryogenic) Burns
Contact with substances such as liquid oxygen and liquid nitrogen can cause cold burns (see *Frostbite* p. 145).

Chemical Burns
Acids and alkalis, found in domestic cleaning products as well as in industry, may cause burns when they come into contact with the skin.

Electrical Burns
Electrical currents and lightning generate heat and burn skin and underlying tissues.

Radiation Burns
Sun rays and light reflected from bright surfaces, (e.g., snow) can damage the skin and eyes.

Very rarely, radiation burns can come from X-rays. An overdose is absorbed by the skin causing burns.

Classification of Burns

Burns are classified according to the area and depth of the injury. These factors will determine what treatment is required and whether the casualty needs hospital attention. However, any casualty with burns covering an area greater than 2.5 cm (1 in) square, involving more than the surface of the skin or burns arising from electrical contact, must be referred to a doctor or hospital.

AREA
The area of a burn gives a rough guide as to whether or not a casualty is likely to suffer shock. The greater the area involved, the greater the possibility of shock, because of greater fluid loss. For example, an otherwise fit adult casualty with a superficial burn covering 9% or more of the body's surface will need hospital treatment (see diagram opposite).

SEVERITY OF BURNS

There are three levels of burning: superficial, intermediate and deep or full-thickness burns. However, it is often difficult to distinguish between the different levels, particularly in the early stages. A large burn will almost certainly contain areas of all three.

Superficial Burns

These burns involve only the outer layers of skin and result in general redness, swelling and extreme tenderness. This type of burn usually heals well.

Intermediate burns

These burns involve the formation of blisters and the area around the burn will be swollen and red. These burns can be infected so you should seek medical aid.

Deep Burns

These burns involve all layers of skin. The skin appears pale, waxy and sometimes, charred. These burns will be relatively pain-free because the nerves are damaged. Deep burns *always* require medical attention.

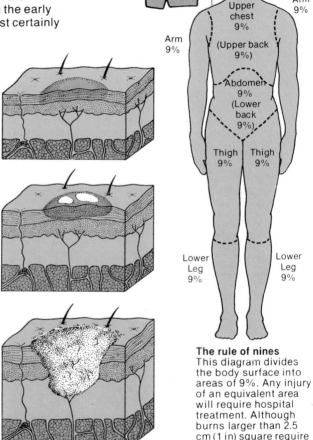

The rule of nines
This diagram divides the body surface into areas of 9%. Any injury of an equivalent area will require hospital treatment. Although burns larger than 2.5 cm (1 in) square require medical attention.

Blisters

Blisters are thin "bubbles" which form on skin damaged by friction or heat. They are caused by tissue fluid (serum) leaking into the burnt area just under the surface of the skin.

During healing, new skin forms at the base of the blister underneath the serum, the serum is reabsorbed and, eventually,

the outer layer of skin peels off. Never break a blister; you will increase the risk of infection.

Unless a blister breaks or is likely to be further damaged, it requires no treatment. If it does need protection, apply a dressing large enough to extend well beyond the edges of the burnt area.

Clothing on Fire

Clothing may be set on fire by standing too close to an electric, gas or open fire or by carelessness in the kitchen. Without prompt help the result is widespread severe burning, shock and possible death. If the accident occurs indoors prevent a conscious casualty from panicking and rushing outside; the movement and/or breeze outside will fan the flames.

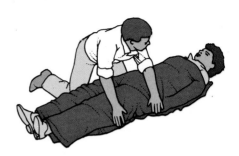

You should lay the casualty down as soon as possible to prevent flames sweeping upwards and quickly put out the flames by dousing the casualty with water or other *non-flammable* liquid. Alternatively, wrap the casualty tightly in

a coat, curtain, blanket (not the cellular type), rug or other heavy fabric then lay the person flat on the ground. This starves the flames of oxygen and puts them out.

Do not use nylon or other inflammable materials to smother the flames.

Do not roll the casualty along the ground as this can cause burning of previously unharmed areas.

If your own clothes have caught fire and help is not immediately available, extinguish the flames by wrapping yourself up tightly in suitable material (see above) and lying down.

Dry Burns and Scalds

These are the most common types of burns both in the home and in industry and they are a major cause of accidental death, particularly amongst children and the elderly.

Burns and scalds must be cooled as soon as possible in order to prevent further damage to underlying tissues and to alleviate pain, swelling and the possibility of shock. The most effective method of cooling is to flood the area gently with cold water for at least 10 minutes.

Any clothing which has been soaked in boiling fluid should be removed as soon as it begins to cool. Cooled, dry, burnt clothing should not be removed because doing so may introduce an infection.

Very small burns or scalds can generally be treated on site. However, if you are in any doubt about the severity of the injury, or if the casualty is an infant or a sick or elderly person, always seek medical advice.

NB Friction burns should be treated as minor burns unless the skin is broken. If the skin is broken see *Minor External Bleeding p. 63)*

General Symptoms and Signs

● Severe pain in and around the injured area if the burn is superficial. The area may be numb if the burn is deep.

● Redness, swelling of area, and sometimes blistering.

● Grey, charred, peeling skin around a severe burn.

● Symptoms and signs of shock (see p. 86). The degree of shock will relate directly to the extent of the injury.

Aim

Reduce the effect of heat, prevent infection, relieve pain and minimise shock. Arrange urgent transfer to hospital if burns are severe or extensive.

General Treatment
FOR MINOR BURNS AND SCALDS

1 Reassure the casualty. Place the injured part under slowly running cold water or immerse it in cold water for 10 minutes — longer if the pain persists.

If no water is available, any cold, harmless liquid such as milk or beer can be used instead.

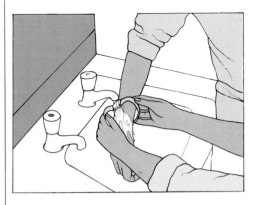

2 Gently remove any rings, watches, belts, shoes or other constricting clothing from the injured area *before* it starts to swell.

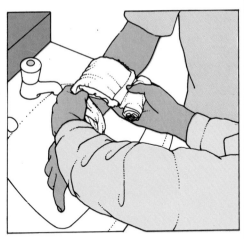

3 Apply a clean, preferably sterile, non-fluffy dressing secured with a light roller bandage (see Dressings pp. 172-5).

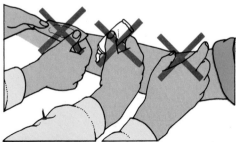

Do Not use adhesive dressings.

Do Not apply lotions, ointments or fat to injury.

Do Not break blisters, remove any loose skin or otherwise interfere with the injured area.

Do Not try to remove any material which is sticking to the skin, for example, bitumen, toffee or melted synthetic fabric.

4 If in doubt about the severity of the injury seek medical aid.

General Treatment
FOR SEVERE BURNS AND SCALDS

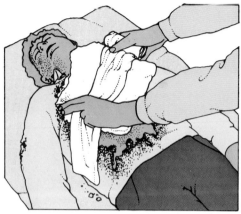

1 Assist the casualty to lie down and protect the burnt area from contact with the ground if possible.

2 Gently remove any rings, watches, belts or constricting clothes from the injured area *before* it starts to swell. Carefully remove any clothing soaked in boiling fluid *after* it has begun to cool. *DO NOT* remove anything that is sticking to the wound.

3 Apply cold water or a cold compress for a few minutes but do not overcool the tissues.

4 Cover the injured area with a sterile, unmedicated dressing or similar non-fluffy material and secure with a light roller bandage (see Dressings pp. 172-5).

Do Not apply lotions, ointments or fat to injury.

Do Not break blisters, remove any loose skin or otherwise interfere with the injured area.

If hot bitumen or other melted substance completely covers a limb, it should be split lengthwise as it cools, to avoid any interference with the circulation.

Burns in the Mouth and Throat

Burns to the mouth and throat usually result from drinking very hot liquid, swallowing corrosive chemicals or inhaling very hot air. These injuries are very serious because the tissues in the throat swell quickly and can close the airway making it difficult, if not impossible, for the casualty to breathe. In this situation it is particularly important to prevent the casualty panicking thereby worsening the situation.

Symptoms and Signs
● Casualty complains of severe pain in the injured area.
● Damaged skin around the mouth.
● Difficulty in breathing.
● Possible unconsciousness.
● Symptoms and signs of shock (see p. 86).

Aim
Maintain airway and breathing; arrange urgent transfer to hospital.

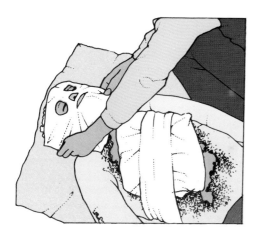

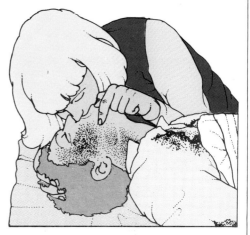

5 For facial burns, make a mask from a clean, dry, preferably sterile, piece of material (a pillow case is useful). Cut holes for the nose, mouth and eyes.

6 Immobilise a badly injured limb (see Fractures, pp. 104–125).

7 To minimise shock treat as on p. 86.

If the casualty is conscious, moisten the lips at frequent intervals.

8 If the casualty is unconscious, turn him on the side and give care of airway, breathing and circulation following the Basic Life Support Flow Chart (see p. 15).

9 Arrange ambulance transport to hospital as a stretcher case, maintaining the treatment position.

Treatment

1 Reassure the casualty.

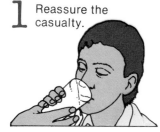

2 If the casualty is conscious, moisten the lips at frequent intervals.

3 Remove any constricting clothing or jewellery from around the neck and chest.

4 If the casualty becomes unconscious, turn him on to the side and give care of airway, breathing and circulation according to the Basic Life Support Flow Chart (see p. 15).

5 To minimise shock, treat as on p. 86.

6 Arrange transfer to hospital immediately maintaining the treatment position; transport as a stretcher case if necessary.

Chemical Burns

Certain substances are irritating to the skin and contact with them can cause severe damage to the tissues; eyes are particularly vulnerable. Apart from the local effects, a few chemicals may be absorbed through the skin and cause widespread and sometimes fatal damage within the body.

Strong corrosives and chemicals will be found in industry but some household goods such as caustic soda, bleaches, household cleaners and paint strippers can cause chemical burns.

While prompt action with this type of burn is important, you should *always* con-sider your own safety before approaching the casualty.

Symptoms and Signs
- Casualty may complain that skin is stinging.
- Skin may appear stained or reddened and blistering and peeling may develop.

Aim
Identify and remove the harmful chemical as quickly as possible. Do not waste time looking for the antidote unless it is immediately available. Arrange urgent transfer to hospital.

Treatment

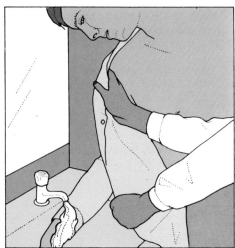

1 Flood the affected area with slowly running cold water for at least 10–15 minutes to prevent further damage to the burned tissue.

NB Make sure the water drains away freely and safely as it will be contaminated by the chemical which caused the burn.

2 Gently remove any contaminated clothing while flooding the injured area; make sure you do not contaminate yourself.

3 Continue treatment for severe burns, (see p. 136).

4 Transfer to hospital immediately; transport as stretcher case if necessary.

Chemical Burns in the Eye

Corrosive chemicals, both liquid and solid, can easily enter the eye and rapidly damage its surface causing severe scarring and even blindness.

Aim
Wash the chemicals away as quickly as possible and transfer to hospital.

Symptoms and Signs
- Intense pain in the affected eye.
- Damaged eye cannot tolerate light.
- Affected eye may be tightly closed.
- The eye may be reddened, swollen or watering excessively.

Treatment

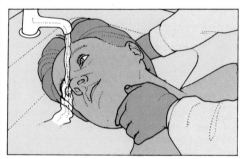

1 Hold the affected side of the casualty's face under gently running cold water for at least 10–15 minutes so that the water drains away from the face. Alternatively let the casualty put the affected side of the face in a bowl of cold water and ask the casualty to blink.

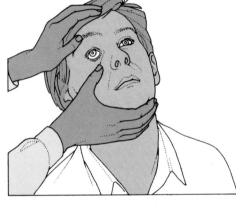

NB Check that both surfaces of the eyelids have been well-irrigated. If the eye is shut in a spasm of pain, you may have to pull the lids firmly, but gently, open.

If this is not possible, sit or lay the casualty down with the head tilted back and turned towards the affected side. Protect the uninjured eye, gently open the eyelid of the affected eye and pour sterile water or saline over it. If these solutions are not available, use a cup of tap water.

2 Lightly dress the eye with a sterile eye pad or, if this is not available, a pad of clean, non-fluffy material.

3 Transfer to hospital immediately.

Electrical Burns

A burn may occur when electricity of a sufficiently high current and voltage passes through the body. Much of the damage occurs at, or close to, the points of entry and exit but, while only small burns may be visible, damage to the underlying tissues may be considerable. Electric shocks can also affect both breathing and heart action (see oxygen lack p. 45).

The most dangerous causes of electrical burns are high-voltage industrial machinery and lightning. Electricity in high-voltage industrial cables can jump or "arc" up to 18 m (20 yd) and kill you. So, do not approach the casualty unless you are officially informed that the current has been switched off (see p. 55).

Symptoms and Signs
- Redness, swelling, scorching or charring of the skin at both the entry and the exit points.
- Possible unconsciousness.
- Breathing and heartbeat may have stopped.
- Symptoms and signs of shock (see p. 86).

Aim
Separate the casualty from the source of injury; maintain airway, breathing and circulation, treat burns and arrange transfer to hospital.

Treatment
1 Place a sterile dressing or pad of clean non-fluffy material over the burn. Secure with a bandage (see *Dressings* pp. 172 – 5).

Do Not apply lotions, ointments or fat to injury.

Do Not break blisters, remove any loose skin or otherwise interfere with the injured area.

2 To minimise shock, treat as on p. 86.

3 If the casualty becomes unconscious, turn him or her on to the side immediately and give care of airway, breathing and circulation according to the Basic Life Support Flow Chart (see p. 15).

4 Transfer to hospital immediately maintaining the treatment position; transport as a stretcher case if necessary.

Sunburn

Direct exposure to the sun's rays may produce redness, itching and tenderness of the skin. It can vary from superficial burning to a more severe reaction in which the skin becomes lobster-red, blistered and painful.

Over-exposure to the sun's rays when it is very windy or the body is wet with sea-water or sweat can result in serious burns. However, sunburn can also occur even on a dull, overcast day in summer and in winter on high mountains when skiing because of the ultraviolet light.

Australia has the highest incidence of skin cancer in the world and research has linked this fact to over-exposure to the sun; in particular to ultra-violet B waves. The most dangerous time for sunburn is in the middle of the day between 10 a.m. and 4 p.m. During this time wear protective clothing as well as sun-screen creams or lotions which will protect the skin against ultra-violet B waves. *Remember to reapply the sun screen after swimming*.

Symptoms and Signs
- Casualty's skin will be red, tender and

swollen with possible blistering.
- Affected skin will feel hot.

Aim
Transfer casualty to a cool place; relieve discomfort and maintain fluids. Seek medical advice if burns are severe.

Treatment

1 Transfer the casualty to the shade and cool the skin by sponging gently with cold water or soaking in a cool bath. Pat the skin dry and keep it protected from further exposure to the sun.

2 Give the casualty sips of cold water at frequent intervals.

3 For extensive blistering, seek medical aid immediately.

Do Not break blisters.

Snow Blindness and Welder's Flash

When the eyes are exposed to glare produced by the reflection of the sun on snow or concrete for too long, the cornea of the eye can be injured. This is a very painful condition and can take as long as a week to subside. It can easily be prevented by wearing dark glasses.

This condition can also result from the ultraviolet light produced by welding. Most protective helmets and goggles worn by welders give complete protection but careless use may expose a worker's eyes to a flash from an adjacent torch.

Symptoms and Signs
These normally appear some time after exposure to glare or welding flash.
- Casualty complains of intense pain in the affected eyes; eyes may feel as if they are full of sand or pepper.
- Affected eyes will be red, watering and sensitive to light.

Treatment

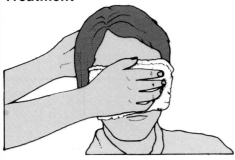

1 Bathe the eyes with cold water (see p. 139).

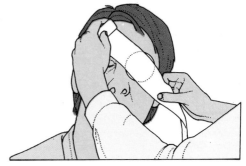

2 Lightly dress both eyes with eye pads or similar pads of clean, non-fluffy material.

3 If in doubt about the severity of the injury, seek medical aid immediately.

EFFECTS OF EXTREMES OF TEMPERATURE

Both extremes of temperature, excessive heat and cold, can damage the skin and other tissues of the body. In severe exposure, death may result.

Our bodies operate most efficiently within a narrow temperature range 36 – 37°C (97 – 99°F) with an average of 37°C (98.6°F). In order to keep a constant temperature, the body must retain its heat when the surrounding temperature is cool, and lose heat when the environment becomes hot.

The capillaries and sweat glands present in the skin are involved in temperature regulation. Part of the brain acts as a thermostat to achieve the balance between the heat gained by the body and the heat lost to the surroundings. In addition to this, the water vapour breathed out from the lungs helps to cool the body. However, this temperature regulation may be inadequate particularly in the very young or the elderly.

Temperature is affected by and can in part be regulated by:
● Insulation in the form of clothing or an artificially controlled environment (e.g., central heating or air conditioning).
● Food intake in the form of high-energy foods which produce heat or fluids which replace fluid lost through evaporation of sweat.
● Physical activity which produces heat. Over-exertion in hot climates can lead to heat exhaustion.

Methods of Producing Heat

Warm clothing

Heated shelter

High-energy foods

Physical activity

The Effects of Cooling

The body temperature falls when the environmental temperature is very low or during immersion in cold water. When this happens the following reactions take place:
● The skin capillaries contract making the person look pale and at the same time reducing the blood flow to the skin so that less heat is lost from the body surface.

● Shivering occurs — the skeletal muscles contract and relax rapidly (without us willing them to do so) and more heat is generated in the muscles.

Two conditions can arise from cooling: *hypothermia* where the whole body is affected by general cooling and *frostbite* where parts of the body, particularly the extremities, are affected locally.

Hypothermia

This is a condition which develops when the body temperature falls below about 35°C (90°F). Moderate hypothermia can normally be reversed and recovery will be complete. However, recovery is unlikely if the body temperature falls below 26 – 24°C (75 – 70°F).
NB A special thermometer is required to read such low temperatures.

Hypothermia occurs when the environmental temperature is very low but it can develop when temperatures are above freezing. It is commonly caused by: prolonged immersion in cold water; inadequate protection against a cold environment, particularly if the casualty is exhausted, wearing wet clothes or at a high altitude; or simply from general exposure to cold by being in an unheated or poorly heated house for a long period.

The ability of the body to protect itself from the cold is lessened by alcohol or drugs. Certain medical conditions such as diabetes may also be a contributory factor.

The onset of the effects of cold may pass unnoticed and their severity may vary with the age and physical condition of the individual, both of which govern the ability to resist chilling.

Symptoms and Signs

General cooling causes the inner body temperature to drop and the casualty passes through several stages of discomfort and disability. Death may occur in a few hours or more rapidly in the case of immersion.

The different stages of hypothermia are as follows:
● Casualty complains of feeling miserably cold.
● Casualty's skin becomes pale, although infants may be pink and appear deceptively healthy (see over).
● Casualty feels abnormally cold to the touch.
● Intense and uncontrollable shivering (rigor) may appear.
● Shivering decreases and may be replaced by lack of muscle co-ordination and slurred speech.
● General comprehension of the situation is dulled and the casualty may become irrational.
● Pulse and respiration rate slow down.
● Loss of consciousness: breathing and heartbeat become increasingly difficult to detect.

NB *Never* assume that a casualty suffering from hypothermia is dead even if breathing and heartbeat appear absent.

Aim

Prevent the casualty from losing any more body heat and help to regain normal body temperature gradually. Arrange urgent transfer to hospital.

The Effects of Hypothermia

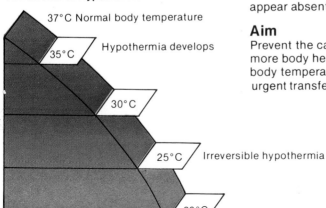

37°C Normal body temperature

35°C   Hypothermia develops

30°C

25°C   Irreversible hypothermia

20°C

Treatment

1 If possible remove casualty from the cold environment or improvise a shelter. Assist the casualty to lie down and place insulating material around casualty to cover body, head and neck but *not* the face, and cover with another sleeping bag or similar material; keep the arms and hands *outside* the first insulating layer.

If the casualty is unconscious, turn him or her on to the side and give care of airway, breathing and circulation, following the Basic Life Support Flow Chart.

NB A casualty with severe hypothermia may have a very slow heartbeat which is difficult to detect and an imperceptible breathing rate. If in doubt, follow the life support chart (see p. 15).

2 Keep the casualty lying flat. If moving is necessary handle him or her gently.

Do Not let the casualty sit up because a fall in blood pressure may occur.

3 When adequate insulation and shelter are available, remove wet clothes.

If adequate insulation and shelter are *not* available, leave wet clothes on the casualty and cover him or her with waterproof material and more insulation.

NB A person in dry clothes standing in a wind free area can tolerate a low temperature over extended periods. However, the combination of cold and wind can produce very low temperatures; the effect is known as the "wind chill factor" and should be taken into account when treating hypothermia.

4 *When medical aid is not readily available*, apply gentle heat to prevent any further drop in body temperature. A companion in a sleeping bag may provide the source of heat, or covered heating bags may be applied to the groin, armpits and sides of the neck but *not to the extremities*. Avoid using hot air as radiant heat.

Do Not rub or massage the limbs or allow the casualty to exercise.

5 Give the conscious casualty warm, sweet drinks.

Do Not give the casualty any alcohol.

6 Transfer to hospital.

NB The natural tendency to "press on" must be avoided. Regrouping on the spot and commencing treatment is more important than a panic evacuation.

HYPOTHERMIA IN INFANTS

Babies can suffer from hypothermia as they have difficulty in regulating their body temperatures. A baby with hypothermia may look very healthy so that its behaviour may be the only indication. Follow the treatment above.

Symptoms and Signs
- The baby is unusually quiet, drowsy and limp.
- The baby will refuse food.
- Usually, the face, hands and feet are bright pink and healthy-looking.

HYPOTHERMIA IN THE ELDERLY

In addition to being less able to regulate their body temperatures, the elderly and infirm are often unable to look after themselves — they go without adequate food and heat and may not feel like moving about. In the aged, hypothermia may be mistaken for a stroke or heart attack. Treat as described above.

Frostbite

Frostbite occurs when the extremities of the body, most frequently the ears, nose, chin, hands and feet, are exposed to prolonged or intense cold. It may be *superficial*, freezing the skin only or *deep*, freezing both the skin and the underlying tissues. In severe cases gangrene of the affected parts may develop.

In the early stages it is not possible to differentiate between the two types. The initial symptoms and signs listed below are common to both. Frostbite may be accompanied by hypothermia; this should be treated before frostbite.

Symptoms and Signs
- Casualty complains of prickling pain in affected part, followed by gradual numbness.
- Movement of the affected part may be impaired.
- The skin feels hard and stiff.
- The skin appears wax-white or a mottled-blue colour.

Aim
Warm the affected area *slowly* and naturally to prevent further tissue destruction. Arrange transfer to hospital.

Treatment

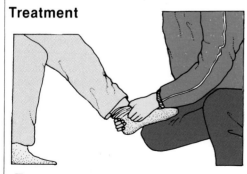

1 Remove to shelter and gently remove any clothing or covering from the affected area.

2 Remove anything of a constrictive nature, such as rings or watches.

3 Immediately re-warm the affected parts by skin-to-skin heat transfer from a warm part of the casualty or yourself. The hands may be placed in the casualty's armpits and the feet may be placed in your armpits. Cover frostbitten ears, nose or face with warm hands until colour and sensation return.

4 Place the injured part in warm water (tolerable to your elbow), if available.

Do Not let the casualty walk on a "defrosted" foot.

5 If re-warming reverses the signs within an hour stop the treatment but do not let the casualty be re-exposed to cold because the circulation has been damaged.

6 Elevate the affected parts to relieve swelling and pain.

7 Lightly cover the affected parts with soft dressings.

8 Transfer to hospital.

Do Not rub or massage the affected parts.

Do Not break blisters or apply ointments or medications to the injured area.

Do Not re-warm by dry or radiant heat.

The Effects of Overheating

During strenuous exercise heat is released in the muscles and distributed to all parts of the body by the blood causing the general body temperature to rise. When this happens, the body reacts immediately to lose heat.
- The skin capillaries enlarge (dilate), so that more blood is carried to the surface allowing heat to be lost. This diversion of blood to the skin makes the person look hot and flushed.
- The sweat glands produce more sweat which evaporates and cools the body.
- Breathing increases and more heat is lost from the lungs.

Two conditions can arise from overheating, heat exhaustion and heatstroke. *Heat exhaustion* usually affects people performing physical exercise in hot, moist climates especially if they do not replace the fluid lost in sweat.

Heatstroke and rapid unconsciousness can occur during exposure to extreme heat or high humidity with no air current. The body temperature may rise as high as 40°C (104°F) because of a person's inability to sweat. A temperature of 42°C (108°F) is considered life-threatening.

Heat Exhaustion

This is a condition caused by loss of water from the body. It is more common in persons unaccustomed to working in a very hot, humid environment although in elderly persons, it may follow a debilitating illness. The condition can be aggravated by a stomach upset with diarrhoea and vomiting.

Symptoms and Signs
- Casualty may feel exhausted but restless.
- Casualty may have a headache and feel tired, dizzy and nauseated.
- Muscular cramps in the lower limbs and abdomen.
- Casualty's face will be pale and the skin will feel cold and clammy.
- Breathing becomes fast and shallow.
- Pulse is rapid and weak.
- Temperature remains normal or falls.
- Casualty may faint on any sudden movement.

Aim
Remove the casualty to a cooler environment and replace lost fluids. Transfer the casualty to medical aid.

Treatment

1 Assist the casualty to lie down in a cool place. Support the legs in a comfortable slightly raised position.

2 If the casualty is conscious, give sips of cold water to drink.

If the casualty is vomiting, seek urgent medical aid because fluids may need to be replaced by intravenous drip.

3 If the casualty is unconscious, turn him into the Lateral Recovery Position and care for airway, breathing and circulation following the Basic Life Support Flow Chart (see p. 15).

4 Seek medical aid.

Heatstroke

Heatstroke is caused by a very high environmental temperature or a feverish illness such as malaria, that leads to a greatly raised body temperature. It develops when the body can no longer control its temperature by sweating and can occur quite suddenly. It can develop in people of any age who have been exposed to heat and high humidity for too long and who are unaccustomed to them; or from prolonged confinement in a hot atmosphere. Anyone suffering from heatstroke should receive urgent medical attention. Heat stroke may be fatal unless it is treated promptly in hospital.

Symptoms and Signs
● Casualty complains of headache, dizziness and of feeling hot.
● Casualty becomes restless.
● Unconsciousness may develop rapidly and become very deep.
● Casualty will be hot with a temperature of 40°C (104°F) or more and will look flushed although skin remains dry.
● Pulse is full and bounding; the breathing may be noisy.

Aim
Reduce the casualty's temperature as quickly as possible and arrange urgent transfer to hospital.

Treatment

1 Move the casualty to a cool environment and remove his outer clothing.

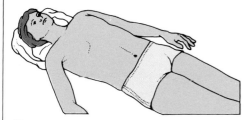

2 If the casualty is conscious, help him to lie down with head and shoulders raised and supported.

If the casualty becomes unconscious, place him in the Lateral Recovery position and care for airway, breathing, circulation following the Basic Life Support Flow Chart (see p. 15).

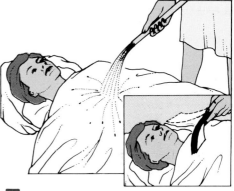

3 Wrap the casualty in a cold, wet sheet and keep it wet. Direct currents of air on to the casualty by fanning with a magazine, book or an electric fan until the casualty's temperature drops to 38°C (101°F).

4 Seek medical aid immediately.

If the casualty's temperature reduces, cover the casualty with a dry sheet and remove to an air-conditioned room if possible.

If the casualty's temperature rises again, repeat steps 2 and 3 above.

POISONING

A poison is any substance which, if taken into the body in sufficient quantity, can cause temporary or permanent damage. Instances of alleged poisoning occur in Australia each year involving both children and adults and some of them are fatal. Whilst some cases are attempted suicide, others are accidental and involve substances in everyday use. Whatever the cause of poisoning, medical aid should always be sought as soon as possible from your nearest Poisons Information Centre (see *Useful Addresses* p. 223, or the local telephone directory) or the local doctor. Only attempt to make the casualty vomit if told to do so by the information centre or doctor; it is likely to be ineffective and you may make the situation worse.

If the Poisons Information Centre tell you to make the casualty vomit, they will suggest that you give the casualty a measured dose of syrup of Ipecac which will make the casualty vomit approximately 20 minutes after taking the recommended dose. Syrup of Ipecac is a useful preparation to keep locked in the family First Aid box and it can be obtained from the local pharmacy. It may need to be replaced after a few months of storage.

THE DIGESTIVE SYSTEM

Food is broken down in the mouth, stomach and intestines by digestive juices secreted by various glands. It is taken in at the mouth and travels down the gullet (oesophagus) until it reaches the stomach. After partial digestion in the stomach, food then passes into the small intestine in small amounts. Here it is broken down into simple substances which are absorbed by the blood. The residue, consisting largely of vegetable fibres, enters the large intestine where accompanying water and mineral salts are absorbed. The final waste products are then eliminated from the body through the rectum at the anus.

The liver acts as a chemical factory which, amongst other functions, inactivates some poisons. The kidneys rid the blood of many impurities.

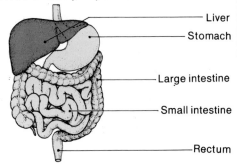

Liver
Stomach
Large intestine
Small intestine
Rectum

How Poisons Enter the Body

Poisons can enter the body in a number of ways either accidentally or intentionally:
● Through the mouth by eating or drinking poisonous substances.
● Through the lungs by inhaling industrial gases, chemical vapours or fumes from fires and petrol engine exhausts.
● By injection into the skin as the result of bites from some animals, insects, poisonous fish or reptiles or by hypodermic syringe.
● By absorption through the skin through contact with poisonous sprays such as pesticides and insecticides.

How Poisons Act

When in the body poisons act in various ways. Once in the bloodstream, some poisons work on the central nervous system preventing breathing, heart action and other vital life processes. Other poisons act by displacing the oxygen in the blood and preventing its distribution.

Swallowed (ingested) poisons also react directly on the food passages resulting in vomiting, pain and often diarrhoea. Corrosive poisons may severely burn the lips, mouth, gullet and stomach thus causing intense pain.

General Symptoms and Signs

These vary depending on the nature of the poison and the method of entry into the body.
● Information from the casualty or an onlooker suggesting contact with a poison. Try to ascertain exactly what was involved and if swallowed, when and how much was taken.
● Presence of a container near the casualty known to hold or have held poison or a poisonous plant.
● Casualty may be delirious and have convulsions without previous history of such conditions.
● Unconsciousness may develop.
● Symptoms and signs of oxygen lack (see p. 45).
● Casualty may be retching or vomiting or suffer from diarrhoea.
● Burns around the casualty's mouth.
● Petrol or Kerosene odour on casualty's breath.

Aim

Maintain and open airway and transfer the casualty to medical aid as soon as possible.

General Treatment

1 Quickly ask the conscious casualty what has happened; remember that the casualty may lose consciousness at any time.

If the lips or mouth show signs of burning, cool them by giving the casualty milk or water to drink.

2 If the casualty is conscious, contact the local Poisons Information Centre or doctor immediately.

If the casualty has swallowed tablets, berries or other non-corrosive material, you will probably be asked to give him or her a measured dose of syrup of Ipecac before transfer to hospital. *Do Not give syrup of Ipecac unless advised to do so by the poison centre or a doctor.*

If the casualty has swallowed a corrosive substance or a volatile fluid such as kerosene or petrol you may be asked to dilute and neutralise the poison with milk or water. If made to vomit, the casualty would suffer more burns because *a substance which burns going down will burn again coming up.*

3 If the casualty is unconscious, turn him or her on to the side and give care of airway, breathing and circulation following the Basic Life Support Flow Chart (see p. 15).

If Expired Air Resuscitation is needed be careful to avoid self-contamination with any poison around the mouth.

If poison may have been absorbed through the skin, remove all contaminated clothing and wash the skin thoroughly under running water.

4 Arrange transfer to hospital immediately. Send any samples of vomit and containers such as bottles or pill boxes found nearby to the hospital with the casualty.

Household Poisons

Many substances found in and about the home can be poisonous. These include liquid soap, some cosmetics, fire-lighters, turpentine, bleach, glue, rat-poison, paint stripper, garden sprays and insecticides. Children are especially at risk from such materials since they may not or cannot be aware of the consequences of eating or drinking them.

The symptoms and signs will vary according to the poison, although vomiting and abdominal pain are likely to occur in most cases. Treat as described on p. 149 and transfer to hospital.

Children are also liable to take medicines and tablets found in medicine cabinets. While most household medicines and tablets are not dangerous if taken as directed, many are poisonous if the dosage is exceeded. Some of the more dangerous medicines include capsules and tablets which look like sweets, for example, certain iron tablets, junior aspirin (especially the coloured ones), tranquillisers and barbiturates.

NB Always make sure that all bottles and jars containing poisonous substances are clearly marked and kept out of reach of children. Avoid the temptation to keep out-dated medicines.

Poisonous Plants

Certain plants, around our gardens as well as in the wild, are dangerous if eaten and some may cause allergic reactions if touched. Children, in particular, are attracted by the bright berries of many of these plants and eat them.

Laburnum, Deadly Nightshade, the Arum Lily, the Castor Oil plant, the Oleander and many flowering bulbs are the more common examples of plants which can poison the system. All toad-stools are likely to be poisonous and many cases of accidental poisoning have occurred when a person has eaten a wild mushroom. Many house plants are poisonous and they should not be left on the floor if young children are playing in the area. A comprehensive list of poisonous plants can be obtained from State departments, botanic gardens or gardening texts. If you suspect that a casualty has eaten a poisonous plant or

Food Poisoning

This is caused by food becoming contaminated by bacteria and being stored or cooked incorrectly. The most common bacteria are: staphylococci, which multiply in the food and produce a poisonous substance (toxin); or salmonellae, which multiply in the bowel and cause a dysentery-like illness. Salmonella is infectious and can be passed through poor personal and kitchen hygiene.

Botulism is an illness which is often fatal which can result from eating food contaminated by a toxic organism called *clostridium botulinum* sometimes found in canned foods. Cans should only be opened if they are in good condition; a dented can is usually safe but one that is bulging outwards at one end may not be.

Some Australian fish can cause severe food poisoning, particularly the Toad fish

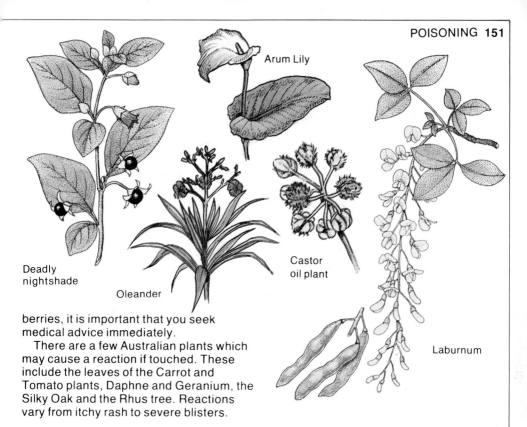

Arum Lily

Deadly
nightshade

Oleander

Castor
oil plant

Laburnum

berries, it is important that you seek
medical advice immediately.

There are a few Australian plants which
may cause a reaction if touched. These
include the leaves of the Carrot and
Tomato plants, Daphne and Geranium, the
Silky Oak and the Rhus tree. Reactions
vary from itchy rash to severe blisters.

or Puffer fish which are frequently caught
by fishermen around the Australian Coastline. Some large fish caught in Australian
tropical waters contain a highly poisonous
substance called *ciguatoxin* which is
tasteless and unaffected by cooking. For
safety eat fish identified by a recognised
fisherman or sold in a shop or restaurant.

Symptoms and Signs

Some of these can appear within two
hours of eating poisonous or contaminated food, whereas others may not
appear for one or two days. Symptoms
and signs will vary according to the poison
or contamination which has entered the
body, but generally includes any or several
of the following.

- Nausea and vomiting or diarrhoea.
- Abdominal cramps or pain.
- Headache.
- Joint pains.

- Numbness and tingling of hands,
fingers or around the mouth.
- Weakness, faintness and, later,
collapse.
- Profuse sweating, with fever later.
- Symptoms and signs of shock (see p.
86).

Aim

Prevent dehydration and seek medical aid
as soon as possible.

Treatment

See general treatment of poisons.

1 Keep the casualty at rest.

2 Give the casualty plenty of fluids.

3 If in doubt about the casualty's
condition, arrange transfer to hospital
or doctor for diagnosis and treatment.

Alcohol Poisoning

Alcohol is a drug that depresses the central nervous system. It affects different people in different ways. One drink usually only produces a slight change in mood. As the intake continues, however, the drug affects the areas of higher reasoning within the brain — those that control restraint and judgement. As the concentration of alcohol in the blood increases, the behaviour of the drinker becomes exaggerated and co-ordination will be impaired. Eventually, the mental and physical abilities are deeply disturbed and unconsciousness will develop.

Aim

Ensure an open airway; arrange transfer to hospital if the casualty is unconscious.

Symptoms and Signs

● Casualty's breath may smell of alcohol.
● Casualty may be vomiting.
● Casualty may be partly conscious or already unconscious. If unconscious you may be able to rouse the casualty, but the casualty will lapse into unconsciousness again quite quickly.

In early stages of unconsciousness:
● Casualty will be breathing deeply.
● Face will be moist and flushed.
● Pulse will be full and bounding.

In later stages of unconsciousness:
● Pulse may become rapid but weak.
● Breathing will be shallow.
● Casualty's face will feel dry and look bloated.
● Eyes will be bloodshot and pupils may be dilated.

Drug Poisoning

This condition is caused by accidental overdose or drug abuse. Drug abuse may be broadly defined as the self-administration of a drug in a manner that is not in accordance with approved medical or social patterns. Drugs can be inhaled, swallowed or injected into the body. A regular drug abuser may show signs of continuous use of hypodermic injections. These marks will usually be on the front of the forearm near the elbow, although other places are used.

Drugs commonly abused are: narcotics (e.g., heroin); depressants (e.g., barbiturates and tranquillisers); stimulants (e.g., amphetamines) and hallucinogens (eg., L.S.D.). In addition there is solvent inhalation (e.g., "glue-sniffing").

Symptoms and Signs

These will vary according to the drug and the quantity taken. Vomiting will not always appear immediately but you should watch for it. The pupils of the eyes may be abnormally dilated or contracted.

Narcotics

These are usually injected but can be taken in tablet form or inhaled.
● Breathing becomes difficult and eventually will cease.
● Casualty may have injection marks on the front of one or both arms.

Depressants

● Breathing will be shallow
● Casualty's skin will feel cold and clammy.
● Weak and rapid pulse.
● Possible unconsciousness.

Stimulants

● Casualty will be excitable and sweating profusely.

Treatment

1 If the casualty is unconscious turn him on to his side and care for airway, breathing and circulation according to the Basic Life Support Flow Chart (see p. 15).

2 If the casualty is conscious, ensure that a responsible adult is available to give any necessary care or help the casualty home. If necessary recommend that the casualty is driven home by someone else because of impaired judgement.

3 If in any doubt about the casualty's condition, arrange transfer to hospital.

● Casualty may be suffering from tremors and hallucinations.

Hallucinogens
● Casualty will be anxious and sweating.
● Casualty may be behaving strangely.

Aspirin Overdose
● Casualty has abdominal pain, and may be vomiting. Vomit may be blood-stained.
● Casualty may be depressed and drowsy.
● Casualty may complain of "ringing" in the ears (tinnitus).
● Difficulty in breathing.
● Casualty will be sweating profusely.
● Full pulse.

Treatment
Follow the general treatment for poisoning. Arrange urgent transfer to hospital and be prepared to resuscitate.

Industrial Poisons

Some people may be in contact with dangerous chemicals or gases at their work places by, for example, the failure of a chemical plant or spillage of corrosive substances.

Amongst the most common industrial poisons are gases. These are usually classed as: irritants (e.g., ammonia and nitrous fumes); toxic gases (e.g., carbon monoxide and hydrogen cyanide gas); and toxic vapours (e.g., those given off by volatile chemicals such as carbon tetra-chloride or trichloroethylene).

There are so many different poisonous substances in use that it is impossible to give a comprehensive list. Any factory using potentially dangerous chemicals or gases must display notices indicating any special action to be taken in case of accidents (see *Accidents Involving Dangerous Chemicals* p. 169). Therefore, if you are called to an industrial accident involving dangerous substances, contact a safety officer or responsible member of staff. Always obey any safety regulations to avoid further injury to yourself and/or the casualty.

Remember that any casualty suffering from the effects of gas or toxic fumes needs air. Take great care to prevent yourself being overcome by any fumes that remain in the area. Never attempt to rescue a casualty trapped in an enclosed space unless equipped with, and practised in the use of, breathing apparatus and life-lines.

Snake Bites

Approximately 500 snake bites are reported every year in Australia although very few people die because of the availability of prompt First Aid and medical care. The majority of snake bites occur on the feet or ankles so that the risk of envenomation can be reduced if people *always* wear sensible clothing, socks and solid shoes when walking in the bush.

Snake venoms vary in their effects on the human body; some lead to changes in the blood which can cause internal bleeding; others work on the central nervous system and lead to progressive paralysis, breathing failure and death.

However, it is rare for death to occur if the casualty receives medical treatment within 8 hours of being bitten, although he or she may require prolonged treatment. If possible make a note of any distinctive markings on the snake. However, most hospitals will have a venom detection kit and a result can often be obtained within 30 minutes and the appropriate anti-venom can be given promptly.

Symptoms and Signs

These will vary but will usually occur between 30 minutes and two hours after envenomation. They generally include
● Two small puncture marks at the site.
● Disturbed vision.
● Nausea and vomiting.
● Headache.
● Drowsiness and fainting.
● Sweating.
● Pain in the abdomen or chest or difficulty in breathing.
● Diarrhoea.
● Symptoms and signs of shock (see p. 86).
● Collapse and breathing failure.

Aim

To delay the absorption of venom into the general circulatory system and arrange immediate transfer to hospital or medical aid. Be prepared to resuscitate.

Treatment

1 Keep calm and reassure the casualty. Assist the casualty to lie down at complete rest.

2 Apply firm pressure over the bitten area using a broad roller bandage. Cover the bite site, extend the bandage down to the extremity of the limb and bandage as high up the limb as possible. Avoid restricting circulation to the extremities (see p. 178).

3 Immobilise the limb completely with a splint, if available. If bitten on the foot or ankle, bind one leg to the other for support; if bitten on the hand or wrist, use an improvised splint (see p. 190) and apply an arm sling (see p. 181).

4 If the casualty becomes unconscious, turn him or her on to the side and care for airway, breathing and circulation according to the Basic Life Support Flow Chart (see p. 15).

5 Avoid moving the casualty if possible and bring medical aid as soon as possible. Alert the nearest hospital or doctor so that preparation for treatment may be commenced immediately.

Do Not wash, cut or suck the bite site, and do not apply an arterial tourniquet.

Marine Animal Bites

Many venomous marine animals occur round the Australian coastline including species of jellyfish, Stone fish, Blue Ringed Octopus and Cone Shell. The Box jellyfish occurs in the Northern Waters and has long, trailing tentacles which discharge venom into the skin through nematocysts (venom organs). It leaves whip-like markings which are excruciatingly painful and the venom is fatal unless prompt First Aid and medical treatment are given. Contact with tentacles of the Portuguese Man-O-War (Blue Bottle) and other species of Jellyfish leaves weals on the skin but the venom is rarely fatal. The Blue Ringed Octopus is normally small and sandy-brown in appearance but iridescent blue rings and stripes appear when it is touched or becomes angry or excited. The venom is injected through a horny beak and causes paralysis which progressively restricts breathing and death may result.

Stone fish and Cone Shells lie buried in sand or coral and rocks and are well camouflaged. Both can envenomate effectively through clothing (including sand shoes) and the venom can be fatal. There is no anti-venom for Cone Shells, however, an effective anti-venom is now available for Stone fish, but C.P.R. may be needed until medical treatment is available. Sting-rays also lie buried in the sand; they have a barbed spine in the tail which is used to inject the venom into the skin. This spine and pieces of the outer cover may be left in the skin and the resulting wound is often long and deep causing profuse bleeding and later, serious infection.

Symptoms and Signs

The symptoms and signs vary according to the venom but often occur within 10 minutes of envenomation.
- Severe or excruciating pain.
- Skin markings which include "ladder" patterns, weals, blisters or red patches with a white centre.
- Nausea, vomiting excessive salivation.
- Muscular cramps or progressive weakness and paralysis.
- Symptoms and signs of shock (see p. 86).
- Collapse and unconsciousness.
- Breathing may be difficult or have failed.

Aim

Relieve pain and limit further envenomation. Arrange urgent medical aid and transfer to hospital by ambulance. Be prepared to resuscitate if necessary.

Treatment

1 If the casualty is in the water, assist him or her to the beach by gripping the arms but avoid any adherent tentacles.

2 Assist the casualty to lie down. If stung by a jellyfish, flood the area of the sting and any remaining tentacles with household vinegar: remaining nematocysts may be picked off with your fingers.

If no vinegar is available, do not use sand, methylated spirits, beer, kerosene or other substitutes because they may cause unfired nematocysts to contract and discharge more venom.

3 With the exception of stonefish and minor jellyfish stings, apply a pressure bandage over the area of the sting and immobilise it as for a snake bite.

4 Stonefish venom should be treated by placing the injury in water as hot as can be tolerated.

5 If the casualty becomes unconscious, turn him on to the side and give care of airway, breathing and circulation according to the Basic Life Support Flow Chart (see p. 15).

6 Arrange urgent transfer to hospital maintaining treatment position.

Other Bites and Stings

SPIDER

All spiders possess fangs and some poison with which to paralyse their prey. However, only the Funnel Web and Red Back spiders have a venom which can cause serious complications if it is injected into human tissues.

The Funnel Web spider is mainly found in and around Sydney and northern New South Wales, and in the southern parts of Queensland. If bitten by a Funnel Web spider, the casualty needs prompt First Aid and medical treatment with anti-venom to avoid collapse, breathing failure and death from cardiac arrest.

The Red Back spider exists all over Australia and is commonly found in dark crevices, under stones or in piles of building materials. If bitten, the venom works very slowly so that there is usually adequate time to seek medical treatment.

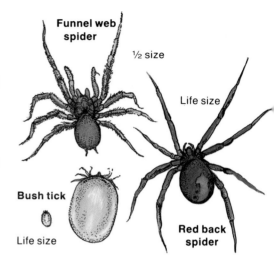

Funnel web spider

½ size

Life size

Bush tick

Life size

Red back spider

SCORPION, CENTIPEDE AND BULL ANTS

Scorpions and bull ants (Inch Ants) are common throughout Australia. They hold their sting in their tails and inject it if disturbed or angry. Centipedes have their sting at the head end but they rarely bite except while being handled.

All of these creatures can inflict a painful bite but the venom is rarely serious for the casualty.

THE BUSH TICK

These are commonly found in humid rainforests in the East and South-eastern areas of Australia, but other species are found in all States. It buries itself behind the ears, above the hairline or other areas with body hair in order to suck blood from its host. If unnoticed, it can cause severe poisoning which leads to paralysis. It should be removed very carefully to avoid leaving the head buried in the skin.

BEE AND WASP STINGS

The most serious sting is caused by the Honey Bee because it can cause allergic reactions in people who become sensitive or allergic to the venom. Some people have become allergic to wasp stings, although this is less common in Australia. If an allergy develops, medical treatment is needed urgently as a life-saving measure because Anaphylactic Shock (see p. 157) can result.

Symptoms and Signs

● Pain at site of bite; often severe if it is scorpion, ant or bee sting.
● Swelling and redness around the bite.
● Nausea or vomiting.
● Headache.
● Disturbed vision.

If the casualty is allergic to the venom, there may be swelling around the face, eyes, mouth and throat which may lead to airway obstruction if medical aid is delayed. A rash may appear over the trunk with wheezing and difficulty in breathing (see *Severe Allergic Reaction*, p. 157).

Aim

Remove the sting if it is still present and try to reduce swelling and relieve pain. Arrange urgent transfer to doctor or hospital.

Treatment

1 Reassure the casualty and help to rest: observe and assess condition.

2 If stung by a bee and the barb is still embedded in the skin, brush or scrape it off sideways. *Do Not* pull the barb or squeeze the poison sac because this will force the remaining poison into the skin.

3 If bitten by a Funnel Web spider, or if known to be an allergic person, treat as for snake bites (see p. 154).

4 If stung by a bee or bitten by an ant, scorpion, centipede or Red Back spider, apply a cold compress or ice pack over the bite site (see p. 176). Elevate and support the injured part.

If the bite is near the mouth, throat or neck, arrange urgent transfer to hospital. Give the casualty ice to suck and apply a cold compress to the neck.

If a tick is found, kill it by applying kerosene, turpentine or methylated spirits and then remove it. If unable to kill it, lever it out carefully with a pair of sharp-pointed scissors keeping the head intact. Avoid pulling on the tick with tweezers; it could cause more poison to be injected.

5 Observe the casualty at 10-minute intervals for any sign of allergic reaction (see *Severe Allergic Reaction*, below).

6 If the casualty loses consciousness, turn him on to the side and care for airway, breathing and circulation according to the Basic Life Support Flow Chart (see p. 15).

7 Arrange urgent transfer to hospital.

Severe Allergic Reaction

A massive allergic reaction, sometimes known as Anaphylactic Shock, can develop within a few seconds or minutes of an injection of a drug or insect sting to which the casualty is sensitive. More rarely, it follows the ingestion of an allergen such as penicillin, in which case the reaction will be slower.

Symptoms and Signs

● Symptoms and signs of shock (see p. 86).
● Nausea or vomiting.
● Casualty complains that chest feels tight.
● Difficulty in breathing — casualty may be wheezing and gasping for air.
● Casualty may be sneezing.
● There may be facial swelling.
● Pulse will be rapid.
● Unconsciousness may develop.
● There may be a blotchy and irritating rash on the neck and chest.

Aim

Arrange urgent transfer to hospital and be prepared to resuscitate.

Treatment

See also treatment for Shock, p. 86.

1 If any prescribed medication is available to treat a known condition, give the recommended dose immediately.

2 Maintain an open airway and help the casualty into the position of greatest comfort and loosen any tight clothing around neck, chest and waist.

3 If the casualty loses consciousness, turn him on to the side and care for airway, breathing and circulation according to the Basic Life Support Flow Chart (see p. 15).

4 Arrange urgent transfer to hospital or doctor.

FOREIGN BODIES

A "foreign body" means any extraneous matter that enters the body either through a wound in the skin (penetrating) or via one of the natural openings of the body (inserted or swallowed).

A penetrating foreign body can be anything that enters the body from a tiny splinter of wood or glass to a large wooden stake or piece of metal. It may be loose and easily removed without causing further pain or injury or it can be embedded. In addition, the latter may be acting as a plug (see p. 62).

Large foreign bodies embedded in the skin may produce a deep wound but small splinters cause little more than minor lacerations.

The main problem with injuries involving penetrating foreign bodies is that foreign bodies are rarely clean so that there is a high risk of infection (see *Wounds and bleeding* p. 58 and *Tetanus Infection* p. 65). Small, foreign bodies may be removed by a First Aider, but embedded objects must be removed only at a hospital.

Loose Foreign Bodies

Most particles of loose grit can be washed out or removed with a clean swab or tweezers. Encourage the casualty to clean the area with soap and water. It is often more comfortable for the casualty to remove the particles him or herself after the wound has been soaked in a correctly diluted solution of antiseptic. After the foreign bodies have been removed, dry the area thoroughly and apply a light, dry dressing for a few hours to protect it.

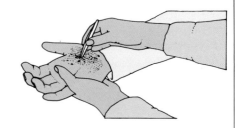

Embedded Foreign Bodies

If particles or objects are deeply embedded in the tissues, dress them using built-up dressings if necessary (see *Wounds and Bleeding*, p. 62). Make the casualty as comfortable as possible and seek medical aid immediately. If the casualty becomes impaled on an immovable object such as a metal railing, support the weight of the limbs or trunk. Call an ambulance immediately and state that cutting tools may be required (see pp. 35 and 62).

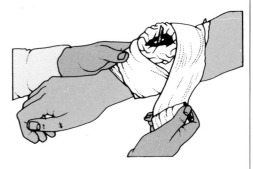

Swallowed Foreign Bodies

Smooth swallowed objects need not necessarily cause alarm. A sharp object, on the other hand, can cause severe damage. In either case, always seek medical aid as soon as possible (see p. 160).

Splinters

Wood and metal splinters which have become embedded in the skin are probably the most common foreign bodies with which you will be confronted. They can generally be removed with special splinter remover or tweezers as described below. However, if the splinter is deeply embedded, seek medical aid as soon as possible.

Symptoms and Signs
- Known contact with pieces of wood, metal or glass.
- Visible indication of embedded foreign body.
- Pain and tenderness in the area.

Aim
Gently remove the splinter.

Treatment

1 If the area around the splinter is dirty, cleanse it using soap and water (see *Wounds and Bleeding*, p. 63).

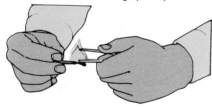

2 Sterilise a splinter remover, needle or tweezers by passing it through a flame.

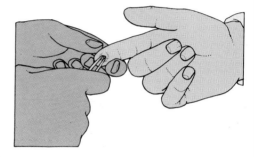

3 If the end of the splinter is exposed, try to lift it clear of the wound with the splinter remover or needle. Hold the tweezers as near to the skin as possible and grasp the splinter. Pull the splinter out in the opposite direction to that in which it entered the skin.

4 If the splinter does not come out easily or begins to break up, treat as an embedded foreign body (see p. 62) and seek medical aid.

Do Not probe the area to reach the splinter.

NB Make sure the casualty's tetanus immunisation is up-to-date (see p. 65) because splinters are rarely clean.

Splinter remover

Fish Hooks in the Skin

Sometimes only the point of the hook enters the skin, in which case the hook can easily be removed. If, however, the barb is caught as well, do not try to remove it but seek medical aid. Only attempt to remove it if medical aid is not immediately available.

Aim

Gently remove the point and treat as a minor wound. Seek medical aid if the barb has penetrated.

Treatment

1 Cut the line from the fish hook.

2 If the barb is not caught in the skin, remove the hook and treat as a minor wound (see p. 63).

3 If the barb is caught in the skin, treat as an embedded foreign body (see p. 62) and seek medical aid.

IF MEDICAL AID IS NOT READILY AVAILABLE

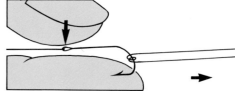

1 Loop a 100mm (4in) length of fishing line around the curve of the hook.

2 Press the eye of the hook down on to casualty's finger with the other hand; this releases the embedded barb. Maintain this pressure and gently pull on the line to withdraw the hook along the entry track. If the eye of the hook extends beyond the fingertip, place packing under it to maintain pressure.

3 Clean the wound and cover with a dressing and seek medical aid.

Swallowed Foreign Bodies

Children in particular often swallow small objects such as pins, coins or buttons. Most small smooth objects are unlikely to damage the intestine or cause choking. However, sharp objects such as pins or needles can damage the intestine. In either case you should seek medical aid or remove the casualty to hospital.

Symptoms and Signs

● History indicating that object has been swallowed.

Aim

Reassure the casualty and transfer to hospital.

Treatment

1 Reassure the casualty and the parents if the casualty is a child.

2 Transfer to hospital.

Do Not give the casualty anything by mouth.

Foreign Bodies in the Nose

These are usually encountered in very young children who try to insert various objects such as pebbles or marbles into their noses. Smooth objects may just be lodged in the nose but a sharp object can easily damage the tissues of the nose. Do not attempt to remove the object but transfer the casualty to hospital.

Symptoms and Signs
- Casualty has difficulty in breathing through the nose.
- Occasionally, nose appears swollen.
- Discharge (often blood-stained) appearing from one or both sides of the nose.

Aim
Reassure the casualty and transfer to hospital as soon as possible.

Treatment
1 Keep the casualty quiet and advise to breathe through the mouth.

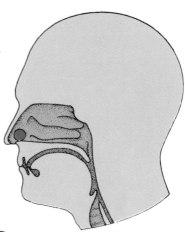

2 Transfer to hospital.

Do Not attempt to remove the foreign body.

Foreign Bodies in the Ear

These are most common in young children. They can cause temporary deafness but deep penetration can damage the eardrum. Alternatively, insects may become lodged in a person's ear.

Symptoms and Signs
- Casualty complains of pain in the ear.
- Casualty may feel vibrations if an insect is inside the ear.
- Hearing on affected side impaired.

Aim
Transfer the casualty to hospital.

Treatment
1 Reassure the casualty.

2 If a foreign body is suspected, *do not* attempt to dislodge it as probing may perforate the eardrum.

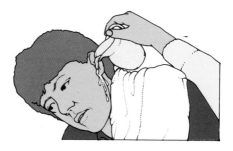

3 If it is an insect, gently flood the ear with tepid water to float it out.

4 Transfer to hospital.

Foreign Bodies in the Eye

All eye injuries are potentially serious because particles may perforate the eye-ball resulting in internal damage and possible infection.

Particles of dust or grit or loose eye-lashes are the most common foreign bodies found in the eyes. They stick to the outer surface of the eyeball or become lodged under the eyelid, normally the upper lid, causing considerable discomfort and inflammation. In most cases these can easily be removed. However, *do not* attempt to remove a foreign body if it is on the coloured part of the eye, or embedded in the eyeball. In these cases, seek medical aid immediately.

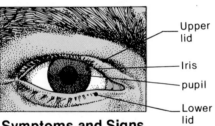

Upper lid
Iris
pupil
Lower lid

Symptoms and Signs

- Casualty's eye is painful and itches.
- Casualty's vision may be impaired.
- Watering of affected eye.
- Casualty's eye is red.

Aim

Remove particle gently. If unsuccessful, Transfer the casualty to hospital.

CONTACT LENSES

Many people now wear contact lenses instead of glasses and occasionally these cause extra problems in an emergency. If conscious help the casualty to remove them, and place them safely in their container and ensure they remain with the casualty. *Never try to remove lenses from a casualty's eye* yourself. If a casualty is known to be wearing lenses, report this to the ambulance officer, nurse or doctor attending the incident.

Treatment

1 Advise the casualty *not* to rub the eye (the casualty will almost certainly be doing so).

2 Ask the casualty to sit down in a chair facing the light and lean back.

3 Stand behind the casualty. Hold the chin in one hand and use the index finger and thumb of your other hand to separate the affected lids. Ask the casualty to look right, left, up and down so that you can examine every part of the eye properly.

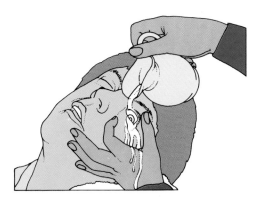

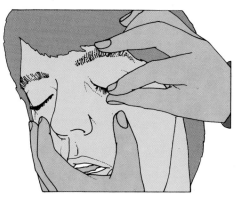

4 If you can see the foreign body try to wash it out with sterile saline solution. If this is not available, irrigate the eye with tap water. Incline the head towards the injured side so that the water will drain out over the cheek *away* from the sound eye; pour water from a jug or place the casualty's head under a tap (see p. 139).

6 If the foreign body is under the upper lid, ask the casualty to look down. Grasp the eyelashes and pull the upper lid downwards and outwards over *the lower lid*. If the lashes of the lower lid do not brush the foreign body off, get the casualty to blink the eye under water in the hope that it will float off.

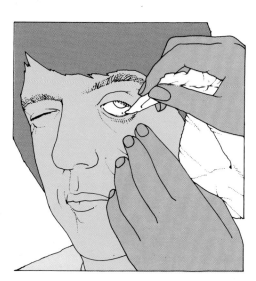

7 If you cannot remove the foreign body, cover the affected eye with an eye pad or a piece of gauze wrapped around a soft pad of cotton wool. Secure it lightly in position and seek medical aid.

If the foreign body is on the coloured part of the eye or it is embedded in or sticking to the eyeball *do not attempt to remove it*. Advise the casualty, not to move the eye. Cover it with an eye pad. Transfer to hospital for treatment.

5 If this is unsuccessful or no water is available and the foreign body is *not* sticking to the eye, lift the foreign body off using a moistened swab or the damp corner of a clean handkerchief.

ACHES

An ache is a continuous dull pain. Some aches are symptomatic of another condition or injury and may be referred from some other part of the body.

While it is not always possible for you to diagnose the cause of the symptoms, you should attempt to provide temporary relief from the pain. However, the administration of medicines is beyond the scope of First Aid. On the other hand, if someone suffering from a minor ache is carrying some pain-killing tablets, the person may be able to deal with the ache in this way.

The aim of all treatment is to relieve discomfort. Treatments for the more common aches are described on the following pages; other conditions such as chest pain caused by heart attacks, are dealt with elsewhere in the book. It is important that you look out for any symptoms or signs mentioned and that you seek medical aid immediately if you notice them.

NB For treatment of minor illness see the companion book *Caring for the Sick*.

Headache

Common causes of headache are: sinusitis, the common cold, stress, eye strain, pressure and lack of sleep or food. However, injuries to the head or spine can also result in headaches.

Symptoms and Signs
● Pain anywhere in the head which may be constant, throbbing or intermittent.

Treatment
1 Place a cold compress (see p. 176) or covered hot-water bottle on the casualty's forehead whichever is preferred.

NB The casualty may take one or two own pain-killing tablets if available.

2 If practical, advise the casualty to lie down in a darkened room.

3 If the headache persists, or if it is accompanied by a feeling of nausea, vomiting, fever, stiff neck, disturbed vision, obvious head injury, confusion or gradual loss of consciousness, seek medical aid.

Migraine

These severe and at times incapacitating headaches sometimes come on for no apparent reason and cannot normally be traced to any particular disorder. However, they may follow lack of food, noise, heat, travelling, or emotional disturbances.

Migraine attacks are more severe than normal headaches but they are not as common and only the casualty will know if it is a migraine attack.

Symptoms and Signs
● Casualty may experience "flickering" vision — this can precede the headache.
● Casualty will be feeling nauseated and may already be vomiting.
● Intense throbbing headache which may only affect one side of the head.
● Casualty cannot tolerate light or noise.
● Casualty may look very pale.

Treatment
As for Headache, above.

Toothache

The most frequent cause of toothache is decay which has penetrated the enamel of a tooth. However, it can also be the result of an abscess, abnormal pressure from an incorrect bite or pain referred from somewhere else, for example, pain caused by inflammation of a facial nerve (neuralgia).

Symptoms and Signs
● Pain in the teeth or jaws, which may be constant, throbbing or intermittent. The pain may be made worse by cold or hot food and drink.

Treatment
1 Advise the casualty not to eat on the affected side and to avoid very hot foods.

NB The casualty may take one or two own pain-killing tablets if available.

2 Advise the casualty to see the dentist or doctor without delay.

Earache

This can be very painful. It is often the result of an infection in or near the ear, for example, a boil in the ear canal or a tooth abcess. The most common cause, however, particularly in children, is middle-ear infection caused by germs spreading from the throat to the middle ear. This type of infection may follow illnesses such as tonsillitis, measles or influenza. Earache can also occur when there is too much wax present in the ear canal or if there is a sudden change of pressure on the eardrum during air travel or underwater swimming.

Symptoms and Signs
● Constant or throbbing pain in the ear.

Treatment
1 To relieve a severe or persistent earache, hold a covered hot water bottle or heated pad against the affected ear.

NB The casualty may take one or two own pain-killing tablets, if available.

2 If earache is caused by a sudden change of pressure advise the casualty to hold the nose and close the mouth and then swallow or blow out the cheeks.

3 If the ache persists or if it is accompanied by discharge, fever, impaired hearing and/or balance, advise the casualty to seek medical aid immediately.

Neck Ache

Mild soreness or stiffness of the neck muscles may be caused by sitting or lying in one position for too long, exposure to draughts or nervous tension but it may also result from a viral illness or an injury such as "Whiplash" (see p. 112).

Symptoms and Signs
● Pain anywhere in the neck increased by movement.

Treatment
1 To relieve pain, hold a covered hot water bottle or heated pad against the affected area and encourage gentle movement of the neck.

NB The casualty may take one or two own pain-killing tablets, if available.

2 If the symptoms persist or if they are accompanied by swelling, feelings of nausea and/or vomiting, headache, confusion and/or loss of consciousness or obvious injury, seek medical aid.

Back Ache

Pain in the back can be a symptom of various disorders. Some involve the back itself, for instance, a strain (see p. 127) poor posture or a displaced disc (see p. 130). In such cases, pain may be caused by disorders elsewhere in the body (e.g., kidney infection).

Symptoms and Signs
● Pain anywhere in the back.

Treatment
1 If caused by a strain, treat as on p. 127. Otherwise place a covered hot-water bottle on the affected area.

NB The casualty may take one or two own pain-killing tablets, if available.

2 If the symptoms persist, there is a raised temperature, the urine has a strong smell or is bloodstained, there is trouble with the bowels and/or bladder, or a loss of movement or sensation in the legs, seek medical aid.

Abdominal Pain

There are many causes of abdominal pain including indigestion, colic, menstrual cramp, constipation and food poisoning. Generally, such pain is not considered serious if it lasts less than half an hour and there are no other symptoms such as headache, vomiting, fever or diarrhoea.

Symptoms and Signs
● Pain anywhere in the abdomen, which may be dull or sharp, constant or intermittent, localised or general.

Treatment
1 To relieve pain, place the casualty in a half-sitting position with the head and shoulders supported. Bend the knees and support in this position.

If menstrual cramps are suspected, the casualty may find walking about relieves the discomfort.

2 Place a covered hot-water bottle or a heated pad over the affected area.

3 If vomiting is likely, place in the Lateral Recovery position (see p. 22).

4 Keep the casualty lying down and comfortable. To minimise shock, treat as on p. 86.

5 If the pain lasts more than half an hour or you are in doubt about the casualty's condition, seek medical aid.

PROCEDURE AT MAJOR INCIDENTS

Major incidents are those in which a large number of casualties are involved. They can be natural, for example an earthquake, or involve human error, as in a road traffic accident. The number of casualties, and the sequence in which they will need to be treated, will vary according to the incident and the types of injury. Casualties may be trapped, thrown some distance or found wandering about in a dazed condition. In a major fire, injuries may be caused by people jumping out of a high building or being trapped in a smoke-filled room.

In any emergency, the way you approach the situation is important (see p. 33). This is especially true in a major incident and because a single First Aider cannot treat all the casualties at once, it is essential that a brief reconnaisance of the scene is made. You will need to find out: exactly what has happened; whether danger still threatens; how many casualties there are and what condition they are in. All this information must then be passed on to the emergency services immediately (see p. 35). If there is no further danger, you should then treat the casualties on site according to the priorities of breathing, bleeding and unconsciousness.

Remember, the general rule for dealing with any casualty in danger is: remove the danger from the casualty and, *only if this is not possible*, remove the casualty from the danger.

Road Traffic Accidents

The general principles for dealing with any major incident can best be illustrated by the procedure for dealing with casualties in a road traffic accident. The most important thing to remember is that you should not attempt to move a casualty unless absolutely necessary — leave it to the emergency services.

Taking risks

In many road traffic accidents casualties may have to be moved in order to save lives. The decision to do so, however, should be carefully considered, because of the risk of spinal injury or severe internal bleeding. Unless casualties are in danger from fire or oncoming traffic, or if they are unconscious and needing care of airway, breathing and circulation, you should carry out a full examination to determine the extent of the injuries before moving them. Then, follow the procedure described on this page.

IMMEDIATE ACTION

- Look for any indication of dangerous substances being present such as Hazchem warnings.
- Instruct someone to telephone the emergency services immediately (see *Calling for Assistance* p. 35).
- Do not pull casualties from the vehicle — this could result in further injuries.

- Minimise the risk of fire by switching off the engine and, if you know how, disconnecting the battery because fires often begin in the wiring under the bonnet or dashboard. Do not allow anyone to smoke near the vehicle. If a diesel truck, bus or car is involved, switch off the fuel supply — there is normally an emergency switch on the outside of the vehicle.

- Instruct bystanders to set up warning triangles at least 200 m (220 yd) from the accident; if no triangles are available, ask them to direct traffic.
- Immobilise the car. If it is on four wheels apply the handbrake, put the car into gear and/or place blocks under the wheels. If the car is on its side and there are passengers inside, *do not try to right it*, just make sure that it will not roll over.
- Look inside the vehicle for any small children who may have fallen out of sight or be hidden under blankets or luggage. Check the area immediately surrounding the vehicle for any passengers who may have been thrown out of the vehicle or who may be wandering about. Ask a conscious casualty how many people were in the vehicle before the accident.

MOVING A CASUALTY

If the situation is such that a casualty needs to be moved then it must be done as gently as possible. When moving a casualty to safety before a full injury assessment can be completed, it is best to drag him or her using the ankle grip or else a wrist grip or elbow grip with the arms extended above the head (see p. 193) but avoid raising the arms or legs unnecessarily. Lifting the casualty is a skilled procedure which should only be used when dragging is impractical (see pp. 192–96).

If a casualty is trapped under a vehicle and has to be removed before the emergency services arrive, because of the danger of fire for example, try to move the vehicle away from the casualty first. If this is not possible, immobilise the vehicle as described left, and move the casualty as gently as possible. Remember to note the exact position of the casualty or vehicle before moving either because the police may need this information later.

In all cases where you have decided against moving the casualty you should always be prepared to do so should the casualty's condition deteriorate or new danger threaten.

DEALING WITH TRAPPED CASUALTIES

Accident victims may be trapped in their vehicles by an impacted steering wheel, for instance. Such a casualty should be watched carefully because, if unconscious, the tongue may fall to the back of the throat and block the airway. To guard against this possibility, the casualty's head should be tilted back and the jaw supported (see p. 17). A trapped casualty must be observed continuously until the arrival of skilled help.

ACCIDENTS INVOLVING DANGEROUS SUBSTANCES

Accidents may be complicated by the spillage of dangerous liquids or the escape of toxic fumes, and any such incident should be approached with great care. Never make any rescue attempt unless you are sure that it is safe to do so; do not endanger yourself by coming into contact with a dangerous substance.

Most vehicles and containers carrying dangerous substances now display notices which signify exactly what is being carried. If you are in doubt about the meaning of the sign keep your distance, especially if there is any spillage. Make a careful note of the code and give the information to the emergency services. Keep bystanders well away from the scene and bear in mind the possibility that poisonous fumes may be given off. If this does occur, stand upwind of the accident so that any fumes are blown away from you.

Hazard Warnings

Vehicles carrying dangerous goods display hazard warning information panels indicating the substance being carried.

Inflammable substances · Poisonous substances · Substances liable to ignite spontaneously

Radioactive substances · Corrosive substances · Compressed gases

Disaster Survival

The basic rules which apply to any house-holder before and during an emergency alert are as follows:
● You should know how and where to turn off your mains supply of electricity, gas and water.
● Keep a torch and First Aid Kit ready in a place known to all members of the house-hold.
● Find out if your neighbours need help, especially if they are elderly, sick or disabled.
● Keep all domestic pets indoors. Give stabled animals and caged animals and birds some food and water.
● Only use your telephone for emergencies.
● Stay tuned to the local radio station and follow all official instructions. Carry a portable radio in case electricity has to be turned off.
● Only leave the house if it is essential and wear protective clothing, including strong shoes.
● Avoid sightseeing; heavy traffic can prevent aid reaching those who need it.

SEVERE STORMS OR CYCLONES

When you hear about a cyclone warning, check that your neighbours know about it and organise the family to help you. Collect all loose items and store them in the house; lock up pets; fuel the car and leave it in a sheltered position; secure the house (lock all doors and windows); fill water containers and TURN OFF electricity, gas and water at the mains.
NB To reduce the risk of damage, leave one window slighly open on the *protected* side of the house.

During the Emergency

When the storm starts, stay calm and remain indoors. Remember that a period of calm may occur as the eye of a cyclone passes overhead; stay indoors until you hear officially that the cyclone has passed and will not return.

After the Emergency

Beware of: fallen power lines, damaged gas main pipes and dangerous debris (e.g., shattered glass or roofing materials).
Leave the electricity, gas and water turned off at the mains until a safety check has been carried out.

FLOODS AND FLASH FLOODS

There are always basic precautions which can be taken. For example if you live in a low-lying area, find out the flood height affecting it in the past. Always keep a supply of new batteries, candles and matches in the house in case electricity fails and keep a supply of instant foods in your cupboard so that meals can be prepared.

When a warning occurs

Listen for official information on your portable radio and make sure that you: have an adequate supply of drinking water (e.g., fill the bath); store valuables such as food, clothing and carpets as high off the floor as possible; ensure that you have enough portable lighting e.g., torches and candles; find the instant food.

Evacuation

● Listen to your radio and follow all official instructions.
● TURN OFF electricity, gas and water at the mains.
● Leave all house doors *open* to minimise structural damage.
● Evacuate *before* flood waters cut across routes.
● Take food, drinking water, blankets, family medicines and First Aid Kits.
● Advise somebody outside the flood area of your destination, the number of people with you, your route and your estimated arrival time.

BUSH FIRES

Ask your local Fire Officer, Fire Brigade or council about any special restrictions, risks, warnings and emergency plans for your area. Take special precautions in the high fire danger period in the summer months. For example: *DO NOT* light fires in the open; clear any combustible material from around the house or rubbish from the guttering; ensure that there is an adequate water supply and that your garden hose reaches all points of your house guttering and outbuildings; check screens on doors, windows and external vents; and, on a fire alert day, ensure that your car is fuelled and ready for prompt evacuation if necessary.

If a bush fire approaches your home:
● TURN OFF electricity and gas at the mains.
● Close all doors and windows.
● Plug all downpipes and fill guttering with water.
● Unless otherwise directed, all fit and able persons should remain to protect the house. Ensure that adequate clothing and footwear are worn in case of close contact with fire.
● Place wet bags, buckets of water and tools around the outside of the house.
● Keep watch and deal with burning twigs, bark or leaves which may spread ahead of the bush fire.
● If asked by Police to evacuate your home, follow instructions promptly.
● If your house catches fire, check the best exit route. Close all doors behind you to contain the fire as long as possible.

If a bush fire approaches in the open:
● Cover as much of your body as possible with fire resistant (woollen) clothing (avoid synthetic fabric) shield from radiant heat and cover your face with a wet cloth to avoid inhaling smoke.
● If in a car, close all windows, cover your body and lie down low until the fire has passed. Leave the car as soon as the fire has passed in case it returns following a change in the wind direction.
● If equipped with a hose, knapsack spray or fire extinguisher, direct flow at the base of the fire and try to restrict all new outbreaks of fire.

Fires

Rapid and clear thinking is vitally important when dealing with fires for your own sake and that of any casualties. Fire spreads very quickly so alert the emergency services immediately giving them as much information as possible. Then, try to get everyone out of the building and make sure that all doors of rooms where there is a fire are shut. *Remember, do not attempt to fight a fire unless you have notified the emergency services and have made sure that you will not be in any danger.*

Modern furniture often contains synthetic materials which, when burning, may give off toxic fumes. So you should never enter a burning building you suspect contains poisonous fumes unless equipped with, and practised in the use of, breathing apparatus. If for any reason you do have to enter a smoke-filled room, make sure you are not endangering yourself and follow the procedure described on pp. 48–9.

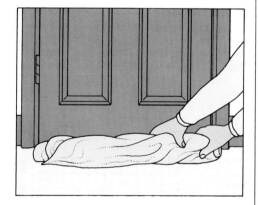

If you are trapped in a burning building, the best thing to do is to go into a room with a window and shut the door. Put a blanket or carpet against the bottom of the door to keep the smoke out and call for help from the window.
NB All the above principles apply if you are involved in an incident where there is a gas leak.

DRESSINGS AND BANDAGES

The type of dressings and/or bandages used and the techniques for applying them vary according to the type of injury sustained and the materials available. Supplies of both dressings and bandages can be bought in sterile packs. However, substitutes can be made from household linen or any other clean, non-fluffy material that is available.

NB As a general rule, fluffy material should *never* be placed directly on to a wound because the fibres will adhere.

DRESSINGS

A dressing is a protective covering which is placed on a wound to help control bleeding, prevent infection and absorb any discharge.

All dressings should be large enough to cover the area of the wound and extend about 2.5 cm (1 in) beyond it. If possible, they should be sterile to avoid introducing bacteria which could cause infection. A dressing should also be absorbent because, if sweat cannot evaporate, the skin around the wound will become moist and the dressing sodden. This will encourage the growth of bacteria and prevent healing.

Dressings help the blood to clot thus assisting the healing process. Although a dressing may stick to a wound, making it difficult to remove later, the benefits of a dressing outweigh any damage done on removal. Many modern dressings are non-adherent and therefore particularly valuable for use on abrasions and burns. Some have a perforated polythene film on one side. This dressing is placed film side down on the wound and permits blood and tissue fluid to flow through the film and in to the absorbent pad above.

Tulle gras dressings, used for serious burns are sealed singly in sterile packets. Each one is covered in a fine film of petroleum jelly or antiseptic cream which reduces the risk of infection and of their adhering to the wound. Always place an absorbent pad over such dressings to help blood and serous fluids leave the damaged tissues.

GENERAL RULES FOR APPLYING DRESSINGS

- If possible, wash your hands.
- Except in an emergency, always wear disposable gloves for any wound cleaning.
- If a wound is not too large and bleeding is under control, clean it and the surrounding skin before applying the dressing (see p. 63).
- Avoid touching the wound or any part of the dressing which will be in contact with a wound.
- Never talk or cough over a wound or the dressing.
- If necessary, cover non-adherent dressings with pads of cotton wool to help control bleeding and absorb discharge. These pads should extend well beyond the dressing and be held in position by a bandage (see p. 177).
- If a dressing slips off a wound before you are able to secure it, renew the dressing — the first one may have picked up germs from the surrounding skin.
- Always place a dressing directly on to a wound, *never* slide it on from the side.
- When the wound care treatment has finished, dispose of used gloves, soiled dressings and other waste into a sealed bag, and then place in a covered bin.

If using antiseptic solution for cleaning a minor wound, *always* follow the instructions on the bottle. If it is too weak, it will be useless against bacteria: if it is too strong, it may burn the skin. *Never* use antiseptic solution on a major wound.

Adhesive Dressings

These dressings consist of an absorbent gauze or cellulose pad held in place by an adhesive backing. The best have a water-repellent adhesive backing which allows moisture to evaporate from the skin. *Waterproof* dressings should *only* be used by food handlers and should not be left on for more than a few hours.

All dressings are supplied in sterile wrappings and they are available in a variety of shapes and sizes.

Always make sure the skin around a wound is clean and dry before applying an adhesive dressing otherwise it will not stick (see p. 63).

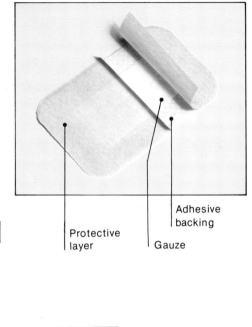

Protective layer

Adhesive backing

Gauze

Method

1 Remove the outer wrapping and hold the dressing, gauze-side down, by the protective strips.

2 Peel back, but do not remove, the protective strips and, without touching the gauze, place the pad on to the wound.

3 Carefully pull off the protective strips and press the ends and the edges down.

Sterile Unmedicated Dressings

These consist of a dressing made up of layers of fine gauze and a pad of cotton wool attached to a roller bandage. Also known as "shell dressings", "field dressings" or "wound dressings", these are the preferred dressings for large wounds. If available, they should be used in preference to any other type of combination dressing and/or bandage on any wound. Sterile dressings are always enclosed and sealed in protective wrappings. *Do not use a sterile dressing if the seal is broken.*

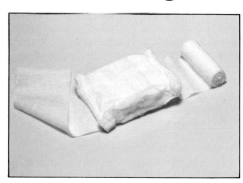

Method

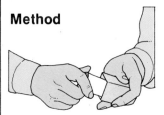

1 Remove the outer wrapping by twisting or pulling apart the outer package and remove the inner wrapping. Alternatively, pull back the tab at the end of the box and remove the inner wrapping.

3 Hold both ends of the bandage with the folded dressing gauze-side down and over the wound; open out the dressing. If necessary, control it by placing your thumbs on the edge of the dressing, then place it on the wound.

5 Secure the bandage by tying the two ends over the pad using a reef knot (see p. 180).

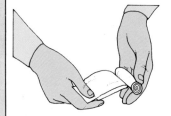

2 Holding the folded dressing and rolled bandage in one hand, unwind the short end of the bandage with the other hand.

4 Wind the short end of the bandage once around the limb and dressing to secure it. Then bandage firmly until the pad is covered (see p. 186)

Gauze Dressings

These consist of layers of gauze which form a soft covering for large wounds. Gauze dressings are used when a light dressing is required. If it is used in place of a serile dressing when the latter is not available, you may need to cover the gauze with a pad of cotton wool and secure it with a light, protective dressing for a healing wound.

Method

1 Remove the outer wrapping. Hold the dressing by the edges over the wound; lower it into place.

2 If necessary, cover the gauze with one or two layers of cotton wool.

3 Secure the pad with a bandage or adhesive strapping.

Adhesive Strapping

If bandages are not available or they are ineffective or difficult to apply, lengths of special adhesive strapping can be used to secure non-adhesive dressings to wounds. Adhesive strapping is available in a variety of lengths and widths.

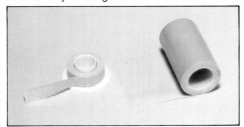

Improvised Dressings

In some emergencies prepared dressings may not be available and you will have to improvise using whatever suitable materials are to hand. Any dry, clean, absorbent material, such as the inside of a clean handkerchief, a freshly-laundered towel or piece of linen or a pad of clean tissues can be used. If possible, avoid placing cotton wool, lint, woollen or fibrous material directly on to a wound; the fibres can become embedded in it.

Improvised dressings to control bleeding should be bulky and held in position using materials that are readily available, for example, a folded scarf.

COLD COMPRESSES

Closed injuries such as bruises and sprains must be cooled to minimise swelling and relieve pain. This is best achieved by placing the injured area under cold running water. However, if the injury is on an awkward part of the body such as the head or chest or prolonged application is required, a cold compress in the form of a cold-water pack or an ice pack may have to be used instead.

APPLYING A COLD-WATER PACK OR COMPRESS

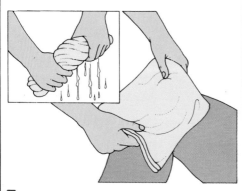

1 Soak a pad of cotton wool, towelling or similar cloth in cold or iced water. Squeeze or wring it out so that it is damp but not dripping, and place it on the injury.

2 To ensure that the cooling effect is maintained, replace pad with a fresh cold-water pack or drip more cold water on to the old one. Continue cooling the injury for 10 minutes, then reassess the injury.

3 If necessary, cover the cold pack with an open-weave bandage to hold it in position.

APPLYING AN ICE PACK

1 Fill a plastic or similar non-porous bag ½ to ⅔ full of crushed or cubed ice; add a little salt to lower the melting temperature of the ice. Exclude all air, seal the bag and wrap it in a damp cloth.

2 Place the pack over the injury; replace as necessary. Continue cooling the injury for a maximum of 10 minutes. Check the skin colour regularly, and remove the ice-pack if reddening occurs.

NB Always wrap ice packs in a damp cloth to avoid burning the skin. You can buy proprietary ice-packs. One is filled with a thick gel which should be kept in a freezer compartment; the gel maintains a stable temperature for a long time. If refrigeration is impractical, a sachet containing Ammonium Nitrate and a small pouch of water is also available. When the water pouch is broken the reaction creates an intensely cold pack which is effective for at least 20 minutes, although it cannot be re-used.

BANDAGES

Bandages are used to maintain direct pressure over a dressing in order to: control bleeding; hold dressings or splints in position; prevent swelling; provide support for a limb or joint; restrict movement; and, occasionally, to assist in lifting or carrying casualties. They should *not* be used for padding when other softer materials are available.

Prepared bandages are made from cotton, calico, elastic net, special paper or other materials. They are of two main types, triangular bandages and roller bandages. In an emergency, bandages can be improvised from any of the above materials or by using tights or stockings, ties, scarves or belts.

When selecting a roller bandage, remember that some are designed for specific purposes. For example, plastic net or elasticated crepe bandages will support a sprained joint, whereas conforming bandages are best used to secure a light dressing in place without pressure.

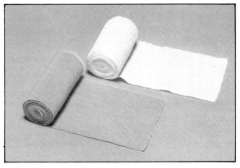

Roller Bandage

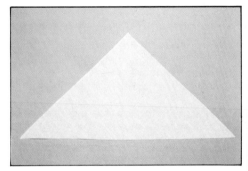

Triangular Bandage

GENERAL RULES FOR APPLYING BANDAGES

● Apply bandages when a casualty is sitting or lying down.

● Always try to sit or stand in front of the casualty and work from the casualty's injured side.

● Before you start bandaging, make sure the injured part is well-supported in the position in which it is to remain.

● If the casualty is lying down, pass all bandages under the natural hollows of the ankles, knees, back and neck. To ease them into position, gently pull them backwards and forwards and move them up or down the body.

● Bandages should be firm enough to hold the dressing in position, control bleeding or prevent movement, but not so tight that they interfere with the circulation (see *Checking Circulation* p. 178).

● Make frequent checks to ensure bandages are not becoming too tight as the tissues swell.

● Where a limb is involved ensure that the fingernails or toe-nails are exposed so that they can be checked for circulation (see overleaf).

● If a bandage is used to control bleeding and maintain direct pressure, tie the knot over the pad or dressing.

● If using bandages to immobilise a limb or part of the body, tie knots in front on the uninjured side of the body unless otherwise specified. If both sides of the body are injured, tie the knots in the centre of the body.

● When using a knot to secure a bandage *always* use a reef knot.

● Always add plenty of padding between the limbs and the body and between the limbs at the bony areas (e.g., the knees and ankles). Pay particular attention to the natural hollows (e.g., the armpits and the thighs), before applying slings and bandages.

Checking Circulation

Immediately after applying a bandage, and at 10-minute intervals thereafter, it is important to check that the circulation and/or nerves have not been affected by the bandage. Check as indicated below, and if any of the warning symptoms and signs are present, adjust or remove the bandage as necessary.

Symptoms and Signs of Affected Circulation

- Casualty experiences tingling or lack of feeling in fingers or toes.
- Casualty is unable to move fingers or toes.
- Casualty's finger or toe-nail beds are unusually pale or blue.
- Pulse is absent or weak in injured limb compared to that of uninjured limb.
- Casualty's fingers/toes are very cold.

Method

Press one of the nails of the bandaged limb until it turns white. When pressure is released, the nail bed should quickly become pink again, showing that blood has returned.

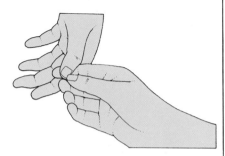

If the nail remains white or blue or the fingers are unnaturally cold, the bandage is too tight.

If no pulse can be felt in the affected limb, the bandage is too tight.

Triangular Bandages

These can be made by cutting a piece of material (linen or calico) not less than 1 m (1 yd) square in half diagonally. Alternatively, they can be bought, in which case they may be wrapped in sterile packages.

Triangular bandages can be used in a number of ways. Open or unfolded bandages can be used as a sling to provide support or protection for the arms or chest or for securing dressings over areas such as the head, hand and foot. Alternatively, they can be folded according to specific requirements (see broad and narrow bandages opposite).

STORING TRIANGULAR BANDAGES

When not in use, Triangular Bandages should be folded neatly and stored away.

1 Make a Narrow Bandage as in steps 1 and 2 opposite.

2 Turn the ends of the bandage into the middle.

3 Continue folding the ends into the middle until a convenient size is reached.

Parts of the Triangular Bandage

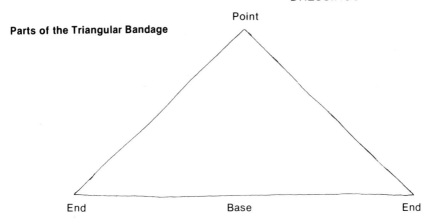

Point

End   Base   End

BROAD BANDAGES

These folded triangular bandages are used for immobilising limbs during transportation or for securing splints.

Method

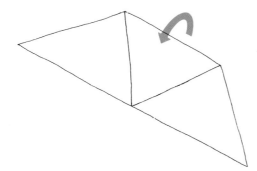

1 Turn in a narrow hem along the base of the bandage and fold the point in towards the base.

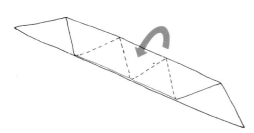

2 Fold the whole bandage in half again in the same direction.

NARROW BANDAGES

These are useful for securing a dressing at a joint if no other bandage is available (e.g., around the ankle or wrist); for applying a figure-of-eight bandage around the feet and ankles when immobilising a fractured leg (see p. 122); and for making a collar-and-cuff sling.

Method

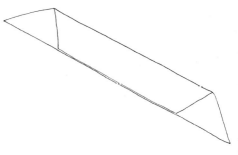

1 Make a broad bandage as in steps 1 and 2, left.

2 Fold the broad bandage in half again in the same direction.

REEF KNOTS

Always secure the ends of a bandage with a reef knot because. it will not slip, it lies flat and is therefore more comfortable for the casualty, and it is easy to untie. Once the knot is tied, the ends should be tucked out of sight or neatly fastened to the bandage. Make sure that the knot does not press on to a bone or into the skin at the back of the neck when used on a sling. If the knot is uncomfortable, place some soft material under it for padding.

Method

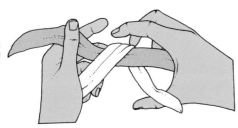

1 Take one end of the bandage in each hand. Carry the left end over the right, and under.

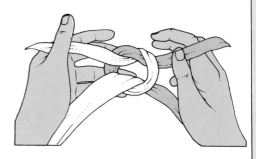

2 Bring the ends up again. Carry the right end over the left and under. Pull the knot tight and carefully tuck the ends in.

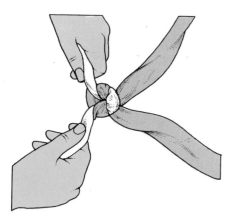

3 To untie a reef knot, select one pair of bandage ends as they emerge from the knot and pull them sharply. Slip the knot apart.

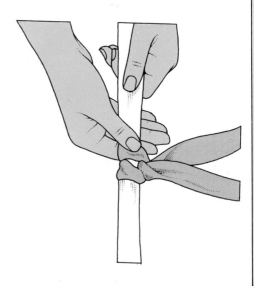

Slings

Slings are used to provide support and protection for injured arms, wrists and hands or for immobilising an upper limb when there are chest injuries. There are two main types: the Arm Sling and the Elevation Sling. A Collar-and-Cuff Sling can also be used to elevate the arm from the wrist. Always apply slings from the injured side so that you can provide extra support if necessary.

ARM SLING

This sling is used where there are injuries to the upper limb and for some chest injuries. It holds the forearm across the chest but it is only effective if the casualty sits or stands.

When an arm sling is in the correct position the casualty's hand will be slightly higher than the elbow. The base of the bandage should lie at the root of the little finger, leaving all fingernails exposed.

Method

1 Ask the casualty to sit down and support his forearm on the injured side with the wrist and hand slightly higher than the elbow.

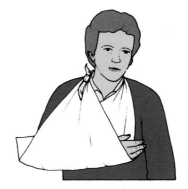

4 Still supporting the forearm, carry the lower end of the bandage up over the hand and forearm and, using a reef knot, tie off on the injured side in the hollow above the collar-bone.

2 Using the hollow between the elbow and the chest slide one end of the triangular bandage between the chest and forearm so that its point reaches well beyond the elbow.

3 Place the upper end over the shoulder on the sound side and around the back of the neck to the front on the injured side.

5 Finally, bring the point forward and secure it to the front of the bandage with a safety pin inserted point downwards.

6 Check the circulation. If it is affected, adjust the bandage and/or the position of the sling.

ELEVATION SLING

This sling is used to support the hand and forearm in a well-raised position if the hand is bleeding, there are complicated chest injuries or there are shoulder injuries.

Method

1 Ask the casualty to sit down and support the injured limb. Place the forearm across the chest with the fingertips almost resting on the opposite shoulder.

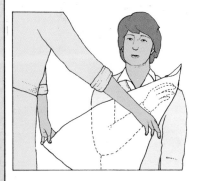

2 Place an open bandage over the forearm and hand with its point reaching well beyond the elbow and its upper end on the shoulder on the sound side.

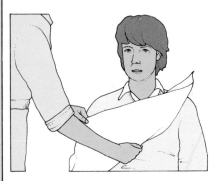

3 Still supporting the forearm, ease the base of the bandage round under the hand, forearm and elbow.

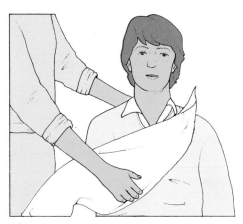

4 Carry the lower end around and across the back and up to the front of the opposite shoulder.

5 Gently adjust the height of the sling, securing the hand with a twist of bandage before completing the knot. Use a reef knot and tie off on the sound side over the hollow above the collar-bone.

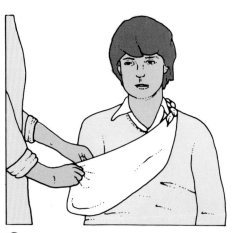

6 Tuck in the point between the forearm and front layer of the bandage. Turn back the fold and adjust any surplus fabric as necessary. Secure fold with a safety pin inserted point downwards.

7 Check the circulation. If it is affected, adjust the bandage and/or the position of the sling.

COLLAR-AND-CUFF SLING

This is used when the upper arm is injured and needs to be supported in a raised position without putting pressure on the elbow (see p. 118).

1 Ask the casualty to sit down and support his or her arm with the fingers pointing towards the opposite shoulder.

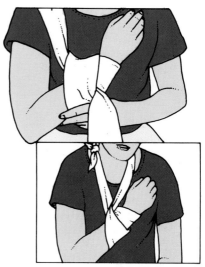

2 Use a narrow fold bandage, belt, tie, or similar material at least 1 metre long. Make a clove hitch; fold two loops over the centre of the fabric length with one loop pointing upwards and the other downwards. Bring both loops together from the outside ensuring that the free ends are between the loops.

3 Slip the clove hitch over the casualty's hand and along the forearm to cover the wrist. Adjust the sling to the most comfortable position and, using a reef knot, tie off the ends on the injured side over the hollow above the collar-bone.

4 Check the circulation and, if it is affected, adjust the finished position of the sling.

IMPROVISED SLINGS

If no triangular bandages are available, slings may be improvised in several ways to provide support.

- Use a scarf, belt, tie or tights to support the limb.

- Pin the sleeve of the injured limb to clothing.

- Turn up the lower edge of the casualty's jacket and pin it to the clothing.

- Support the injured limb in the fastening of a jacket or waistcoat.

Hand/Foot/ Knee Bandage

Method

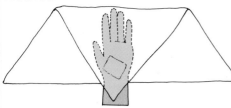

1 Keeping the injury uppermost, place a bandage under the casualty's hand with the base at the casualty's wrist and the point away from the casualty. Bring the point up over the hand to the wrist.

NB For a small hand or foot you may need to fold in a hem along the base of the bandage.

2 Carry the ends around the hand, cross them and finally, tie off below the point using a reef knot.

3 Bring the point down over the knot and secure.

4 Check the circulation.

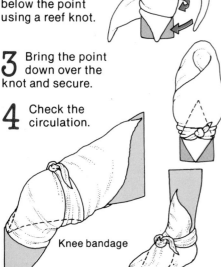

Knee bandage

Foot bandage

Scalp Bandage

This is used to hold dressing in place over a scalp wound but it is *not* used to control bleeding.

Method

1 Fold in a hem along the base of a triangular bandage. Place the base on the forehead so that the centre of the base is above, but close to, the eyebrows and the point hangs down at the back of the head.

2 Carry the ends round to the back of the head passing just above the ears.

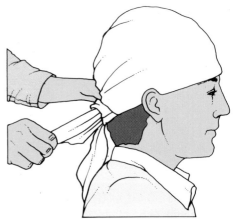

3 Cross the ends above the point of the bandage in the nape of the neck and bring them around to the front. Using a reef knot, tie off on the forehead close to the hem.

4 Steady the head with one hand and with the other, gently draw the point of the bandage down to take up the slack. Turn up the point, and secure to the bandage on top of the head with a safety pin.

Roller Bandages

A roller bandage can be used to keep dressings in position, to apply pressure to control bleeding or to support a sprain or strain. Standard roller bandages are made of cotton, gauze or synthetic fibres and are usually supplied in 5 m (5 yd) rolls. "Conforming" bandages hold dressings lightly but firmly in place and, because they mould to the shape of the limb, they maintain an even pressure.

Roller bandages are available in many different sizes. The size and type used will vary according to the part of the body to be bandaged and the size of the casualty (see chart below for details of sizes).

Before applying a roller bandage make sure it is tightly rolled and of a suitable width. Position yourself in front of the injury and support the injured part in the position in which it is to remain. Hold the bandage with the "head" uppermost and unroll only a few inches of the bandage at

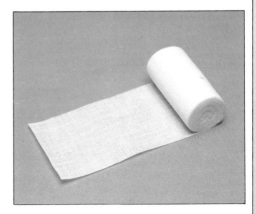

a time. To bandage a left limb hold the bandage in the right hand; to bandage a right limb hold it in the left hand. Always work from the inner side outwards, and from below the injury upwards.

Average Sizes of Roller Bandages for Use on Adult Casualties	
Part to be bandaged	Width
FINGER	2.5 cm (1 in)
HAND	5 cm (2 in)
ARM	5 or 6 cm (2 or 2½ in)
LEG	7.5 or 9 cm (3 or 3½ in)
TRUNK	10 or 15 cm (4 or 6 in)

Parts of a Roller Bandage

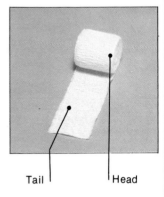

Tail | Head

When partly unrolled, the roll is called the head and the unrolled part the free end, or tail.

Applying a Roller Bandage

The most common method of applying a roller bandage is to use simple spiral turns as shown below.

Method

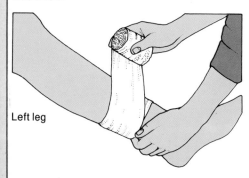

Left leg

1 Begin by placing the tail of the bandage on the limb and make a firm oblique turn to hold it in position.

2 Make a series of spiral turns working up the limb. Allow each successive turn to cover two-thirds of the previous layer and leave the free edges parallel.

3 Finish off with a straight turn and secure the end.

4 Check the circulation.

Securing a Roller Bandage

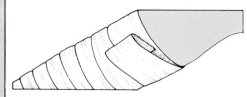

1 Finish off above the dressing. Fold in the end of the bandage.

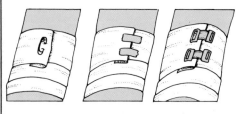

2 Secure with a safety pin, adhesive tape or a bandage clip.

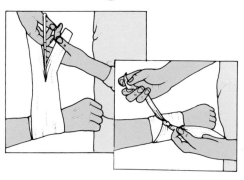

If pins, tape or clips are not available, gauze bandages can be tied. Leave about 15 cm (6 in) or more of the bandage free – the amount you leave will depend on the size of the part being bandaged – and split it down the centre. Tie a knot at the bottom of the split and using a reef knot tie the ends around the limb.

Figure-of-Eight Bandage

This is used to support a soft tissue injury on an arm or leg where even pressure is required.

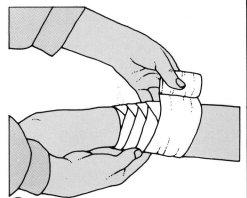

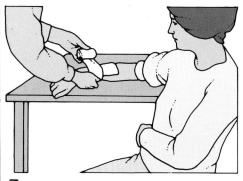

1 Hold the bandage with the roll uppermost and start to fix it around the limb below the wound with a firm turn.

2 Working from the inside outwards progress up the limb using a figure-of-eight pattern. Fasten off the bandage with a small safety pin inserted with point downwards.

Bandaging Around a Foreign Body or Open Fracture

Great care should be taken *not* to apply pressure on the protrusion and always use a roller bandage if one is available.

1 Build up dressings around a foreign body or fracture site.

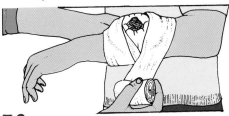

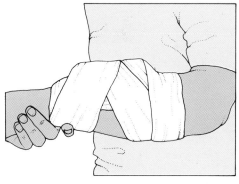

If bandaging around a foreign body, pass the bandage diagonally under the limb and up over the upper half of the built-up dressings avoiding the protrusion. Pass the bandage above and below the dressings until the pad is secure

If bandaging around an open fracture wound, place the tail of the bandage on the lower part of the built-up dressings and make the diagonal turns *above* and *below* the padding to avoid pressure on the underside of the fracture.

Elbow/Knee Bandage

The method for bandaging an elbow can be adapted for bandaging a knee.

Method

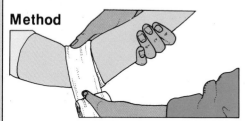

1 Ask the casualty to support the limb in the most comfortable position. Place the tail of the bandage on the inside of the elbow and make one straight turn, carrying the head over the tip of the elbow and around the limb.

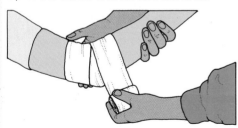

2 Take the bandage around the upper arm, covering half of the first turn, then around the forearm, covering the other edge of the first turn and touching the edge of the second turn.

3 Continue turns alternately above and below the first turn, allowing each to cover a little more than two-thirds of the previous turn. Avoid any unnecessary turns; they may add pressure on the inside of the joint.

4 Finish off with a straight turn above the elbow and secure the end.

5 Check the circulation.

Hand/Foot Bandage

The method for bandaging a hand can also be used for bandaging a foot.

Method

1 Ask the casualty to support the hand with the palm held downwards. Fix the tail of the bandage at the wrist by making one straight turn.

2 Carry the head of the bandage diagonally across the back of the hand towards the base of the little finger, then take it around the palm of the hand under the fingers to the base of the fingernails.

3 Carry the head of the bandage up across the top of the fingers to the root of the nail of the little finger. Then, bring it down around the palm again and diagonally across the back of the hand towards the wrist.

4 Continue making these figure-of-eight turns until the hand is covered. Finish off by making a straight turn at the wrist and secure the end.

5 Check the circulation.

Tubular Gauze Bandage

Made of a roll of seamless gauze, these bandages are in many ways easier and quicker to apply than traditional bandages. They require a special applicator and can be purchased as a finger dressing set. The bandage conforms gently to the part being covered and is equally suitable for fingers and toes.

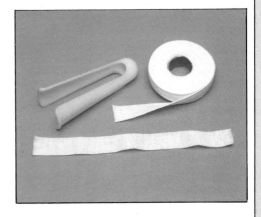

Method

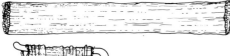

1 Cut a length of tubular gauze which is approximately three times the length of the area to be covered. Then, push the whole length of the gauze on to the applicator.

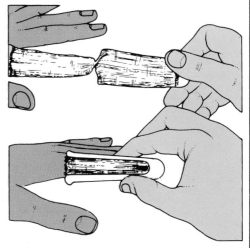

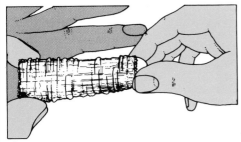

2 Gently push the applicator over the dressing on the finger. Holding the end of the gauze in position with one hand, gently pull back the applicator with the other, leaving the length of tubular gauze in position on the limb.

3 Holding the end of the gauze on the limb, pull the applicator back slightly and twist once or twice at the end of the finger. Push it back on the limb again, rotating the applicator slightly. Withdraw the applicator again leaving two layers of gauze on the finger.

Do Not twist the gauze more than twice as you may impede the circulation.

4 Secure the end of the gauze with adhesive strapping.

SPLINTS

These are used to hold fractured or injured limbs steady while a casualty is being transferred to hospital. Ideally a sound leg can be used to support an injured one by tying bandages around both limbs. This is called "body splinting". However, if this is not possible, or greater support is needed for a long and/or rough journey, then a splint will be required.

The basic requirement of any splint is that it is long enough to extend well beyond the joints above and below the injury and that it is well-padded. When placed against a limb, extra padding should be inserted where the bones touch it (e.g., at the ankles), and in the natural hollows (e.g., under the knees).

For information on when and how to use splints, see *Fractures*, pp. 121–25.

There are many different types of splint available commercially, examples are: the inflatable plastic, wood, wire frame, cardboard and traction splint. However, splints can be improvised using any material which is rigid, and long and broad enough to support the injured limb such as boards, fencing slats, sticks and rolled-up newspapers. A pillow or rolled blanket may be used to splint a lower leg or ankle fracture. **NB** Always use improvised splints or body splinting methods unless you have received special training in the use of commercial splints.

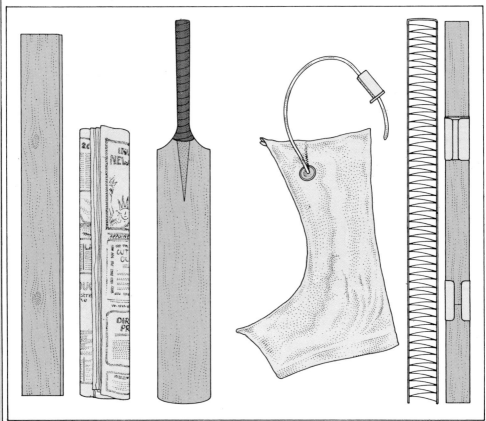

FIRST AID KITS

While bandages and dressings can be improvised it is far better to have proper equipment on hand. These materials should always be kept in a clean, dry, airtight container. Do not keep the container in a damp atmosphere such as a bathroom, and make sure that it is clearly labelled.

Below is a suggested list of contents for a family First Aid Kit. This should be taken as the minimum you should have in a kit although you may add to the list if you wish. For example it may be advisable to keep extra triangular bandages and several 25 g (1 oz) packs of cotton wool.

FAMILY FIRST AID KITS

10 assorted adhesive strip dressings
1 metre adhesive dressing strip
3 Sterile combine dressings
3 Sterile non-adherent dressings
3 Sterile packets of tulle gras dressing
1 Large sterile wound dressing (B.P.C. No. 15)
1 Medium sterile wound dressing (B.P.C. No. 14)
1 Anti-irritant solution for bites and stings
1 Roll of cotton wool
3 Assorted roller bandages (50 mm and 75 mm)

1 Tubular-gauze finger dressing set
4 Triangular bandages
1 Antiseptic solution
1 Pair blunt/sharp-ended scissors
1 Pair splinter forceps
1 Splinter remover
1 Bottle syrup of Ipecac
1 25 mm roll of hypo-allergenic tape
6 Assorted safety pins
1 Cold pack/ice pack

ROAD EMERGENCY FIRST AID KIT

A First Aid Kit suitable for a roadside emergency should contain additional life-saving bulky dressings but requires fewer materials for the treatment of minor wounds. In a major road accident, First Aid should be confined to Basic Life Support techniques rather than minor treatments. For example, if C.P.R. is needed it will depend on your skill as a First Aider not on the contents of your First Aid Box. Bulky dressings are likely to be needed to control severe bleeding and light-weight dressings and conforming bandages will be needed to cover serious wounds. Triangular bandages may be needed to support fractured limbs. The Australian Red Cross Society recommends the following materials as a minimum for a road emergency First Aid Kit.

1 Small wound dressing (B.P.C. No. 13)
2 Medium wound dressings (B.P.C. No. 14)
1 Large wound dressing (B.P.C. No. 15)
2 Conforming bandages (7.5 cm)
2 Conforming bandages (5 cm)
2 Sterile combine dressings (10 x 10 cm)
2 Sterile combine dressings (20 x 20 cm)
2 Non-adherent dressings
12 Adhesive dressing strips
1 Foil rescue blanket
1 Pair blunt/sharp-ended scissors
8 Safety pins
4 Calico triangular bandages
Notebook and pencil/pen
First Aid instruction leaflet or manual

Optional items
Roll of cotton wool
Packet of tissues

HANDLING AND TRANSPORT

The comfort, safety and well-being of the casualty are among your primary considerations and you must always make sure that the condition will not be made worse by careless handling or movement. The most important rule to remember is that you should *never move a severely injured or ill person unless there is immediate danger to life or if skilled help is not readily available*. It is better to leave the casualty undisturbed, send for help and provide First Aid treatment on the spot.

If the casualty's life is endangered by fire, falling debris or poisonous gases, move the casualty as quickly as possible without endangering yourself. Otherwise it is important if the casualty is unconscious to turn him or her on to the side promptly and give care of airway, breathing and circulation following the Basic Life Support Flow Chart (see p. 15). If the casualty is conscious, carry out a quick examination (see pp. 36–40).

There are various methods of carrying casualties using support from one or more helpers, such as hand-seats and chair carries, blanket lifts and stretchers.

The method used depends on: the nature and severity of the injury; the number of helpers and the facilities available; the casualty's build; the distance to shelter; and the route to be travelled.

Never attempt to move a seriously injured casualty on your own if help is available. Always make sure that everyone involved, including the casualty, if conscious, knows exactly what is going to happen and what they must do before you begin and always give a preparatory word of command before each stage.

If the casualty is to be removed to hospital you should arrange for an ambulance, although, if the injuries are minor or only involve upper limb injuries, the casualty may be taken in a car. Whichever method of transport is used, the aim is always the same — to enable the casualty to reach the destination without deterioration or discomfort. Wherever possible, the position in which the casualty is found or has been placed should not be changed and the general condition watched carefully throughout.

LIFTING CASUALTIES

This is a skill and, if it is done correctly, even a very heavy casualty can be lifted without undue strain. However, it is important that you should not attempt to lift too heavy a weight and that you always obtain assistance from any available bystanders to avoid injury to yourself.

There are two principles of lifting: first, you should always use the most powerful muscles of the body, the thigh, hip and shoulder; second, the weight should be kept as close to your body as possible.

It is very important that the correct

posture for lifting is adopted. Feet should be placed comfortably apart to ensure a stable, balanced posture and a firm stance. Keep your back straight and head erect and hold the casualty close to your body using your shoulders to support the weight. Use your whole hand to strengthen the grasp. If the casualty begins to slip, do not injure your own back by trying to prevent the casualty falling. Let the casualty slide slowly and gently to the ground without causing more damage to the injured area.

Carries for One First Aider

If help is available, *do not* attempt to move a seriously ill or injured casualty on your own.

CRADLE METHOD
To carry lightweight casualties or children, pass one arm under the casualty's thighs and the other around the trunk above the waist and lift.

DRAG METHOD
This method involves pulling the casualty along the ground without lifting. It should *only* be used where a casualty is unable to stand and must be moved quickly from a source of danger.

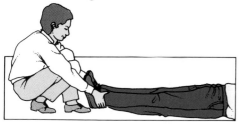

1 Grip the casualty's ankles and, crouching as low as possible, lean backwards and drag the casualty along the ground without raising the legs.

2 Alternatively, grip the casualty's wrists, crouch down low and drag the casualty as above.

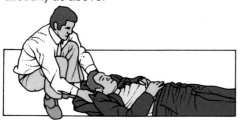

If the casualty is wearing a jacket or coat, unbutton it and pull it back up under the casualty's head. Pull the casualty along the ground in the same way with the head supported on the clothing.

HUMAN CRUTCH
This is used to support a conscious casualty who is able to walk with assistance. It should *not* be used if an upper limb is injured.

1 Stand at the casualty's injured side, if any. Place the casualty's nearest arm around your neck and hold the hand with your free hand.

2 Put your other arm around the casualty's waist and grasp the clothing at the hip. The casualty may be given additional support from a walking stick or staff.

3 Co-ordinate your steps with the casualty to give a broad base of support.

Carries for Two First Aiders

FOUR-HANDED SEAT

This method is used to carry a conscious casualty who can assist the bearers by using one or both arms to hold on.

1 Stand facing each other behind the casualty. Make a seat by grasping your own left wrists with your right hands and your partner's right wrist with the free hand and stoop.

2 Instruct the casualty to place an arm around each of you at the neck, to sit back on to your hands and to steady himself during transport.

3 Rise together, step off with the outside feet and walk with ordinary paces.

TWO-HANDED SEAT

This method is used to carry a casualty who is unable to assist the bearers.

1 Squat facing each other on either side of the casualty. Each should pass the arm nearest the casualty's body under and around the back just below the shoulders and, if possible, grasp each other's wrists, otherwise, grasp the casualty's clothing.

2 Raise the casualty's legs slightly, pass your other arms under the middle of the thigh and grasp each other's wrists.

3 Rise together, step off with the outside feet and walk with ordinary paces.

FORE-AND-AFT CARRY

This method can be used to place the casualty on to a chair or a carrying chair.

1 Supporting the casualty on both sides, both First Aiders should help the casualty to sit up and fold the arms across the chest.

2 One person moves around behind the casualty and places the arms through and under the casualty's armpits and grasps the casualty's wrists.

Do Not use this method if you cannot grasp the casualty's wrists.

3 The other person remains at the casualty's side and places one arm around the casualty's back and the other under the thighs.

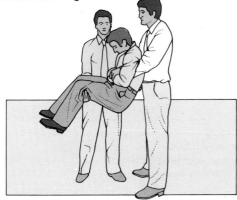

4 Working together casualty is lifted on to the chair or stretcher.

CHAIR METHOD

When a conscious casualty with no serious injuries is to be moved up or down stairs or along passageways, the casualty can be seated on an ordinary chair and carried by two people. However, the passages must be cleared of any obstructions or dangers such as loose matting before you start.

1 Test the chair to ensure that it is strong enough to support the casualty then, sit the casualty down and secure in position with broad bandages. Stand facing each other, one in front of the chair and one behind.

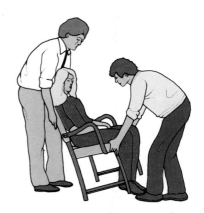

2 The person behind the chair should support the back of the chair and the casualty; the other should hold the chair by the front legs. Slowly tilt the chair backwards to seat the casualty securely then lift it together.

3 With the casualty facing forwards, move slowly along the passage or down the stairs.

If the stairs or passage are wide enough, you can stand facing the chair, each supporting the back and the top of a front leg of the chair.

LIFTING A CASUALTY IN A WHEELCHAIR

Wheelchair-bound casualties can be transported where they sit by adapting the chair method.

1 Locate the brakes (ask the casualty) and apply securely.

2 Sit the casualty well back in the chair.

3 Examine the wheelchair to find out which parts are fixed — arm rests and side supports are often removable and will detach if you use them to lift the chair. Supporting the chair from either side, lift by holding the fixed parts, *never* by the wheels.

4 Carry the chair as described on p. 195.

STRETCHERS

These are used to carry a seriously ill or injured casualty to an ambulance or similar shelter to minimise the risk of further injury. There are a variety of stretchers in general use such as: the standard stretcher; the pole-and-canvas stretcher; the Jordon Frame stretcher; the scoop stretcher; the carrying sheet; the carrying chair; the ambulance stretcher; the Neil Robertson stretcher; and the paraguard stretcher.

Most stretchers can be used to transport casualties with any injury and should be rigid enough to carry casualties with suspected spine fracture without additional boards. All equipment must be tested *before* it is used.

TESTING A STRETCHER

To ensure that a stretcher is capable of taking the weight of a casualty, one person should lie on the stretcher and each end of the stretcher should be lifted in turn. Then, both ends should be lifted at the same time.

NB If possible, this should not be carried out in front of the casualty.

THE STANDARD STRETCHER

The "standard" or Furley stretcher consists of poles, handles, traverses, runners and a canvas bed. The traverses are jointed so that the stretcher can be opened and closed. When closed, the poles lie close together with the canvas bed folded on top. This is then kept in position by two transverse straps. If slings are carried they are laid along the canvas held by the straps.

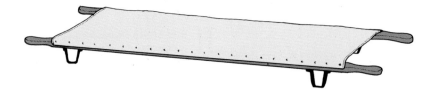

Opening the stretcher

1 Place the stretcher on its side with its runners towards you and the studs or buckles securing the straps uppermost. Unfasten any straps.

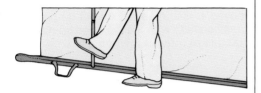

2 Push the traverses fully open with your heel and place the stretcher on its runners.

Closing the stretcher

1 Turn the stretcher on its side with its runners towards you and the studs or buckles which secure the straps uppermost. Push the joints of the traverses inwards with your heel to release them.

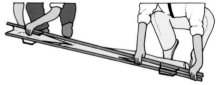

2 Push the poles together pulling the canvas out from between them. Fold the canvas neatly on to the poles and secure with the straps.

POLE-AND-CANVAS STRETCHER

This is one of the most commonly used stretchers. It consists of a canvas or plastic sheet about 200 cm (80 in) long and 50 cm (20 in) wide and two long poles. The canvas can be folded and slid under the casualty where the casualty lies (see p. 202). The poles are passed through sleeves down the side of the canvas to form the stretcher. Spacer bars may be placed over the ends of the poles to keep them apart and the stretcher firm.

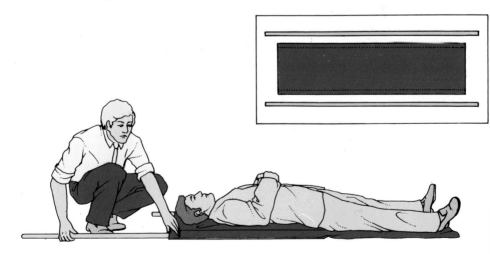

JORDON FRAME STRETCHER

The Jordon Frame is used to lift a casualty without twisting or bending the body. It consists of a tubular frame made to standard stretcher dimensions, plus 10 flexible plastic gliders. The gliders lock on to 12 spigots which are evenly spaced alongside each frame section. Small legs keep the frame slightly raised off the ground. The advantage of a Jordon Frame is that a casualty may be placed on it at the accident site and remain on the frame during ambulance transport and within hospital treatment areas. If a spinal injury is suspected, you should wait for trained ambulance assistance to im-mobilise the casualty before a Jordon Frame is used.

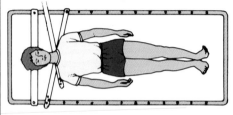

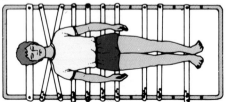

1 Assemble tubular frame around the casualty then slide the widest plastic glider under the head. Insert the remaining gliders evenly under the trunk and limbs. The gliders may be crossed under the shoulders for extra support. Use all 10 gliders and select any 10 of the 12 available spigots to ensure maximum support for the weight of the body; work from the head downwards to the feet.

2 Once on the frame the casualty can be lifted using a side-lift or end-lift within a confined space. Always check that every glider is still firmly attached to its spigot every time the casualty is lifted.

SCOOP STRETCHER

The scoop or orthopaedic stretcher is an adjustable stretcher used to lift casu-alties on to an ambulance stretcher without altering the position in which they were found. It is not used to carry a casualty any distance. The length can be adjusted to suit any size of casualty and because the casualty does not have to be moved, it is particularly useful for picking up a casualty with a suspected spine fracture or internal injuries.

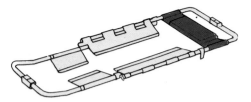

Scoop stretcher

1 Bring the stretcher to the casualty's side and adjust the length.

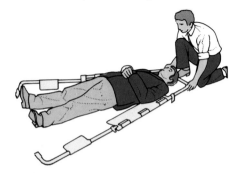

2 Uncouple both ends of the stretcher and gently slip each half of the stretcher under the casualty; rejoin the head sections.

3 Place the head pad in position.

4 While one First Aider stays at the casualty's head, the other should rejoin the foot section. Secure the head pad to the stretcher.

5 Working from either side of the stretcher, lift the stretcher and casualty and place on the trolley bed. Leave the stretcher in position or uncouple and remove it if other casualties are to be moved.

AMBULANCE STRETCHER

This is a fully-adjustable stretcher bed on wheels made of light metal which is carried in many ambulances.

Ambulance stretchers should always be kept prepared for immediate use. A canvas sheet from a pole and canvas stretcher is laid on the stretcher bed and two blankets are placed on top (see p. 201).

NEIL ROBERTSON STRETCHER

Made of stout canvas and bamboo this stretcher is designed for lifting casualties in the *upright* position through small hatches, such as manholes or pot-hole entrances, or for lowering casualties from heights as in mountain rescue.

The casualty is placed on the stretcher. Rope at the base acts as "stirrups" to hold the casualty's feet. The strap at the top is passed around the casualty's forehead to hold the head in position. The upper flaps are wrapped around the casualty's chest and secured with the two short straps, leaving the arms outside. The casualty's arms are then secured with the long strap. The lower flaps are strapped round the lower limbs.

The ring at the head of the stretcher is used for hoisting. Another length of rope is attached to the ring at the foot of the stretcher to guide the stretcher.

The stretcher should be stored in a place where it is most likely to be needed together with a suitable length of rope, preferably made of a rot-proof fibre.

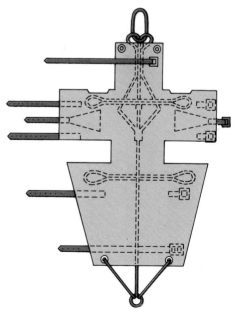

PARAGUARD STRETCHER

This stretcher is similar to the Neil Robertson stretcher and is used for the same purposes. However, it is lighter, less cumbersome and more durable than the Neil Robertson and can be folded up and carried on the back. The main advantage of the paraguard stretcher is that it will bend in the middle so you can negotiate obstacles.

IMPROVISED STRETCHERS

Stretchers may be improvised as follows:
● Turn the sleeves of two or three coats inside out. Pass two strong poles through the sleeves and button up the coats. The poles may be kept apart by

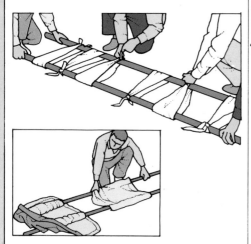

strips of wood tied to the poles at each end of the stretcher.
● Tie broad bandages at intervals around two strong poles.
● Make holes in the bottom corners of one or more sacks and pass strong poles through them; keep them apart as above.
● Spread out a rug, piece of sacking, tarpaulin or a strong blanket and roll up two strong poles in the sides
● Use a hurdle, broad piece of wood, door or shutter and add a rug, clothing, or hay or straw covered with a piece of stout cloth or sacking.
NB Always test an improvised stretcher (see Testing a stretcher p.196).

Preparing a Stretcher

To protect and keep the casualty warm, blanket the stretcher according to the number of blankets available.

WITH ONE BLANKET

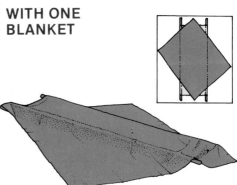

1 Place the blanket diagonally over the stretcher so that there are two opposing corners at the ends of the stretcher.

2 After placing the casualty on the stretcher, bring the point of the blanket at the foot of the stretcher up over the casualty's feet and tuck a small fold between the ankles.

3 Fold the point of the blanket at the head around the head and neck. Bring the right side of the blanket over the casualty and tuck it in. Then bring the left side of the blanket over and tuck it in.

WITH TWO BLANKETS

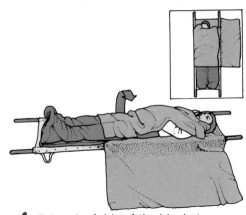

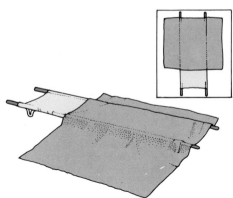

1 Place the first blanket lengthwise across the stretcher with one edge covering half the handles at the head and leaving slightly more to one side of the stretcher than the other.

4 Bring the folds of the blanket over the legs and feet and tuck them in.

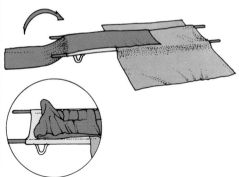

2 Fold the second blanket lengthwise into three and place on the stretcher with the upper edge about one third of the way down the stretcher leaving enough at the bottom end to fold in over the feet.

3 After placing the casualty on the stretcher bring the foot of the top blanket up over the casualty's feet and tuck a small fold between the ankles to prevent rubbing.

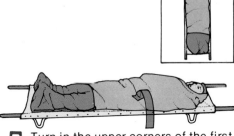

5 Turn in the upper corners of the first blanket and bring the shorter side over the casualty and tuck it in. Finally, bring the long side of the blanket over the casualty and tuck it in.

Loading a Stretcher

Ideally five people will be required to load a casualty on to a stretcher — four to lift the casualty and one to move the stretcher. However, there are methods of moving a casualty using two or three bearers if there are not enough people available or space is limited. The First Aider in charge of the casualty should assemble a squad of four bearers, decide which method of lifting is to be used, make it clear to each person what is to be done and give *all* the directions.

If you are unloading a stretcher in order to place a casualty on to a bed or examination couch reverse the loading procedure.

LOADING A CASUALTY ON TO A POLE-AND-CANVAS STRETCHER

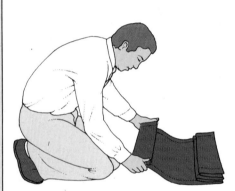

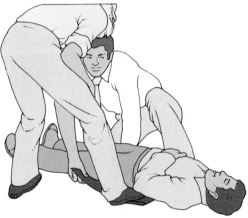

1 Working from top and bottom fold the canvas sheet into a concertina-shape; make three complete folds from the top and four from the bottom. Slide the folded canvas under the casualty through the hollow of the back.

2 Each person should place one foot on the top pile of folds, pull the casualty's clothing taut from the waist down and gently work the canvas down under the buttocks and legs. Repeat for the top part of the body until the canvas is extended.

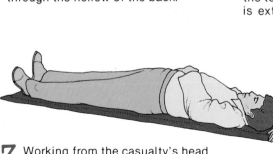

3 Working from the casualty's head, slide the poles into the sleeves and place spacer bars over the ends if they are to be used. Lift the stretcher as described on pp. 206 – 7.

PLACING A BLANKET UNDER THE CASUALTY

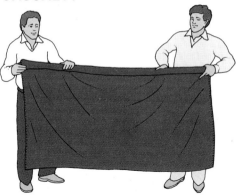

1 Test the blanket. Lay the blanket on the ground. One person should lie down on the blanket while two others attempt to lift it.

2 Roll a blanket or rug lengthwise for half its width; place the roll in line with and against the injured side of the casualty (or most severely injured side if both are injured).

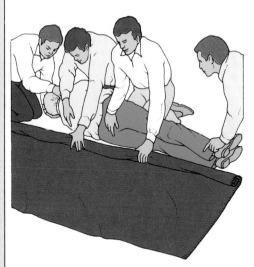

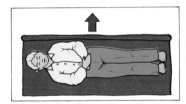

3 All four people should work together and turn the casualty slowly and gently on to the side away from the blanket. Move the rolled portion of the blanket or rug up against the casualty's back.

4 Gently turn the casualty on to the back over the roll of the blanket and far enough on to the opposite side to allow the blanket to be unrolled. Turn the casualty on to the back again.

NB This method can also be used to load a casualty on to a pole-and-canvas stretcher.

BLANKET LIFT

1 Stand so that two people face each other on either side of the trunk, and two face each other at the lower limbs. Tightly roll the two edges of the blanket up against the casualty's sides.

If poles of sufficient length and rigidity are available, the edges of the blanket can be rolled around them. It will make the casualty easier to lift and prevent the blanket sagging.

2 With backs straight, squat and grasp the blanket with palms downwards and fingers at the inner side of the rolled blanket edge. The two people nearest the casualty's head should each place one hand level with the head and the other at the waist. The people at the lower limbs should place one hand level with the hips and the other at the ankles.

3 Working together, carefully and evenly lift the casualty high enough to enable a fifth person to push the stretcher underneath.

4 Working together again, carefully and evenly lower the casualty on to the stretcher.

If a fifth person is not available or if it is not possible to push the stretcher under the casualty, place the stretcher in line with the casualty as close to the head as possible. Carefully lift the casualty and move with short even side paces until the casualty is directly over the stretcher then lower the casualty on to it.

MANUAL LIFTS

If a blanket is not available you will have to lift the casualty using one of the following methods.

For Four People

1 Three people should place themselves on the left of the casualty: one facing the knees, one facing the hips and the third facing the shoulders. The person in charge of the casualty should be on the casualty's right facing the middle person.

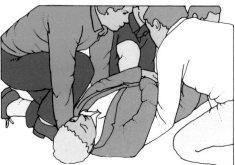

2 Everyone should go down on their left knees and place their forearms beneath the casualty paying particular attention to the site of the injury. The person in charge should grasp the left wrist of the person at the shoulders with the left hand and the right wrist of the person opposite with the right hand. The person at the shoulders should support the head and shoulders and ensure an open airway and the fourth person should support the lower limbs.

3 When the order "lift" is given by the person in charge raise the casualty gently, slowly and evenly and place on the other three people's knees.

4 If a fifth person is not available to move the stretcher, the person in charge should disengage, get the prepared stretcher and place it under the casualty. It should be positioned so that the casualty's head will be just clear of the top traverse when lowered on to it. The person should then resume the original position and rejoin hands.

5 When the order "lower" is given, work together and gently raise the casualty slightly from everyone's knees. Then slowly and evenly lower the casualty on to the stretcher bed.

For Three People

1 Place the stretcher in line with the casualty as near the head as possible. One person should kneel on one knee on the injured side of the casualty level with the knees and place the hands under the casualty's legs. The other two should kneel on opposite sides of the casualty's chest and grasp each others' wrists under the shoulders and hips.

2 On the order "lift", gently and evenly raise the casualty and stand up. Then, moving with side paces, carry the casualty head first over the stretcher.

3 When the order "lower" is given, gently, slowly and evenly lower the casualty on to the stretcher.

If the casualty is seriously injured and must be kept rigid all three people should work from the same side. They should raise the casualty and tilt the body towards them as they lift.

LOADING A CASUALTY IN THE RECOVERY POSITION

1 Prepare the stretcher as on p. 200 but place one extra rolled blanket down one side of the stretcher to support the casualty in the Recovery Position.

2 Bring the casualty's arms down by the side; three people should stand on the casualty's left at the head to ensure an open airway, at the hips and the knees while a fourth person supports the casualty's trunk from the other side.

3 Follow the procedure described left and opposite.

Carrying a Stretcher

When the casualty has been placed on the stretcher everyone should take up their positions at each end of the stretcher. At least two trained people will be required to carry a stretcher and the person in charge of the casualty should always remain at the casualty's head. If bystanders are available they should be used to help carry the stretcher to spread the load. However, there should be at least one trained person at each end of the stretcher.

Unless a casualty is suffering from shock, the head should be kept higher than the feet. So as a general rule the casualty should always be carried feet first. However, there are a few exceptions:

● When going up stairs or hills when the lower limbs are *not* injured.

● When going down stairs or hills when the casualty's lower limbs *are* injured or the casualty is suffering from hypothermia.

● When carrying a casualty to the side or foot of a bed.

● When loading a casualty into an ambulance.

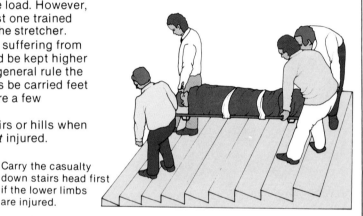

Carry the casualty down stairs head first if the lower limbs are injured.

For Four People

1 Keeping your backs straight everyone should squat and grasp the handles with the inner hands, palms inwards. On the order "lift", all rise together holding the stretcher with arms fully extended and keeping it level.

2 At the order "Advance", move off together but walk out of step to avoid bouncing the stretcher.

3 When you reach the ambulance, working together, gently and evenly lower the stretcher to the ground with the casualty's head nearest the ambulance.

CROSSING UNEVEN GROUND

A stretcher should, if possible, be carried by four people when crossing uneven ground. Secure the casualty to the stretcher with a harness or broad bandages before you start. Keep the stretcher as nearly level as possible; this can be done by each person adjusting the height of the stretcher individually.

If crossing very uneven ground for a short distance, all four people should stand at the side of the stretcher facing inwards. Grasp the poles with one hand and place the other about 75 cm (30 in) in from the end of the stretcher; then, move with side paces and *not* cross-over steps.

CROSSING A WALL

Always avoid crossing a wall, if possible, even if it means carrying a stretcher further. However, if there is no gap, follow the procedure described below.

1 Lower the stretcher in front of the wall and turn inwards. Lift the stretcher and rest it on the wall, with the front runners beyond the wall.

2 The two people at the front should cross the wall one at a time while the others steady the stretcher.

3 Everyone should lift the stretcher and move it forwards until the rear runners are close to the approach side of the wall. The remaining people should then cross the wall one at a time while the others steady the stretcher.

4 Finally, lower the stretcher to the ground then carry it in the usual way.

Miscarriage

A miscarriage or "spontaneous abortion" is the loss of the embryo or foetus at any time before the 28th week of pregnancy. It is usually due to abnormality or death of the foetus and is therefore a protective mechanism that avoids the full development and birth of an abnormal baby.

About 20 per cent of all pregnancies end in miscarriage. Although some women may experience a "threatened" miscarriage involving little or no pelvic pain and only slight "spotting" of blood from the vagina, complete miscarriages always include the very real danger of severe vaginal bleeding. Incomplete miscarriage is serious because products of the conception are retained in the womb and it can result in severe bleeding.

Symptoms and Signs
- Vaginal bleeding and, if severe,
- Symptoms and signs of shock (see p. 86).
- Cramp-like pains in the lower abdomen or pelvic area; these may be severe.
- Passage of the foetus and other products of conception.

Aim
Reassure and comfort casualty and arrange removal to hospital.

Treatment
1 Reassure the casualty and keep her warm. Lay her down with head and shoulders raised and knees slightly bent.

2 Check pulse (see p. 85) and breathing rate (see p. 12).

3 Place a sanitary towel or clean towel over the vagina.

4 Remove to hospital immediately.

EMERGENCY CHILDBIRTH

A woman may go into labour unexpectedly at a time and place where she is unable to put her arrangements for confinement into practice. Also, a few women make no preparation at all.

It is important to remember that childbirth is a natural process and that the majority of births do not threaten the life of either mother or baby. In most cases, there is adequate time to arrange transport to hospital, or for the assistance of a doctor or midwife, but it is nonetheless essential that you clearly understand what you can do and what you should not do, before expert help arrives.

In a normal birth, the baby's head will emerge first. Rarely, however, the baby's position in the womb is reversed. This is known as a *Breech Birth* (see p. 214) and it requires urgent medical attention.

Never try to delay a birth in any way. Allow the delivery to proceed without interfering until the baby's head has emerged.

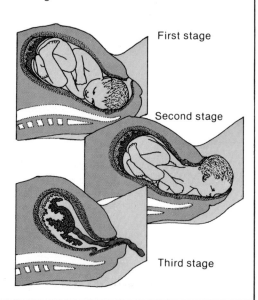

First stage

Second stage

Third stage

The First Stage

The first indication that labour has started is when the mother notices a low backache. A "show" of blood-stained mucus is a sign that the neck of the womb (cervix) has softened and dilated and the mucus plug has come away. At this stage the womb (uterus) contracts every 10 to 20 minutes, dilating the neck of the womb and the birth canal.

This stage may take 15 to 16 hours for a first child and about 10 hours for the second or any subsequent pregnancies. You should have ample time to call an ambulance and have the mother safely transported to hospital.

Towards the end of the first stage, the cramp-like contractions become more painful and more frequent. The "waters" will break indicating that the bag containing the amniotic fluid in which the baby lies has ruptured. Half a litre (1 pint) or more of liquid may escape in a sudden rush, although sometimes a constant trickle is all that is evident. When this occurs, it means that the baby is on its way, the second stage of labour has begun and the mother needs help.

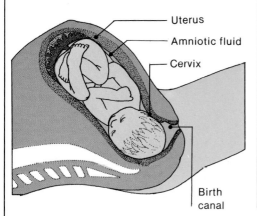

- Uterus
- Amniotic fluid
- Cervix
- Birth canal

The Knee-Elbow Position
Very rarely the cord protrudes into the birth canal after the waters have broken. If this occurs, place the mother in the Knee-Elbow position, to reduce pressure on the cord, and remove to hospital immediately.

The Second Stage

It is during this stage that the baby will be born. It generally lasts about one hour for a first baby and thirty to forty-five minutes for any subsequent births. Always remember that from the first sign of labour there is plenty of time to get ready so do not fuss.

Do not move the mother. Remain calm and if this is not already being done, immediately despatch someone to call for an ambulance. Instruct them to give the ambulance control details of the

stage of labour that has been reached, together with the name, if any, of the hospital into which the mother is booked and the address where she can be found (see *Calling for Assistance*, p. 35).

Once the contractions are approximately two minutes apart and the mother is pushing down and straining hard with contractions, she needs help immediately. It is now essential that a warm, quiet environment be arranged for the delivery of the baby.

Preparing for the Birth

The prospective mother is likely to be very nervous and excited. It is most important that she should be reassured of your ability to deal with the situation. This is best done by talking calmly to her and making the whole thing appear as an everyday occurrence.

All unnecessary people should be asked to leave the room, but make sure you are not left alone with the mother.

Usually there will be a female relative or a neighbour you can ask to help, and the father, if available, may want to stay.

Protect the mattress or floor with any plastic sheeting that may be available, but remember that towels or newspaper can be used as a substitute. If the mother is not at home or near a bed, she can lie down on the floor, the seat of a car, or any flat surface. In a public place, if there

PREVENTING INFECTION

Lack of scrupulous cleanliness and infection can jeopardise the lives of both the mother and the baby. No person who has a cold, sore throat or septic hands should help with the delivery. You and your assistant should both wear masks. If none are available, you can improvise by tying clean handkerchiefs around your faces. If possible, scrub your hands, nails and forearms thoroughly under running water for four minutes. Do not dry them and if they become soiled, wash them again in the same way.

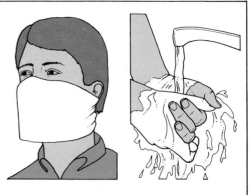

Delivery

are people around, ask them to stand with their backs to her to afford some privacy.

Lay the mother on her back with her knees drawn up and her head and shoulders comfortably supported. Ask her to remove any clothing that will interfere with the delivery. Cover her with blankets for as long as is possible and put cotton, lint or any suitable sheeting under her buttocks for warmth, and to absorb any subsequent mess. Fold a blanket in three and wrap it in a sheet to make a pack to cover the top half of her body during the delivery.

For the baby

Make sure there is some form of heating available. Prepare a cot and have a blanket, shawl or towel ready to wrap up the baby. A cot can be improvised from linen baskets, drawers or boxes. Place it in a corner away from any draughts.

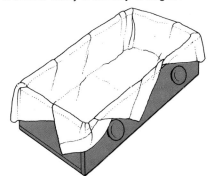

For the delivery

Fill some jugs with hot water and find a clean basin, and a plastic or stout paper bag to hold the soiled swabs, etc. Have scissors and sterile ligatures ready in case you need to cut the umbilical cord. Boil the scissors for ten minutes to sterilise them. If there are no ligatures available, boil three 25 cm (10 in) pieces of string (for ten minutes) or soak in methylated spirits (for ten minutes). You will also need sterile dressings (see p. 174) to dress the cord after cutting.

During contractions, the labouring mother should be encouraged to grasp her knees, bend her head forward, hold her breath and push, and then to relax between contractions.

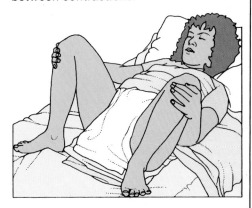

Eventually the perineum will become distended, a bulge will appear and, during the contractions, you will see the baby's head at the entrance to the birth canal — it will recede between contractions. This indicates that the birth is imminent.

More of the baby's head will appear with each contraction. You must steady the baby's head as it emerges because while in the birth canal it is subjected to great pressure during contractions. If it is allowed to "shoot out" the sudden change of pressure could rupture a blood vessel in the baby's brain. This may result in brain damage. *Do not* pull on or twist the baby's head.

Check as soon as possible whether or not the umbilical cord (a soft thick, gelatinous-looking rope) is around the baby's neck. If it is, it can usually be gently eased over the head. *Do not* pull it.

If the bag of fluid in which the baby is lying inside the mother has not broken before the birth, there may be a covering (membrane) over the baby's face as it emerges. This must be torn as soon as possible to prevent asphyxia and to allow the fluid to escape.

Procedure for delivery

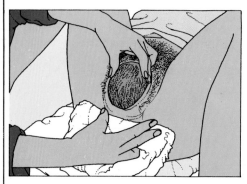

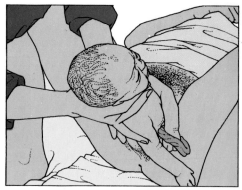

1 Place a clean pad over the back passage (anus). If a bowel movement occurs wipe it from front to back to avoid soiling the birth canal.

Do Not put your fingers into the birth canal.

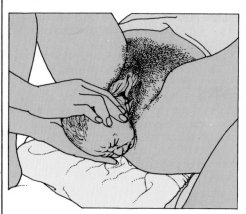

3 When the widest part of the head has passed through the birth canal, tell the mother to open her mouth and pant. Support the baby's body as it is born.

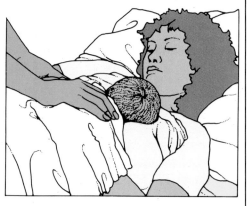

2 Gently support the baby's head as it emerges and steady it to prevent it "shooting" out.

If there is a covering over the baby's face, tear it with your fingers to prevent asphyxia.

Check the position of the umbilical cord. If it is around the baby's neck, gently ease it over the head.

4 Once the baby is born, lift it on to the mother's abdomen and clear out its mouth (See *Care of the Newborn Baby*, opposite).

Do Not pull the cord in any way; remember that it is still attached to the mother. (There is no need to cut the cord at this stage.)

Hold the baby very carefully because it will be very slippery. Lay it down so that the head is lower than the body. Make sure the mother and baby are covered and warm.

Care of the Newborn Baby

As soon as the baby has emerged, open its mouth and wipe away any blood or fluid with a swab. By this time it will probably be crying and it is quite possible for you to clean it up a little more. Wrap up the baby in something soft and warm. Make sure that its head is pointing down, so that any fluid or mucus can drain from the mouth and nose, and ensure the airway is kept clear.

The baby can be allowed to suck at the breast if the mother desires.

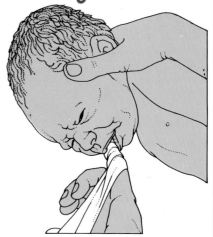

THE NON-BREATHING BABY

Occasionally, the baby does not cry and if it is not breathing, there may be an obstruction in the airway. This is usually mucus and must be cleared immediately.

1 Carefully clear the baby's airway wiping the mouth and nose.

Do Not smack the baby.

2 If the baby fails to respond and is either blue or white and completely limp, then care for airway, breathing and circulation according to the Basic Life Support Flow Chart (see p. 15).

The Third Stage

At any time between 10 and 30 minutes after the birth of the baby, the *afterbirth* should separate from the mother's womb. When it is about to be expelled, the mother will experience mild contractions. Encourage her to hold her breath and push the afterbirth out. She will find this easiest if she is lying down with her knees up and apart. *Do not* pull the afterbirth or cord while it is being expelled.

There is no need to separate the afterbirth from the cord, this can safely be left until medical aid is available. Keep it intact, preferably in a polythene bag, as it will have to be checked for completeness when the mother reaches hospital.

Even a small piece left inside the mother can cause complications later.

When the afterbirth has been expelled, clean up the mother and lay a sanitary towel or clean cloth over the vagina. Make her as comfortable as possible and encourage her to rest. A small amount of bleeding is normal. Severe bleeding rarely occurs, but, if this does happen, remember skilled help is on the way, so keep calm. Gently massage the mother's abdomen just below the navel to stimulate the uterus to contract. The uterus will harden as it contracts but continue massage until skilled help arrives.

Breech Delivery

This is where the baby's position in the womb is reversed. It is not a common condition but it is one which requires urgent medical attention.

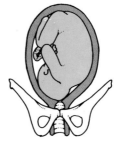

Normal (Head down)   Breech (Head up)

Treatment

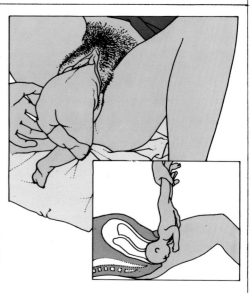

1 If the mother is on a bed, lay her across the bed with her buttocks at the edge and her legs and feet over the side. Place two boxes or stools under her feet to support the legs.

2 Gently support the baby as it appears. Keep its body warm so as not to stimulate breathing by excessive cooling before the head emerges.

3 Allow the baby to hang from the birth canal during delivery. If the head is retained for more than three minutes after the shoulders have appeared, grasp the feet and lift baby over the mother's abdomen to free mouth and nose.

4 Clean any mucus from the baby's mouth and nose to open the airway.

5 Wait for the rest of the head to emerge. Too rapid a delivery may cause brain damage, and once the mouth and nose are free, there is no need to hasten the rest of the delivery.

Dealing with the Cord

In most instances no harm will result if the umbilical cord is left attached to the baby until mother and baby reach hospital. If the cord is very short or removal to hospital will be delayed, it may be necessary to cut the cord. Wait until: after the afterbirth has been delivered; the cord has stopped pulsating; or until at least ten minutes after the birth.

1 Using two of the sterile ligatures, or prepared pieces of string (see p. 211), tie the cord very firmly in two places: 15 cm (6 in) and 20 cm (8 in) from the baby's abdomen. If the ligature nearest the baby is not tied very firmly the baby may bleed to death when the cord is cut.

2 Cut the cord between the two ties using sterilised scissors.

3 Place a sterile dressing over the cut end at the baby's abdomen.

Do Not put powder or disinfectant of any kind on the cut end of the cord.

4 Ten minutes after cutting, inspect the cord to make sure there is no bleeding. Tie the remaining ligature around the cord about 10cm (4 in) from the baby's abdomen.

5 Dress the cord again with another sterile dressing and secure it by tying a folded napkin around the baby.

If there is no sterile dressing available, do not tie anything around the baby.

If the cord has to be cut before the afterbirth has been expelled, cover the end of the umbilical cord attached to the afterbirth with a sterile dressing. **Always keep the afterbirth so that it can be inspected later.**

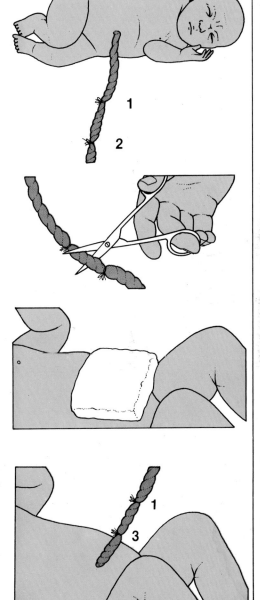

INDEX